Contents

Introduction

Lessons for Theme 1: Silly Stories

Lessons for Theme 2: Nature Walk

Lessons for Theme 3: Around Town: Neighborhood and Community

Lessons for Theme 4: Amazing Animals

Lessons for Theme 5: Family Time

Lessons for Theme 6: Talent Show

Blackline Masters

Teaching Masters and Practice Masters

Letter Cards

Sound/Spelling Cards

Blending Strategies and Routines

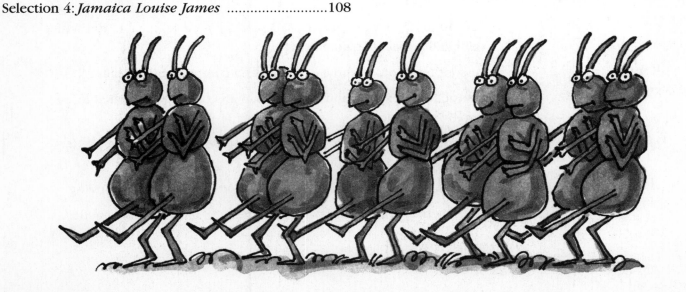

Teachers' greatest challenges tend to be fitting in special instruction during an already busy day, having appropriate materials and organizing them quickly, and maintaining structure and concentration when interruptions and distractions are frequent.

Houghton Mifflin Reading's materials for reaching all learners are a time-saving system of instruction for meeting those challenges. With this group of handbooks you can turn your attention to specific needs in your classroom—to advanced children, children who are struggling below level, or children who are learning English—while other children work independently. The Challenge, Extra Support, and English Language Learners handbooks are each tied to the core instruction in *Houghton Mifflin Reading*. For independent work, the *Classroom Management Handbook* provides meaningful activities related to literature selections and to core skills.

As a group, the handbooks for reaching all learners:

- help you manage your classroom and organize your time effectively

- provide excellent, additional instruction

- give you the resources you need to help *all* students achieve grade-level expectations

Extra Support Handbook Overview

The *Extra Support Handbook* provides support to enable lower-performing children to achieve grade-level expectations and to participate effectively in the instruction and reading opportunities in *Houghton Mifflin Reading*. Lessons in the handbook coincide with the daily skill instruction in your *Houghton Mifflin Reading* Teacher's Edition, providing critical support for children prior to core instruction. Handbook lessons are specifically designed for children needing extra support:

- Lessons are presented in a five-day plan for preteaching and reteaching key skills and previewing core literature.

- Lessons focus on essential decoding and comprehension skills.

- Instruction is explicit and systematic, with concepts presented in easy, step-by-step order.

- Learning is scaffolded through teacher modeling, visual examples, and interactive guided practice.

- Lessons include regular checks to monitor students' understanding.

- The Practice/Apply step provides meaningful independent practice.

Your goal is to advance these children to greater proficiency and ultimately to on-level reading independence.

The *Extra Support Handbook* is one of several options in *Houghton Mifflin Reading* for providing extra support for children. Your Teacher's Edition provides suggestions for each major anthology selection and includes a Resources section for support at the theme level. However, the *Extra Support Handbook* targets key skills in greater depth and gives students familiarity with skills before they participate in the core lesson—an important tool for building fluency and confidence.

Identifying Children Who Need Extra Support

Children who will benefit from Extra Support instruction include those who struggle to read on-level fiction or nonfiction, or who are in a Title 1 or similar program. These children may have difficulty with decoding or comprehension or both. They may be able to decode simple words but need help learning to decode longer words. Some may lack fluency, being unable to read rapidly and accurately and simultaneously grasp the meaning of the text.

Evaluating Children's Needs At the start of the year, and periodically throughout the year, you can evaluate children's instructional needs using the diagnostic assessments included in *Houghton Mifflin Reading*. These instruments include the Baseline Group Test, Leveled Reading Passages, Phonics Decoding Screening Test, and others. More information on diagnostic assessment can be found in the *Teacher's Assessment Handbook*. In general, children who need extra support will likely fall into one of the following groups:

- **Benchmark Group** These children's difficulties tend to be temporary or intermittent. In general, they are meeting their learning goals and are not performing far below grade-level expectations. You can determine specific difficulties using the Monitoring Student Progress boxes in the Teacher's Edition. Often, the Reteaching Lessons in the Resources section of the Teacher's Edition will provide the support these childen need. In some cases, these children may need the more ongoing support provided by the lessons in this handbook.

- **Strategic Group** Diagnostic assessment will show that these children's proficiencies are consistently below level, and this will be confirmed by your ongoing observations. These children need the regular, structured preteaching and reteaching support provided in this handbook. They should be evaluated regularly to make sure that they are progressing toward meeting grade-level expectations.

- **Intensive Group** These children are likely to be reading far below expectations. Diagnostic testing may reveal significant lack of decoding or comprehension skills. These children should receive intensive intervention or an individualized education plan. In the meantime, they can benefit from the lessons included in this handbook.

Frequent, positive feedback supports children's belief that they can do well. Make sure children who are struggling have opportunities for success.

Houghton Mifflin Reading includes a variety of assessments to help you determine the cause of reading difficulties, the degree of severity, and develop various grouping plans for instructing children at risk. At the beginning of the year, you'll use diagnostic tools to identify your children's skill proficiencies. Assessment tools in the Teacher's Edition and the *Teacher's Assessment Handbook* include:

> Diagnostic Checks
> Selection Tests
> Reading Fluency Tests
> Observation Checklists
> Selection Comprehension Charts
> Reading-Writing Workshops

Once you have diagnostics underway, the *Classroom Management Handbook* provides guidance for managing groups for differentiated instruction.

Lesson Structure

The number of Extra Support lessons are related to the frequency of word identification and comprehension lessons in the core program. Preteaching prepares students for whole-class instruction; reteaching after core instruction provides more practice. Further, each daily lesson includes a literature focus in the form of guided previews or through revisiting selections or ancillary literature. Lessons are not intended to substitute for core instruction, but are in addition to it.

The handbook provides multiple ways of explaining a concept, flexibility in pacing, levels of complexity, and frequent checks of children's understanding.

Five-day Instructional Plan

DAY 1	DAY 2	DAY 3	DAY 4	DAY 5
Preteach Phonics skill(s)	**Preteach** Comprehension skill	**Reteach** High-Frequency Words; Grammar skill	**Reteach** Phonics skills	**Reteach** Comprehension skill
Preview Phonics Library, first selection	**Preview** Anthology selection Segment 1	**Preview** Anthology selection Segment 2	**Review** Phonics Library, second selection	**Revisit** Anthology and Phonics Library selections

A consistent pattern of preteaching, reteaching, and revisiting skills is built into instruction day to day, and week to week. Consistency, repetition, and predictability help children progress more quickly. Skill focus instruction is modeled step-by-step for children. Appropriate examples are used to help them comprehend the skill. Children's understanding is monitored carefully with reminders to check that every child comprehends.

An application of the skill is presented and modeled, using the Teaching Master. This master introduces the skill in an interactive, visual way. The teacher guides children through the process, and then students practice and apply the skill on their own.

Teacher support for each selection includes:

Skill focus

- Easily scanned objectives and materials

- Guided instruction

- Visual examples

- Guided practice using the Teaching Master

- Support for Practice Master

- Teaching Master and Practice Master facsimile reference

Literature focus

- Literature citation

- Support for preview and review

See the Walkthrough on the following pages for more information.

To the Teacher

This walkthrough will familiarize you with the five-day instructional plans for Extra Support. Each plan is based on a selection in this level of *Houghton Mifflin Reading*. Days 1 and 3 are presented here for *Julius* from Theme 1, *Silly Stories,* and show the basic features of a typical lesson.

Instruction Labels

Preteach or Reteach labels note when to use the lesson in relation to core instruction. The type of Skill Focus lesson is shown and a suggested amount of time to spend on it.

Objectives/Materials

Skill Focus objectives are listed each day. Most of the materials are provided at the back of the handbook; literature needed for the Literature Focus is listed.

Additional Resources

The Get Set for Reading CD-ROM builds background and summarizes the Anthology selection. Children can log on to the Education Place site for activities. The theme audiotape helps with listening and comprehension skills. The Lexia Phonics CD-ROM provides phonics intervention.

Guided Practice

After teaching the skill, this section allows you to gradually turn the responsibility for practice to the children and to give immediate feedback. When two skill lessons are taught on Day 1, the guided practice and Teaching Master are provided for the first skill, while the practice/apply and Practice Master are provided for the second skill. (See Practice/Apply description on the facing page.)

THEME 1/SELECTION 2
Julius

Day 1

PRETEACH
SKILL FOCUS: PHONICS   10–15 MINUTES

Short Vowels *o, u, e*

Teach

Recite and repeat the chant shown. Invite children to join in.

> **CHANT**
> Net, not, nut
> Leg, log, lug
> Pep, pop, pup
> Deck, dock, duck

Have children repeat the first line. Write *net, not,* and *nut* on the board. Tell children they will learn about the vowel sounds they hear.

Point to the word *net.* Say *net,* stretching /ĕ/. Underline the letter *e* in *net,* and tell children that the letter *e* can stand for /ĕ/. Have children repeat the word *net,* listening for /ĕ/. Follow a similar procedure with the words *not* and /ŏ/ and *nut* and /ŭ/.

Blend

Use Blending Routine 1.

Spread out the letter cards *c, d, e, g, k, l, n, o, p, p, t, u k.* Say *nut,* stretching out the sounds. Tell children to choose the corresponding letters for each sound in *nut.* Have them blend the sounds for *nut* with you.

Make more words with short vowel sounds, calling on children to build the words in the chant. Have them say sound in a word, and then blend them together.

Guided Practice

Display or **distribute** Teaching Master ES1-3 and discuss the illustration. Point to the words and phrases under the picture. Ask children to use what they know about the sounds for letters as they read the words with you.

Ask children to help you check the list to see if all the items were purchased. Read each item and have children find it on the checkout counter. Label the items.

Check children's ability to read and write short *o, u* and *e* words by having them read aloud their labeled items.

Objectives
- recognize and say the short vowel sounds *o, u, e*
- blend and read short *o, u,* and *e* words

Materials
- Teaching Master ES1–3
- Letter Cards *c, d, e, g, k, l, n, o, p, p, t, u*
- Phonics Library: *Big Hog's House Hunt*

Technology

Get Set for Reading CD-ROM
Julius

Education Place
www.eduplace.com
Julius

Audio CD
Julius
Audio CD for **Silly Stories**

Lexia Phonics CD-ROM
Primary Intervention

Visual Support

Chalkboards and notebook art help organize instruction for visual learning and promote active student involvement.

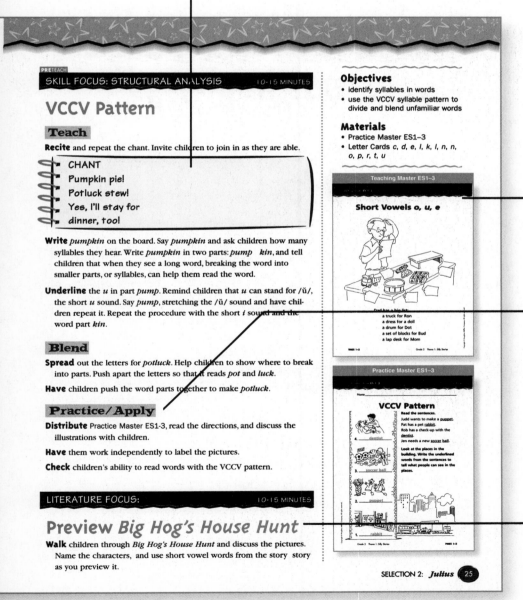

PRETEACH

SKILL FOCUS: STRUCTURAL ANALYSIS 10-15 MINUTES

VCCV Pattern

Teach

Recite and repeat the chant. Invite children to join in as they are able.

> CHANT
> Pumpkin pie!
> Potluck stew!
> Yes, I'll stay for
> dinner, too!

Write *pumpkin* on the board. Say *pumpkin* and ask children how many syllables they hear. Write *pumpkin* in two parts: *pump kin*, and tell children that when they see a long word, breaking the word into smaller parts, or syllables, can help them read the word.

Underline the *u* in part *pump*. Remind children that *u* can stand for /ŭ/, the short *u* sound. Say *pump*, stretching the /ŭ/ sound and have children repeat it. Repeat the procedure with the short *i* sound and the word part *kin*.

Blend

Spread out the letters for *potluck*. Help children to show where to break into parts. Push apart the letters so that it reads *pot* and *luck*.

Have children push the word parts together to make *potluck*.

Practice/Apply

Distribute Practice Master ES1-3, read the directions, and discuss the illustrations with children.

Have them work independently to label the pictures.

Check children's ability to read words with the VCCV pattern.

LITERATURE FOCUS: 10-15 MINUTES

Preview *Big Hog's House Hunt*

Walk children through *Big Hog's House Hunt* and discuss the pictures. Name the characters, and use short vowel words from the story story as you preview it.

Objectives
- identify syllables in words
- use the VCCV syllable pattern to divide and blend unfamiliar words

Materials
- Practice Master ES1-3
- Letter Cards *c, d, e, l, k, l, n, n, o, p, r, t, u*

Teaching Master ES1-3

Short Vowels o, u, e

a truck for Ron
a dress for a doll
a drum for Dot
a set of blocks for Bud
a lap desk for Mom

Grade 2 Theme 1: Silly Stories

Practice Master ES1-3

VCCV Pattern

Read the sentences.
Judd wants to make a puppet.
Pat has a pet rabbit.
Rob has a check-up with the dentist.
Jen needs a new soccer ball.

Look at the places in the building. Write the underlined words from the sentences to tell what people can see in the places.

4. dentist
3. soccer ball
2. puppet
1. rabbit

Grade 2 Theme 1: Silly Stories

SELECTION 2: *Julius* 25

Blackline Masters

The Teaching Master and Practice Master are shown for reference. See the following pages for descriptions of the masters.

Practice/Apply

Children use the Practice Master to work on the skill independently. When a single skill is taught on Day 1, the Practice Master provides an additional opportunity beyond the Teaching Master to teach and assess the skill. When two skill lessons are taught on one day, the Practice Master provides the only application of the second skill.

Literature Preview

The Phonics Library selection walkthrough is targeted at the day's reading in the core program, and follows the previewing suggestions in the Teacher's Edition.

Blackline Masters

Shown here are the Teaching Master and Practice Master for Day 1 of *Julius*.

Skill Title

To familiarize children with the academic language for the skills they are learning, the skill title is shown on both the Teaching and Practice masters.

Teaching Master

The Teaching Master is used as a verbal guide to model the process and practice expected of children for applying the skill. Teaching Masters can be held up or displayed for guiding children through the activity, or they can be copied and distributed so that children can follow along individually.

Short Vowels *o, u, e*

Dad has a big list:
　　a truck for Ron
　　a dress for a doll
　　a drum for Dot
　　a set of blocks for Bud
　　a lap desk for Mom

Practice Master

Children practice the skill with a brief activity to check mastery. As they explain their answers, you have the opportunity to make corrections immediately and give positive feedback.

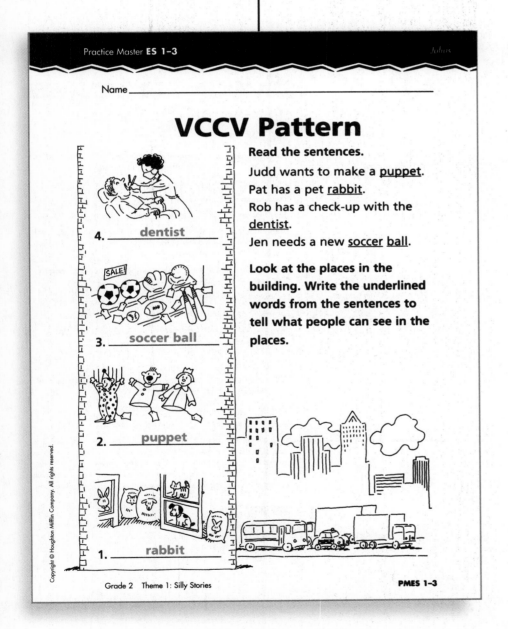

Visual Support

Usually an illustration or illustrations are added that can help reinforce the skill concept or help with word identification.

Skill Focus: Reteach

Day 3 lessons reteach high-frequency words and grammar skills. Notice the Reteach labels and the skill titles, along with the suggested amount of time for instruction.

3-Step Approach

Reteach lessons rely on a **Teach/Practice/Apply** lesson approach, using multiple examples for reinforcement.

Directive Verbs

For ease of use, the beginning verb of each paragraph is boldfaced.

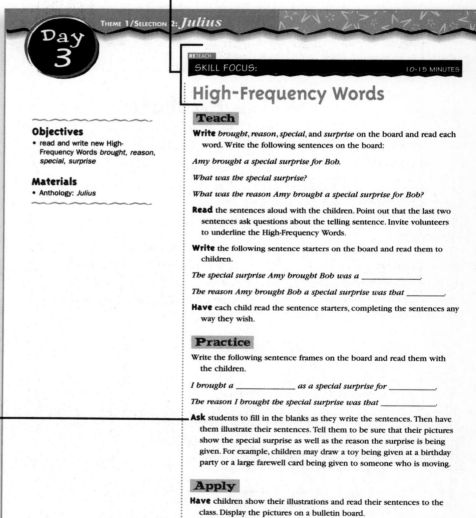

THEME 1/SELECTION 2: *Julius*

Day 3

RETEACH

SKILL FOCUS: 10-15 MINUTES

High-Frequency Words

Objectives
- read and write new High-Frequency Words *brought, reason, special, surprise*

Materials
- Anthology: *Julius*

Teach

Write *brought, reason, special,* and *surprise* on the board and read each word. Write the following sentences on the board:

Amy brought a special surprise for Bob.

What was the special surprise?

What was the reason Amy brought a special surprise for Bob?

Read the sentences aloud with the children. Point out that the last two sentences ask questions about the telling sentence. Invite volunteers to underline the High-Frequency Words.

Write the following sentence starters on the board and read them to children.

The special surprise Amy brought Bob was a _____.

The reason Amy brought Bob a special surprise was that _____.

Have each child read the sentence starters, completing the sentences any way they wish.

Practice

Write the following sentence frames on the board and read them with the children.

I brought a _____ as a special surprise for _____.

The reason I brought the special surprise was that _____.

Ask students to fill in the blanks as they write the sentences. Then have them illustrate their sentences. Tell them to be sure that their pictures show the special surprise as well as the reason the surprise is being given. For example, children may draw a toy being given at a birthday party or a large farewell card being given to someone who is moving.

Apply

Have children show their illustrations and read their sentences to the class. Display the pictures on a bulletin board.

Suggestions for grouping and planners for coordinating small group instruction can be found in the *Classroom Management Handbook*, along with selection-based independent activities.

RETEACH

SKILL FOCUS: GRAMMAR 10-15 MINUTES

Naming Parts of Sentences

Teach

Write the following sentences on the chalkboard:

<u>My grandfather</u> lives in the city of Los Angeles.

<u>My parents, puppy, and I</u> live in Riverside.

Explain to children that the *naming* part of a sentence names *someone* or *something*. Read the sentences to children. As you read each one, ask *Who or what is this sentence about*? Have volunteers draw a line under the naming part of each sentence.

Practice

Write the following sentences from *Julius* on the board:

"<u>Maya's Granddaddy</u> lived in Alabama."

"<u>He</u> lived in Alaska in the winter."

"<u>Julius</u> made a big mess in the house."

"<u>Maya</u> liked red felt."

Ask children to identify the naming part of each sentence. If they are having trouble, guide them with the question, *Who or what is this sentence about?*

Apply

Make up other simple sentences about the story. Write them on sentence strips. Have children work in pairs to identify the naming parts of the sentences. Encourage children to make up new naming parts for each sentence.

Objectives
- identify the naming parts of sentences
- put sentence parts together to make complete sentences

Materials
- Anthology: *Julius*

LITERATURE FOCUS: 10-15 MINUTES

Preview *Julius* Segment 2

Refer to the bottom of page 60 in the Teacher's Edition and preview with children Segment 2 of *Julius* (pages 60-73). Note the suggestions in the Extra Support boxes on the Teacher's Edition pages 67, 71, and 72.

SELECTION 2: *Julius* 29

Literature Preview

On Day 3, children preview Segment 2 of the Anthology selection; they have previewed Segment 1 on Day 2. Use the Teacher's Edition to preview the segment as noted. For Days 1, 4, and 5, children preview the Phonics Library or revisit the Anthology and Phonics Library selections.

Theme 1

Silly Stories

Selections

1 Dragon Gets By

2 Julius

3 Mrs. Brown Went to Town

Day 1

Objectives

- recognize and say the short vowel sounds *a*, *i*
- blend and read short *a* and short *i* words

Materials

- Teaching Master ES1–1
- Practice Master ES1–1
- Letter Cards *a, b, f, h, i, m, n, p, s, t, t*
- Phonics Library: *Len and Linda's Picnic*

Technology

Get Set for Reading CD-ROM

Dragon Gets By

Education Place

www.eduplace.com
Dragon Gets By

Audio CD

Dragon Gets By
Audio CD for **Silly Stories**

Lexia Phonics CD-ROM

Primary Intervention

PRETEACH

SKILL FOCUS: PHONICS   25–30 MINUTES

Short Vowels *a, i*

Teach

Recite and repeat the chant shown. Tell children to join in as they are able.

> /ă/ - /ă/ - /ă/, at
>
> Pat has a bat.
>
> /ĭ/ - /ĭ/ - /ĭ/, it.
>
> Kit has a mitt.

Ask children what Pat has. Write *bat* on the board. Then ask what Kit has and write *mitt* on the board. Tell children that today they will learn about the vowel sounds they hear in words like *bat* and *mitt*.

Point to the word *bat*. Say *bat*, stretching the /ă/ sound. Then say: *Get your mouth ready to say* bat. *Now say it*. Have children repeat *bat* several times.

Underline the letter *a* in *bat*, and tell children that the letter *a* can stand for the /ă/ sound. Have children repeat the word *bat*, listening for the /ă/ sound. Follow a similar procedure with the word *mitt* and the /ĭ/ sound.

Blend

Use Blending Routine 1.

Model how to blend the sounds together for *bat*. Have children blend the sounds as you repeat them.

Give three children the letter cards *b, a, t*. Have them say their letter sound when you point to them in order. Then have children move together to form the word *bat*. Have children blend the sounds to say the word.

Repeat the process with these words: *mitt, tap, him, sit, fan*.

Guided Practice

Display or **distribute** Teaching Master ES1-1. Read the directions at the top of the page and discuss the illustrations. Ask children to use what they know about the sounds for letters as they make each of the words and read them with you.

Read the second set of directions and have children complete the sentences.

Ask children to find other short *a* and short *i* words in the sentences. *(Kitty, Brad, Cindy, cat, Jack, Jill, Phil, Fran)*

Practice/Apply

Distribute Practice Master ES1-1 and read all of the directions with children.

Have them work independently to blend and write the words with the short *a* and short *i* sounds and complete the sentences.

Check children's ability to read short *a* and short *i* words by having them read aloud the completed sentences.

LITERATURE FOCUS: 10-15 MINUTES

Preview *Len and Linda's Picnic*

Walk children through *Len and Linda's Picnic* and discuss the illustrations, naming the characters *Len* and *Linda*. Emphasize short *a* and short *i* words from the story such as *Linda*, *chin*, *hand*, *sad*, *visit*, *glad*, *big*, *pad*, *list*, *packed*, *until* and *dip*.

Tell them that they will read this story with the rest of the class.

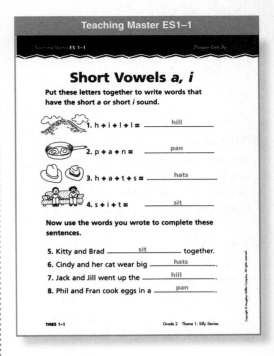

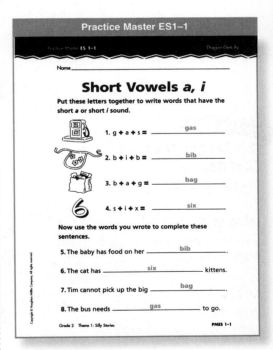

Day 2

PRETEACH

SKILL FOCUS: COMPREHENSION   25-30 MINUTES

Objectives
- tell who the story is about
- tell where the story takes place
- tell what happens in the beginning, middle, and end

Materials
- Teaching Master ES1–2
- Practice Master ES1–2
- Anthology: *Dragon Gets By*

Story Structure

Teach

Explain to children that a story is about characters and it takes place somewhere. A story also includes events that happen in the beginning, middle and end.

Tell children to suggest the name of a familiar story such as *Little Red Riding Hood* and then ask them to answer these questions:

- Who is the story about? (Little Red Riding Hood)

- Where does the story take place? (Little Red Riding Hood's house, the woods, her Grandmother's house)

- What happens in the beginning? (Little Red leaves her house to go visit her sick Grandmother)

- What happens in the middle? (She stops in the woods to pick flowers and meets the wolf who disguises himself as Little Red Riding Hood and eats up Grandmother)

- What happens in the end? (When Little Red Riding Hood gets to Grandmother's, the wolf tries to eat her too, but she is saved by a woodcutter.)

Explain to children that stories are made up of characters, places and events that answer the questions *Who? Where?* and *What happens?*

Guided Practice

Display or **distribute** Teaching Master ES1–2 and identify the chart as a story map. Explain to children that they can use a story map to write down the important parts of a story.

Read *The Tortoise and the Hare* with children. Have them share what they remember about this story to complete the story map with you.

Practice/Apply

Distribute Practice Master ES1–2 to children and read aloud the directions. Be sure children understand that they need to tell who is in the story and where it takes place. They also need to tell what happens at the beginning, in the middle, and at the end of the story.

Have children read the story and work in pairs to complete the story map.

Check children's comprehension of the story by going over their responses in the story map.

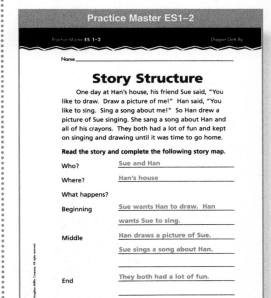

LITERATURE FOCUS: 20-30 MINUTES

Preview *Dragon Gets By*

Segment 1

Refer to the bottom of page T47 in the Teacher's Edition and preview with children Segment 1 of *Dragon Gets By* (pages 19-25).

Note the suggestions in the Extra Support boxes on the Teacher's Edition page T49.

Segment 2

Refer to the bottom of page T47 in the Teacher's Edition and preview with children Segment 2 of *Dragon Gets By* (pages 26-30).

Note the suggestions in the Extra Support boxes on the Teacher's Edition pages T52 and T53.

Teaching Master ES1–2

Teaching Master **ES 1–2**   *Dragon Gets By*

Story Structure
The Tortoise and the Hare

One afternoon by the pond, Hare began making fun of how slowly Tortoise walked. Tortoise didn't mind. In fact, he said he would race Hare around the pond. Hare agreed, and Tortoise began his slow and steady walk.

Hare looked at Tortoise and said, "He is so slow, I have time for a nap. Then I'll catch up with him and beat him to the finish line."

So Hare napped, and Tortoise walked on. When Hare woke up, he ran as fast as he could around the pond. But Hare was too late. Tortoise slowly crossed the finish line to win the race!

Who?	Tortoise, Hare
Where?	By the pond
What happens?	
Beginning	Tortoise challenges Hare to a race.
Middle	Hare decides to take a nap.
End	Hare loses the race.

TMES 1–2   Grade 2   Theme 1: Silly Stories

Practice Master ES1–2

Practice Master **ES 1–2**   *Dragon Gets By*

Name _____

Story Structure

One day at Han's house, his friend Sue said, "You like to draw. Draw a picture of me!" Han said, "You like to sing. Sing a song about me!" So Han drew a picture of Sue singing. She sang a song about Han and all of his crayons. They both had a lot of fun and kept on singing and drawing until it was time to go home.

Read the story and complete the following story map.

Who?	Sue and Han
Where?	Han's house
What happens?	
Beginning	Sue wants Han to draw. Han wants Sue to sing.
Middle	Han draws a picture of Sue. Sue sings a song about Han.
End	They both had a lot of fun.

Grade 2   Theme 1: Silly Stories   **PMES 1–2**

Day 3

Objectives
• read and write new High-Frequency Words *bought, front, kitchen, roll, until*

Materials
• Anthology: *Dragon Gets By*

RETEACH

SKILL FOCUS: 10-15 MINUTES

High-Frequency Words

Teach

Write bought, front, kitchen, roll, and until in a column on the board and read each word. Then write yard, food, later, table, and under in a second column. Have volunteers draw lines to connect the words in each column that go together. Lines should be drawn as shown below.

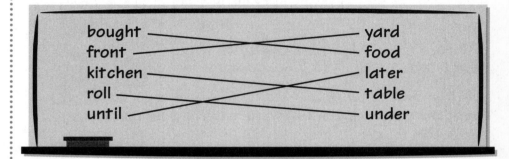

Have children read the pairs of words with you. Then ask them to dictate a sentence using each pair of words. For example, a child might say, "Henry bought food at the store." Write the dictated sentences on the board, an overhead transparency, or chart paper. Allow each student to contribute at least one sentence. Then read the sentences together.

Practice

Have children work in pairs. Give each child five index cards. Ask them to write one High Frequency Word on each card. Each pair of students should combine their cards into one stack. Have children mix up the cards and then place them face down in rows. Have children play concentration by matching up pairs of words. After getting a matching pair, a player writes a sentence using the word shown on the cards. Play continues until all cards have been matched and a sentence has been written for each word.

Apply

Invite each pair of children to present their sentences to the class by reading them aloud. Have the partners exchange papers with children from other pairs. Ask each pair of children to present the other children's sentences to the class by reading them aloud.

What Is a Sentence?

Teach

Write the following sentence on a sentence strip.

The dragon ate doughnuts for breakfast.

Cut it into two parts: 1) The dragon 2) ate dough-nuts for breakfast. Read each part separately. Point out that either of the two sentence parts do not make complete sense alone. Then put the two parts of the sentence together. Help children to see that now the words communicate a complete thought about what the dragon ate for breakfast.

Tell children that a sentence communicates a complete thought. Remind them that a sentence begins with a capital letter and ends with a punctuation mark. Use other examples of sentences and sentence fragments, and help children identify the differences.

Practice

Give each child two index cards, and have children write the word *yes* on one and *no* on the other. Tell them that you will read groups of words about the story *Dragon Gets By.* If the group of words is a sentence, tell children to raise the *yes* card. If the group of words is not a complete sentence, have them hold up the *no* card.

Dragon drove the car. *(yes)*
A balanced diet. *(no)*
Started to eat. *(no)*

Apply

Have children make up phrases and sentences of their own. As children read them, have classmates hold up the yes or no card to show which groups of words are sentences, and which are not.

Objectives
- identify complete and incomplete sentences
- make up complete and incomplete sentences

Review *Dragon Gets By*

Ask children to review *Dragon Gets By.* Have them retell the story, including who is in the story, where it takes place, and what happens at the beginning, in the middle, and at the end of the story. You might want children to complete a story map before they retell the story.

Day 4

RETEACH

SKILL FOCUS: PHONICS   25-30 MINUTES

Short Vowels *a, i*

Objectives

- listen to and blend phonemes
- say the short vowel sounds *a, i* in short vowel patterns
- read and write words with the short vowels *a, i*

Materials

- Phonics Library: *An Ice Cream Crash*
- Sound/Spelling Cards: *apple, igloo*

Teach

Tell children to listen to and blend these sounds: /l/ /ă/ /s/ /t/. Have children repeat the sounds and say the word. (last) Then tell children to change the /ă/ sound to an /ĭ/ sound. Ask what the new word is. (list)

Display the Sound/Spelling Card *apple* and remind children that the letter *a* can represent the short *a* sound: /ă/. Have children repeat the sound after you, /ă/, /ă/, /ă/. Write the word *cap* on the board. Use Blending Routine 2 to help children blend the word. For each sound, point to the letter(s), say the sound, and have children repeat it. Have children say the sound for *c*, /k / then the sound for *a*, /ă/ then blend /ă/ /ă/ /ă/ Finally, have them say the sound for p, /p/, and blend /k//ă/ /ă/ /ă/ /p/. Point out that *cap* has the short *a* vowel sound. Ask children to name other words with the short *a* vowel sound. Write their suggestions on the board. Examples: *crab, lamp, gas, wax, ant, plant, damp*.

Display the Sound/Spelling Card *igloo,* and review the short *i* vowel sound. Then write *sit* on the board and follow the same blending procedure as above using the word *sit*. Ask children to name other words with the short *i* vowel sound such as *his, mix, swim, twig, sick, hint, hill*, and *quit*. Write children's suggestions on the board.

Practice

Ask children to fold a piece of paper in half and write *cap* at the top of one column and *sit* at the top of the second column. Point out that *cap* has the short *a* vowel sound and that *sit* has the short *i* vowel sound. Have children work individually to write more short *a* and short *i* words in the appropriate columns. Have children read their lists to the class. If children need help, have them think about the letter sounds and blend the word. Example: /th/ /ĭ/ /ĭ/ /ĭ/ /n/, thin.

cap	sit
flat	grin
nap	wig
slam	thing
small	pit

Apply

Have children choose one word *pop*, *bug*, or *let*. Tell them to build four different words using the word they chose, replacing the first or last letter each time. Have children share their words with the group.

Preview *An Ice Cream Crash*

Walk children through *An Ice Cream Crash*. Read the first page of the story and ask children to name the characters.

Tell children to use picture clues to figure out where the story takes place and what happens.

Tell them they will read this story with the rest of the class.

Day 5

Objectives

- identify the characters, setting and plot
- complete a story map

Materials

- Anthology: *Dragon Gets By*
- Phonics Library: *Len and Linda's Picnic, An Ice Cream Crash*

SKILL FOCUS: COMPREHENSION   25-30 MINUTES

Story Structure

Teach

Ask children to suggest the name of a familiar fairytale or fable, for example, *The Three Little Pigs*. Choose one of children's suggestions and ask the following questions:

> *Who are the characters in the story?*
> *Where does the story take place?*
> *What happens at the beginning of the story?*
>   *in the middle of the story? at the end?*

Draw the following story map on the chalkboard:

> Story Map
> Characters
> Settings
> Plot

Fill in the map with children's responses to the questions. Remind children the *characters* are the people or animals in the story; the *setting* is the time and place the story occurs; and the *plot* is the sequence of events, which often includes a problem and resolution.

Practice

Work with children to identify the characters, setting, and plot of the story *Dragon Gets By*. Begin by walking through the story with them, pointing out Dragon, the main character; the different settings, such as Dragon's kitchen, the car, and the grocery store; and the plot. Support understanding of the plot by asking such questions as the following:

What happens at the beginning of the story? (Dragon realizes that he has no food, so he goes shopping to buy some.)

What happens in the middle of the story? (Dragon buys so much food that it won't fit in the car. So he eats the food. Then he is so big that he can't fit in the car. So he pushes the car home.)

What happens at the end of the story? (When he gets home, he is hungry. But his cupboards are bare. So he must go shopping again.)

Apply

Guide children as they work to complete a story map for the story *Dragon Gets By*. You might want to have some children draw pictures to demonstrate their understanding of the characters; setting; and beginning, middle, and ending events of the story. Invite children to use their story maps to retell the story. When finished, display children's completed story maps for others to see.

LITERATURE FOCUS: 10-15 MINUTES

Revisit *Dragon Gets By*, *Len and Linda's Picnic*, and *An Ice Cream Crash*

Page through all the stories with children and ask them who the characters are, where the story takes place, and what happens in the beginning, middle and end of each story.

Tell children to look through *Dragon Gets By* for the following high-frequency words: *bought*, *front*, *kitchen*, *roll* and *until*.

Have children look for words with the short *a* and short *i* sounds in *Len and Linda's Picnic* and *An Ice Cream Crash*.

Day 1

Objectives

- recognize and say the short vowel sounds *o, u, e*
- blend and read short *o, u,* and *e* words

Materials

- Teaching Master ES1–3
- Letter Cards *c, d, e, g, k, l, n, o, p, p, t, u*
- Phonics Library: *Big Hog's House Hunt*

Get Set for Reading CD-ROM
Julius

Education Place
www.eduplace.com
Julius

Audio CD
Julius
Audio CD for **Silly Stories**

Lexia Phonics CD-ROM
Primary Intervention

PRETEACH

SKILL FOCUS: PHONICS   10-15 MINUTES

Short Vowels *o, u, e*

Teach

Recite and repeat the chant shown. Invite children to join in.

> CHANT
> Net, not, nut
> Leg, log, lug
> Pep, pop, pup
> Deck, dock, duck

Have children repeat the first line. Write *net*, *not*, and *nut* on the board. Tell children they will learn about the vowel sounds they hear.

Point to the word *net*. Say *net*, stretching /ĕ/. Underline the letter *e* in *net*, and tell children that the letter *e* can stand for /ĕ/. Have children repeat the word *net*, listening for /ĕ/. Follow a similar procedure with the words *not* and /ŏ/ and *nut* and /ŭ/.

Blend

Use Blending Routine 1.

Spread out the letter cards *c, d, e, g, k, l, n, o, p, p, t, u k*. Say *nut*, stretching out the sounds. Tell children to choose the corresponding letters for each sound in *nut*. Have them blend the sounds for *nut* with you.

Make more words with short vowel sounds, calling on children to build the words in the chant. Have them say sound in a word, and then blend them together.

Guided Practice

Display or **distribute** Teaching Master ES1-3 and discuss the illustration. Point to the words and phrases under the picture. Ask children to use what they know about the sounds for letters as they read the words with you.

Ask children to help you check the list to see if all the items were purchased. Read each item and have children find it on the checkout counter. Label the items.

Check children's ability to read and write short *o, u* and *e* words by having them read aloud their labeled items.

SKILL FOCUS: STRUCTURAL ANALYSIS · 10-15 MINUTES

VCCV Pattern

Teach

Recite and repeat the chant. Invite children to join in as they are able.

> CHANT
> Pumpkin pie!
> Potluck stew!
> Yes, I'll stay for
> dinner, too!

Write *pumpkin* on the board. Say *pumpkin* and ask children how many syllables they hear. Write *pumpkin* in two parts: *pump   kin*, and tell children that when they see a long word, breaking the word into smaller parts, or syllables, can help them read the word.

Underline the *u* in part *pump*. Remind children that *u* can stand for /ŭ/, the short *u* sound. Say *pump*, stretching the /ŭ/ sound and have children repeat it. Repeat the procedure with the short *i* sound and the word part *kin*.

Blend

Spread out the letters for *potluck*. Help children to show where to break into parts. Push apart the letters so that it reads *pot* and *luck*.

Have children push the word parts together to make *potluck*.

Practice/Apply

Distribute Practice Master ES1-3, read the directions, and discuss the illustrations with children.

Have them work independently to label the pictures.

Check children's ability to read words with the VCCV pattern.

LITERATURE FOCUS: · 10-15 MINUTES

Preview *Big Hog's House Hunt*

Walk children through *Big Hog's House Hunt* and discuss the pictures. Name the characters, and use short vowel words from the story story as you preview it.

Objectives

- identify syllables in words
- use the VCCV syllable pattern to divide and blend unfamiliar words

Materials

- Practice Master ES1–3
- Letter Cards *c, d, e, l, k, l, n, n, o, p, r, t, u*

Teaching Master ES1–3

Short Vowels o, u, e

Dad has a big list:
a truck for Ron
a dress for a doll
a drum for Dot
a set of blocks for Bud
a lap desk for Mom

TMES 1-3 · Grade 2 Theme 1: Silly Stories

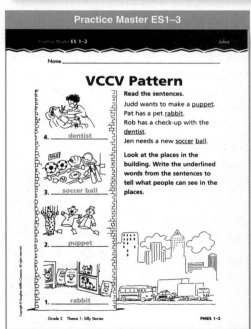

Practice Master ES1–3

VCCV Pattern

Read the sentences.
Judd wants to make a <u>puppet</u>.
Pat has a pet <u>rabbit</u>.
Rob has a check-up with the <u>dentist</u>.
Jen needs a new <u>soccer</u> <u>ball</u>.

Look at the places in the building. Write the underlined words from the sentences to tell what people can see in the places.

4. dentist
3. soccer ball
2. puppet
1. rabbit

Grade 2 Theme 1: Silly Stories · PMES 1-3

Day 2

Objectives
- distinguish between fantasy and realism
- identify realistic and make-believe elements of a story

Materials
- Teaching Master ES1–4
- Practice Master ES1–4
- Anthology: *Julius*

Fantasy and Realism

Teach

Write the following sentences on the board and read them aloud:

1. Lisa fed peanuts to the baby elephant at the petting zoo.

2. The baby elephant said, "Thank you for the peanuts, Lisa."

Ask children which sentence they think could really happen. Repeat the first sentence and affirm by saying, *This sentence tells about something that can happen in real life.*

Point to the second sentence and say: *Real elephants cannot talk. This sentence tells about something that is make-believe or could not happen in real life. Something that is make-believe is called a fantasy.*

Explain to children that some stories tell mostly about things that could happen in real life, and some stories tell mostly about things that are make-believe.

Guided Practice

Display or **distribute** Teaching Master ES1–4 .

Read the story once with children, pausing at the end of each paragraph to help them complete the chart.

Discuss the completed chart with children. Lead children to conclude that a story can have realistic and fantasy elements, but that it takes only one make-believe character or event to make a story a fantasy.

Practice/Apply

Distribute Practice Master ES1–4 to children. Explain to children that they will read a story, *Ana's Pets*, and then answer some questions about it. Remind children that they can look at the story to help them with their answers.

Have children work independently to complete the Practice Master.

Check children's comprehension when they share their answers.

Preview *Julius*

Segment 1

Refer to the bottom of page T123 in the Teacher's Edition and preview with children Segment 1 of *Julius* (pages 44-51).

Note the suggestions in the Extra Support boxes on the Teacher's Edition pages T125 and T126.

Segment 2

Refer to the bottom of page T123 in the Teacher's Edition and preview with children Segment 2 of *Julius* pages 52-61).

Note the suggestions in the Extra Support boxes on the Teacher's Edition pages T131 and T132.

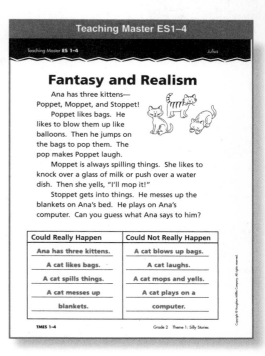

Teaching Master ES1–4

Fantasy and Realism

Ana has three kittens—Poppet, Moppet, and Stoppet! Poppet likes bags. He likes to blow them up like balloons. Then he jumps on the bags to pop them. The pop makes Poppet laugh.

Moppet is always spilling things. She likes to knock over a glass of milk or push over a water dish. Then she yells, "I'll mop it!"

Stoppet gets into things. He messes up the blankets on Ana's bed. He plays on Ana's computer. Can you guess what Ana says to him?

Could Really Happen	Could Not Really Happen
Ana has three kittens.	A cat blows up bags.
A cat likes bags.	A cat laughs.
A cat spills things.	A cat mops and yells.
A cat messes up blankets.	A cat plays on a computer.

TMES 1–4   Grade 2   Theme 1: Silly Stories

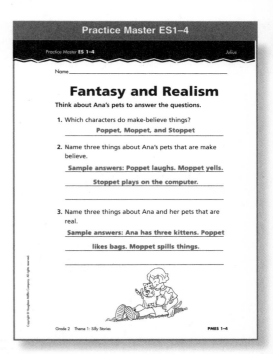

Practice Master ES1–4

Name_____

Fantasy and Realism

Think about Ana's pets to answer the questions.

1. Which characters do make-believe things?
   Poppet, Moppet, and Stoppet

2. Name three things about Ana's pets that are make-believe.
   Sample answers: Poppet laughs. Moppet yells.
   Stoppet plays on the computer.

3. Name three things about Ana and her pets that are real.
   Sample answers: Ana has three kittens. Poppet
   likes bags. Moppet spills things.

Grade 2   Theme 1: Silly Stories   PMES 1–4

Day 3

SKILL FOCUS: 10-15 MINUTES

High-Frequency Words

Teach

Write *brought, reason, special,* and *surprise* on the board and read each word. Write the following sentences on the board:

Amy brought a special surprise for Bob.

What was the special surprise?

What was the reason Amy brought a special surprise for Bob?

Read the sentences aloud with the children. Point out that the last two sentences ask questions about the telling sentence. Invite volunteers to underline the High-Frequency Words.

Write the following sentence starters on the board and read them to children.

The special surprise Amy brought Bob was a _____.

The reason Amy brought Bob a special surprise was that _____.

Have each child read the sentence starters, completing the sentences any way they wish.

Practice

Write the following sentence frames on the board and read them with the children.

I brought a _____ as a special surprise for _____.

The reason I brought the special surprise was that _____.

Ask students to fill in the blanks as they write the sentences. Then have them illustrate their sentences. Tell them to be sure that their pictures show the special surprise as well as the reason the surprise is being given. For example, children may draw a toy being given at a birthday party or a large farewell card being given to someone who is moving.

Apply

Have children show their illustrations and read their sentences to the class. Display the pictures on a bulletin board.

Objectives

- read and write new High-Frequency Words *brought, reason, special, surprise*

Materials

- Anthology: *Julius*

Naming Parts of Sentences

Teach

Write the following sentences on the chalkboard:

<u>My grandfather</u> lives in the city of Los Angeles.

<u>My parents, puppy, and I</u> live in Riverside.

Explain to children that the *naming* part of a sentence names *someone* or *something*. Read the sentences to children. As you read each one, ask *Who or what is this sentence about*? Have volunteers draw a line under the naming part of each sentence.

Practice

Write the following sentences from *Julius* on the board:

"<u>Maya's Granddaddy</u> lived in Alabama."

"<u>He</u> lived in Alaska in the winter."

"<u>Julius</u> made a big mess in the house."

"<u>Maya</u> liked red felt."

Ask children to identify the naming part of each sentence. If they are having trouble, guide them with the question, *Who or what is this sentence about?*

Apply

Make up other simple sentences about the story. Write them on sentence strips. Have children work in pairs to identify the naming parts of the sentences. Encourage children to make up new naming parts for each sentence.

Objectives
- identify the naming parts of sentences
- put sentence parts together to make complete sentences

Materials
- Anthology: *Julius*

Review *Julius*

Ask children to review and retell *Julius*. After the retelling, have children list in a two-column chart story events that could really happen and story events that could not happen in real life.

Day 4

Objectives

- listen to and blend phonemes
- say the short vowel sounds *o, u, e*
- read and write words with the short vowel sounds *o, u, e*

Materials

- Sound/Spelling Cards: *ostrich, umbrella, elephant*

Short Vowels *o, u, e*

Teach

Remind children of the short o vowel sound, /ŏ/. Say the word *hop*, stressing each sound: /h/ /ŏ/ /p/. Ask children to blend the sounds and say the word. Say the following words, and have children hop if they hear the short *o* vowel sound: *cot, stop, go, sob, hat*. Do the same for short *u* and short *e*, having children tug if they hear short *u* in *jump, fun, cute, nut,* and *home*. Have children nod their heads yes if they hear /ĕ/ in *pen, goat, mess, peg,* and *feed*.

Display the Sound/Spelling Card *ostrich*. Review the short o sound: /ŏ/, and have children repeat it. Write the word *pop* on the board.

Use Blending Routine 2. Point to the letter(s), say the sound, and have children repeat it. Have children say the sound for p, /p/, then the sound for o, /ŏ/ then blend /p/ /ŏ/ /ŏ/ /ŏ/. Have them say the sound for p, /p/, and blend /p/ /ŏ/ /ŏ/ /ŏ/ /p/.

Display the Sound/Spelling Card *umbrella*. Review the short *u* sound. Write *bug* on the board and follow the blending procedure as above. Display the Sound/Spelling Card *elephant*. Review the short *e* sound. Write *jet* on the board, and use the blending procedure as above.

Practice

Write *pop, bug,* and *jet* as headings of a three-column chart. Read each word with children. Point out that *pop* has the short *o* vowel sound, *bug* has the short *u* vowel sound, and *jet* has the short *e* vowel sound. Work with children to generate words under the appropriate heading. Have children read the words.

pop	bug	jet
shop	truck	tent
frog	nut	desk

Apply

Have children choose one word *pop, bug,* or *jet*. Tell them to build four new words using the word they chose, replacing the first or last letter each time. Have children share their words with the group.

SKILL FOCUS: STRUCTURAL ANALYSIS   10-15 MINUTES

VCCV Pattern

Teach

Display a basket, a button, and a pencil. Have children name the items, clap out the syllables, and say the number of syllables in each word. (2) Explain that breaking words into syllables can help them figure out how to read longer words.

Write *basket* on the chalkboard. Divide it into syllables using the VCCV pattern. Mark a V under each vowel and a C under each consonant. Point to the vowel-consonant-consonant-vowel pattern. When a word follows this letter pattern, it can be divided into syllables between the consonants. Divid the word with a slash. Cover *ket* and point out that *bas* is a closed syllable, so the *a* has a short vowel sound. Blend the first syllable, *bas*. Do the same for the second syllable, *ket*. Uncover and blend the syllables together to read the entire word, *basket*. Repeat the procedure with the words *button* and *pencil*.

Practice

Write the following words on the board: *rabbit, signal, helmet*. Tell children to copy the words and use the VCCV pattern to decode them. Select a child to give verbal clues or pantomime an action elicit one of the words from the other children. For example, a child might hop across the room to get the other children to guess *rabbit*. After children identify the word, have them label it with the VCCV pattern and-divide it into syllables. Repeat with other groups of words like *catnip, traffic, attic*; *foggy, funny, dentist*; and *cactus, picnic, muffin*.

Apply

Tell each child to write three sentences using a word from the board in each one. Have children label the VCCV patterns in their sentences.

LITERATURE FOCUS: 10-15 MINUTES

Preview *Robin's Farm*

Walk children through *Robins' Farm* and discuss the illustrations.

Ask children to look at the pictures to decide whether this story is real or a fantasy.

Objectives
- identify the number of syllables in words
- use the VCCV pattern to divide unfamiliar words into syllables
- blend words with the VCCV pattern

Materials
- Phonics Library: *Robin's Farm*
- a basket, a button, and a pencil

Day 5

Objectives
- identify realistic and make-believe elements of a story
- give examples of fantasy and realism

Materials
- Anthology: *Julius*
- Phonics Library: *Big Hog's House Hunt* and *Robin's Farm*

Fantasy and Realism

Teach

Use the sentences below to discuss with children what is real and what is fantasy. For each statement, ask, *Can a human or animal really do this? Can this happen in real life?* Remind children that those things that animals and people can do are real and those that they cannot do are *fantasy*.

I will travel by airplane to visit my mother.

I will fly on a pink pig to visit my mother.

The bear jumped over the log.

The bear jumped over the moon.

Practice

Walk through the story of *Julius* with children. As they look at each of the pictures, ask questions such as the following:

Page 46: *Do you think a pig could be shipped in a crate?* (Yes)

Page 48: *Do you think a pig could eat peanut butter?* (Yes) *Do you think a big pig would live in a house?* (No)

Page 50: *Do you think a pig could make too much noise?* (Yes) *Do you think a pig would stay up late to watch movies?* (No)

As you walk through pages in the story, help children to see that the author includes both fantasy and realism.

Apply

Have children make up sentences to add to the story of *Julius* that include real and make-believe events. Tell children to illustrate their sentences.

Revisit *Julius, Big Hog's House Hunt,* and *Robin's Farm*

Page through all the stories with children and discuss the elements of fantasy and realism in each. Ask children to compare the animals in *Big Hog's House Hunt* and *Julius* to the animals in *Robin's Farm*.

Have children look through *Julius* for the following high-frequency words: *brought, reason, special,* and *surprise*. Have them also look for words with the VCCV pattern such as *butter, messes,* and *better*.

Ask children to look for words with the short *e, o* and *u* sounds in each story.

Day 1

Objectives
- recognize and say the long vowel sounds *a* and *i* in CVCe patterns
- blend and read words with the long vowels *a* and *i*

Materials
- Teaching Master ES1–5
- Practice Master ES1–5
- Letter Cards *a, e, g, i, k, l, m, t*
- Phonics Library: *Jane's Mistake*

**Get Set for Reading
CD-ROM**
Mrs. Brown Went to Town

Education Place
www.eduplace.com
Mrs. Brown Went to Town

Audio CD
Mrs. Brown Went to Town
Audio CD for **Silly Stories**

**Lexia Phonics
CD-ROM**
Primary Intervention

Long Vowels CVCe: *a, i*

Teach

Recite and repeat the chant shown. Invite children to join in as they are able.

> CHANT
>
> Mike rides a bike.
>
> Kate shuts the gate.
>
> Jake makes a cake.
>
> Nate sets a plate.

Ask children what Mike rides. Write *bike* on the board. Then ask what Kate shut and write *gate* on the board.

Point to the word *bike*. Say *bike*, stretching the long *i* sound. Have children repeat *bike*.

Underline the letter *i* in *bike*, and tell children that sometimes the letter *i* can stand for /ī/. Point out the CVCe pattern, explaining that the first vowel is usually long and the *e* is silent. Have children repeat the word *bike*, listening for the long *i* sound.

Follow a similar procedure with the word *gate* and /ā/.

Blend

Use Blending Routine 1.

Point to the first set of letters *k, i, t, e*, noting with children the CVCe pattern.

Have children listen as you sound out each letter. When you get to the final *e*, hold a finger against your lips. Then model how to blend the sounds together to make *kite*.

Give four children the letter cards *k, i, t, e*. Have children sound out each letter as you point to them. Then have children move together to form the word *kite*. Ask children to blend the sounds to say the word.

Have children identify the vowel sound in *kite* as being long or short.

Repeat the process with *time, late* and *game*.

Guided Practice

Display or distribute Teaching Master ES1–5 and read the directions at the top of the page with children. Have children read sentences and then tell which word to circle.

Read the second set of directions with children. Help them to write the circled words in the appropriate columns.

Practice/Apply

Distribute Practice Master ES1–5 and read the directions with children.

Have them work independently to put the words together to write words with the short *a* and short *i* sounds and long *a, i* sounds in the CVCe pattern and to fill in the words in the appropriate columns.

Check children's ability to read the words by having them read their answers aloud.

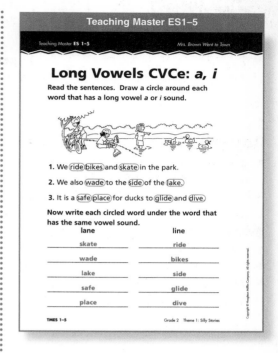

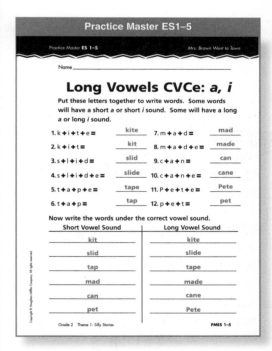

Preview *Jane's Mistake*

Walk children through *Jane's Mistake* and discuss the illustrations.

Explain to children that they will have a chance to read some long *a* and long *i* words in this story. As an example, call on volunteers to read words from the first page of the story. Have the class tell if the word contains a long *a* or a long *i* sound.

Tell children that they will read this story with the rest of the class.

Day 2

Objectives
- make predictions based on personal knowledge and story details

Materials
- Teaching Master ES1–6
- Practice Master ES1–6
- Anthology: *Mrs. Brown Went to Town*

Predicting Outcomes

Teach

Write the following number sequences on the board: 1, 2, 3, __
2, 4, 6, __

Have children examine the pattern and predict the number that comes next. Repeat with several other number sequences. Discuss how children predicted the next number by using what they know about numbers and the clues in the patterns.

Tell children that they make many predictions throughout the day, often without thinking about it. As an example, have children look out the window and describe the weather. Then ask a question that requires them to make a prediction, for instance: *Do you think it will rain today? Do you think the sun will come out today?* Encourage children to explain their predictions.

Explain that children can also make predictions when they read. Tell them that making predictions can help readers to better enjoy and understand a story.

Guided Practice

Display or distribute Teaching Master ES1–6 and discuss the picture with children. Read the story and the question with them. Tell children to use what they know to predict what might happen next.

Discuss each prediction with children. Then record reasonable suggestions on the chart.

Practice/Apply

Distribute Practice Master ES1–6 to children and read aloud the directions. Make sure children understand that they should write three things that might happen next.

Check children's ability to predict outcomes by having them share their answers with the rest of the class. Have them use specific information from the story to justify their predictions.

Preview *Mrs. Brown Went to Town*

Segment 1

Refer to the bottom of page T191 in the Teacher's Edition and preview with children Segment 1 of *Mrs. Brown Went to Town* (pages 72-81).

Note the suggestions in the Extra Support boxes on the Teacher's Edition pages T193 and T195.

Segment 2

Refer to page T191 in the Teacher's Edition and preview with children Segment 2 of *Mrs. Brown Went to Town* (pages 82-89).

Note the suggestions in the Extra Support boxes on the Teacher's Edition pages T198 and T200.

Teaching Master ES 1–6

Predicting Outcomes

Anita likes to run. For a month, she has run the track after school. She has practiced very hard for her first meet. On the day of the meet, there are four other runners to race with. At the starting bell, she takes off and feels great!

What might happen?

1. _____ Anita comes in first.
2. _____ Anita practices for many years.
3. _____ Anita wins a gold medal.

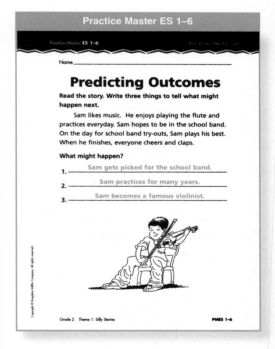

Practice Master ES 1–6

Name _____

Predicting Outcomes

Read the story. Write three things to tell what might happen next.

Sam likes music. He enjoys playing the flute and practices everyday. Sam hopes to be in the school band. On the day for school band try-outs, Sam plays his best. When he finishes, everyone cheers and claps.

What might happen?

1. _____ Sam gets picked for the school band.
2. _____ Sam practices for many years.
3. _____ Sam becomes a famous violinist.

Day 3

SKILL FOCUS   10-15 MINUTES

High-Frequency Words

Objective
- read and write new High-Frequency Words *different, floor, letter, move, poor, word*

Materials
- Anthology: *Mrs. Brown Went to Town*

Teach

Write the following High-Frequency Words and definitions on the board.

different – unusual or not the same

floor — part of a room that is on the ground and that you walk on

letter — a note written to someone

move — to change from one home to another

poor — unlucky or unfortunate

word — a small unit of spoken or written language that has meaning

Read the words and their meanings to children. Then ask children to think of and say sentences with each of the High-Frequency Words as defined on the board.

Practice

Write the following sentence frames on the board.

My _____ is different because it is _____.

I slipped on a _____ that was on the floor.

I wrote a long letter to _____ to tell her about _____.

I wish I could move to _____.

My poor _____ lost a _____.

_____ did not speak a word.

Have children complete and then illustrate each sentence.

Apply

Invite children to share their illustrations and sentences with the class. Have them exchange papers with someone who sits close to them. Then ask children to pick their favorite sentence from the paper they now have. Tell them to read their favorite sentence to the class. Ask them to tell why they like that sentence. For example, children may say their favorite sentence was funny or that the illustration was good.

Action Parts of a Sentence

Teach

Write the following sentences on the chalkboard:

My aunt and uncle <u>live on a farm</u>.

The goats and cows <u>graze on grass</u>.

The chickens and pigs <u>eat a special feed</u>.

Explain that the *action* part of a sentence tells what the naming part of the sentence *is* or *does*. Read the sentences. Then ask, *What words in the sentence tell what the naming part of the sentence is or does?* Have children underline the action parts of the sentences.

Practice

Write these sentences from *Mrs. Brown Went to Town* on the board:

"Mrs. Brown <u>lives in the barn</u>."

"The animals on her farm <u>live in the house</u>."

"They <u>slide down the stairs</u>."

Ask children to identify the action part of each sentence. Guide them with: *What words tell the naming part of the sentence?*

Apply

Write other simple sentences related to the story on sentence strips. Divide the sentence strips into the naming part and the action part. Have children identify action parts of the sentences. Have them put the sentence parts together to make complete sentences.

Objectives

- identify action parts of sentences
- put sentence parts together to make complete sentences

Review *Mrs. Brown Went to Town*

Ask children to review and retell *Mrs. Brown Went to Town*. Then ask children to use what they already know and information from the story to predict what might happen to Mrs. Brown and her animals beyond the end of the story.

Day 4

Objectives

- listen to and blend phonemes
- say the long vowel sounds *a* and *i* in the CVCe pattern
- independently read and write words with the long vowels *a* and *i* in the CVCe pattern

Materials

- Phonics Library: *The Big Surprise*
- Sound/Spelling Cards: *acorn, ice cream*

Long Vowels CVCe: *a, i*

Teach

Tell children to listen closely to these words: *pal, fast, math*. Ask children what sound they hear in the middle of each word. /ă/ Next, ask children to listen to these words: *cave, blaze, grape*. Ask children what sound they hear in the middle of each one. /ā/ Repeat this procedure with *kit, mill, brick* and *five, ride, prize*. /ĭ/ and /ī/

Write the word *can* on the board. Use Blending Routine 2 to help children blend the word. For each sound, point to the letter(s), say the sound, and have children repeat it. Have children say the sound for *c*, /k/, then the sound for *a*, /ă/, then blend /k/ /ă/ /ă/, /ă/. Finally have them say the sound for *n*, /nnn/ and blend /k/, /ă/, /ă/, /ă/, /nnn/, *can*.

Write *cane* on the board and tell children that the *e* at the end of *cane* signals a long vowel sound. Have students blend the sounds to read the word. When students get to the vowel, underline the *a* and point out the *a*-consonant-*e* pattern, which signals a long *a* vowel sound. Then display the Sound/Spelling Card *acorn*, say the long *a* sound, /ā/, and have children repeat the sound back to you. Point out the *a_e* spelling of the long *a* sound. (You may want to cover the other long *a* spellings with self-stick notes.)

Write the word *dim* on the board and blend it sound by sound. Then write *dime* on the board and blend the sounds. Tell children that the *e* at the end of *dim* signals a long *i* vowel sound. Underline *i* and point out the CVCe pattern (i_e). Then display the Sound/Spelling Card *ice cream*, say the long *i* sound, /ī/, and have children repeat the sound back to you. Point out the *i_e* spelling of the long *i* sound. (You may want to cover the other long *i* spellings with self-stick notes.)

Practice

Write *mane* and *dime* as headings of a two-column chart on the board. Read each word with children. Remind children that *mane* has the CVCe pattern with the long *a* sound and that *dime* has the CVCe pattern with the long *i* sound. Ask children to fold a piece of paper in half and write *mane* at the top of one column and *dime* at the top of the second column. Have them write words that have the CVCe pattern with the long *a* sound in the column under *mane*. Have them write words that have the long *i* sound in the column under *dime*.

Have children read their lists to the class. If children need help, have
them think about the letter sounds and blend the word.
Example:/t/ /ā/ /ā/ /ā/ /p/, *tape*.

Apply

Have children write two sentences, one with at least one word that has
the CVCe pattern with the long *a* sound and the other with at least
one word that has the CVCe pattern with the long *i* sound. Have
children read their words and write them on the chart paper.

Invite children to read their sentences to the class. Then have them
exchange papers. On the paper children now have, ask them to use
one color to circle any words that have the CVCe pattern with the long
a sound and another color to circle any words that have the CVCe
pattern with the long *i* sound. Have children read the sentences to the
class. Ask them to name which words they circled and explain the
pattern that goes with each color.

LITERATURE FOCUS: 10-15 MINUTES

Preview *The Big Surprise*

Walk children through *The Big Surprise* and discuss the illustrations,
naming the characters and using words from the story.

Ask children to predict, based on the pictures, who gets surprised and
why.

Tell children they will find out if their predictions are correct when they
read the story with the rest of the class.

Day 5

Objectives

- make predictions based on what you know about story characters
- make predictions about the story characters in similar situations

Materials

- Anthology: *Mrs. Brown Went to Town*
- Phonics Library: *Jane's Mistake, The Big Surprise*

Predicting Outcomes

Teach

Explain to children that authors often give us clues about characters by showing the way they act or the things they do. Explain, too, that these clues can often help us predict how the character might act or what the character might say in another situation.

Have children recall the wolf in *The Three Little Pigs*. Ask what the wolf would have done if there had been a fourth pig. Point out that based on what readers know about the wolf, the wolf would have tried to blow down the house of the fourth pig.

Practice

Have children think about the story, *Mrs. Brown Went to Town*. Ask them how the animals behave once Mrs. Brown leaves home. Record children's suggestions. Here are some examples.

How the Animals Act

They get into mischief.

They slide down the stairs.

They wear her clothes.

They make a mess.

Ask, *Based on what you know about how the animals behave, how do you think they might act if they were to come to school when no one was there?*

Help children to see that based on their behaviors when Mrs. Brown leaves, the animals would probably misbehave at school. Invite children to suggest things the animals might do. (Sit at the teacher's desk, swing too high on the swings on the playground, draw pictures in the storybooks, and so on.)

Apply

Have children work in pairs and brainstorm ways in which the animals might behave at other places, such as a grocery store or a clothing store, if no one was around. Help them to see that the author of *Mrs. Brown Went to Town* helps the reader understand who the characters are and how they behave. Therefore, the readers can predict how the animals might act in another similar situation.

LITERATURE FOCUS: 10–15 MINUTES

Revisit *Jane's Mistake, Mrs. Brown Went to Town,* and *The Big Surprise*

Page through all the stories with children and brainstorm different possible outcomes for each story.

Tell children to look through *Mrs. Brown Went to Town* for the following high-frequency words: *different, floor, letter, move, poor* and *word*.

Ask children to look for and say aloud words with long vowels *a, i* in the CVCe pattern in each of the stories.

Have children read aloud selected sentences or pages from the stories.

Theme 2

Nature Walk

Selections

Day 1

SKILL FOCUS: PHONICS   10–15 MINUTES

o, u, e in CVCe Patterns

Objectives

- associate the long vowel sound with *o, u,* and *e* in CVCe patterns
- blend and read words with the long vowels *o, u,* and *e*

Materials

- Teaching Master ES2–1
- Letter Cards: *c, e, e, h, l, m, n, o, s, t, u, v*
- Phonics Library: *Miss Pig's Garden*

Technology

Get Set for Reading CD-ROM
Henry and Mudge and the Starry Night

Education Place
www.eduplace.com
Henry and Mudge and the Starry Night

Audio CD
Henry and Mudge and the Starry Night
Audio CD for **Nature Walk**

Lexia Phonics CD-ROM
Primary Intervention

Teach

Recite the chant. Repeat it, inviting children to join in.

> CHANT
> Look at every pretty rose.
> Steve will use these,
> And Eve will use those.

Say *rose* and *those*, stretching out the long *o* sound. Have children repeat /ō/ and name the vowel sound: long *o*. Say *use*, stretching out the long *u* sound. Have children repeat /ū/ and name the vowel sound: long *u*. Say *Steve, eve,* and *these*, stretching out the long *e* sound. Have children repeat /ē/ and name the vowel sound: long *e*.

Display *rose, those, use, Steve, Eve, these,* and read them with children. Point to the final *e* in each word and to the vowel and consonant before it. Display the pairs *cub* and *cube* to show how the final *e* changes the short *u* to a long one.

Blend

Display the letters *c, u, t, e*. Have children name the letters. Point out the vowel *u*, consonant *t*, and final *e*—the VCe pattern. Have children listen as you say the sound for each letter, /k/ /ū/ /t/ and then hold a finger against your lips for final *e*. Use Blending Routine 1, and have children blend the sounds to say the word *cute*.

Give four children the letter cards *h, o, l, e*. Point to a card, and have that child say the sound for the letter, or hold a finger to the lips signaling a silent letter. Then have children move together to say the word *hole*. Continue with the words *eve, hose, note, stove, use,* and *mule*.

Guided Practice

Display or **distribute** Teaching Master ES2-1 and discuss the pictures with children.

Read the sentence and boxed words with children. Help them to complete the sentences.

Check children's ability to read long vowel words with the VCe pattern.

Two Sounds for *g*

Teach

Recite the chant. Repeat it, inviting children to join in.

> **CHANT**
> Gordon the goat ate the garden.
> Gene the giraffe ate the hedge.

Say *Gordon, goat, garden*, emphasizing /g/, and have children repeat them. Write the three words, underlining each *g* and repeating /g/. Tell children that /g/ is called the hard *g* sound.

Say *Gene, giraffe, hedge*, emphasizing /j/, and have children repeat them. Write the words, underlining *G* in *Gene*, *g* in *giraffe*, and *dge* in *hedge*. Point out that only the sound /j/ is heard in the *dge* combination. Tell children that /j/ is called the soft *g* sound.

Blend

Display the letters *h, u, g*. Have children name the letters, say the sound for each: /h/ /ŭ/ /g/, and use Blending Routine 1 to say the word *hug*.

Add final *e* to *hug*, reminding children that it is silent. Have them blend the word *huge* with you: /h/ /ū/ /j/. Write these words: *budge, green, rag, rage, stingy, ginger.* Have children blend them and identify words with hard *g* (green, rag) and words with soft *g*. (budge, rage, stingy, ginger)

Practice/Apply

Distribute Practice Master ES2–1 and read the directions. Have children work independently to read the sentences, circle the words with *g*, and write them under the correct sound for *g*.

Check children's ability to associate the letter *g* with two sounds.

Preview *Miss Pig's Garden*

Walk children through *Miss Pig's Garden* and discuss the illustrations. Have them say the vowel sound in *rose* and the sound for *g* in *garden*.

Objectives
- identify the two sounds for *g*
- read and write words with *g*

Materials
- Practice Master ES2–1
- Letter Cards: *e, g, h, u*

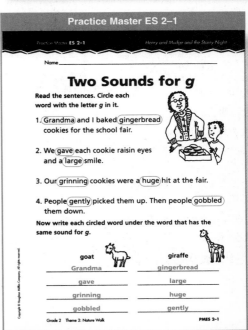

Day 2

Objectives
- compare and contrast characters in a story
- use a Venn diagram to compare story characters

Materials
- Teaching Master ES2–2
- Practice Master ES2–2
- Anthology: *Henry and Mudge and the Starry Night*

Compare and Contrast

Teach

Ask volunteers to tell how they are like another family member. They may describe similar facial features, similar interests, similar talents. List a few ideas on the board.

Continue by asking volunteers to name some differences between themselves and family members. Children may note different hair colors, different interests, different ages, and so on. Select ideas to list in a different section of the board.

Draw on the board a large Venn diagram to show how a volunteer's similarities and differences can be shown. Example:

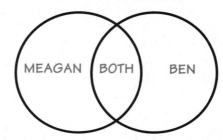

Explain that people have similarities and differences, and so do story characters. Tell children that it can be interesting to think about how characters are alike and different.

Guided Practice

Display or **distribute** Teaching Master ES2–2. Discuss the illustration.

Have children name the labels in the Venn diagram and tell where to write information about Goose, about Duck, and about both.

Read aloud the following story:

Read Aloud

> *Goose and Duck both live at Wildwood Lake. They are good swimmers. Every day Goose swims from a little island in the middle of the lake to the shore. Duck swims from the shore to the little island in the middle of the lake. As they pass each other, they nod and say hello. Goose nods her long neck and calls HONK HONK. Duck nods her short neck and calls QUACK QUACK.*

Have children recall details to help you fill out the Venn diagram.

Practice/Apply

Distribute Practice Master ES2–2 and read the directions with children.

Have children read the sentences independently or with a partner.

Call on volunteers to name one way in which Snowflake and Midnight are alike, and to tell where they will write that detail. (in the middle section, under "Both")

Have children complete the page independently.

Check their responses by calling on volunteers to name ways in which the characters are alike and ways in which they are different.

LITERATURE FOCUS: 20–30 MINUTES

Preview *Henry and Mudge and the Starry Night*

Segment 1

Refer to the bottom of page T47 in the Teacher's Edition and preview with children Segment 1 of *Henry and Mudge and the Starry Night* (pages 133–149).

Note the suggestions in the Extra Support boxes on the Teacher's Edition pages T51 and T54.

Segment 2

Refer to the bottom of page T47 in the Teacher's Edition and preview with children Segment 2 of *Henry and Mudge and the Starry Night* (pages 150–157).

Note the suggestions in the Extra Support box on the Teacher's Edition page T58.

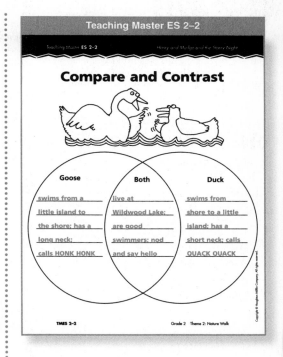

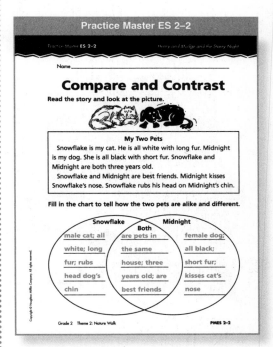

Day 3

Objective

• read and write new High-Frequency Words: *beautiful, even, quiet, straight, year*

SKILL FOCUS: 10–15 MINUTES

High-Frequency Words

Teach

Write *beautiful, quiet,* and *straight* in a three-column chart on the board and read each word.

Have children brainstorm a list of things that could be *beautiful, quiet,* and *straight.* Possible answers include:

beautiful	quiet	straight
flowers	libraries	measuring
people	nighttime	rulers
songs	mice	straight pins

Draw a four-column chart on the board with the headings *Fall, Winter, Spring,* and *Summer.* Label the chart *Favorite Time of Year.* Underline the word *Year.* Read the title of the chart and the names of the four seasons. Conduct a survey to find out which season each child likes best. Mark the chart to show the results of the survey.

Write *even* on the board and read it to children. Point out that this word has many meanings. Explain that today the class is going to use the word *even* to stress that something is true. Write this sentence on the board: *Everyone at school was dressed in a costume, even the principal.* Read the sentence aloud. Ask a volunteer to tell what the sentence is trying to point out as being true. (The principal is wearing a costume like everyone else in the school.)

Practice

Write the following sentence frames on the board, and read them with children.

> I think a _____ is beautiful.
> I think a _____ is quiet.
> I think a _____ is straight.
> I think the best time of year is _____.
> I like animals, even _____.

Have them copy the sentences and draw pictures to illustrate how they would complete each one.

Apply

Have children read their sentences, share their illustrations, and trade papers. Have them read one of the sentences from that paper, substituting the name of the child who wrote the sentence for the word *I*, and changing the verb. For example: *Juan thinks a horse is beautiful.*

SKILL FOCUS: GRAMMAR   10–15 MINUTES

Telling Sentences and Questions

Teach

Tell children that you are thinking of an object in the room. Invite children to ask you things about the object to try to guess what it is. As you play, record some of children's questions and your responses.

Explain to children that sentences that ask something are *questions*, and they end with a question mark. Explain that sentences that tell something are *telling sentences* and they end with a period. Have volunteers point to the question and the telling sentence on the chalkboard.

Practice

Read aloud sentences from *Henry and Mudge and the Starry Night.* Instruct children to stand if the sentence is a question, and to clap their hands if the sentence is a telling sentence.

Apply

Have children work independently to write three telling sentences and three questions about the story.

LITERATURE FOCUS   10–15 MINUTES

Review *Henry and Mudge and the Starry Night*

Have children review and retell *Henry and Mudge and the Starry Night.* Then have them choose two story characters and discuss how they are alike and different. You might want children to write their ideas in a Venn diagram.

Objectives
- identify telling sentences and questions
- recognize differences in intonation
- form telling sentences and questions

Materials
- Anthology: *Henry and Mudge and the Starry Night*

RETEACH
SKILL FOCUS: PHONICS   10–15 MINUTES

o, u, and e in CVCe Patterns

Teach

Tell children to listen to and blend these sounds:/h//ō//p/. Have children repeat the sounds and say the word. (hope) Repeat with *cube* and *eve*.

Write *hope* on the board. Underline the *o* and point out the *o-consonant-e* pattern. Remind children that this pattern usually signals a long *o* vowel sound and that the *e* is silent. Use Blending Routine 2 to help children blend the sounds. Have children say the sound for *h*, /h/, then the long vowel sound for *o*, /ō/ then blend /h/ /ō ō ō/. Finally, have them say the sound for *p*, /p/, and blend /h/ /ō ō ō/ /p/, *hope*.

Display the Sound/Spelling Card *ocean*, say the long *o* sound, and have children repeat it. Point out the *o_e* spelling of the long *o* sound. (You may want to cover the other long *o* spellings with self-stick notes.)

Write the word *mule* on the board. Underline the *u* and tell children that the *u*-consonant-e pattern often signals a long *u* sound. Repeat the Blending Routine 2 procedure.

Display the Sound/Spelling Card *unicorn*, say the long *u* sound, and have children repeat it. Point out the *u_e* spelling of long *u*. Write the word *Pete*, and point out the *e*-consonant-e pattern which signals a long *e* sound.

Practice

Write this sentence on chart paper: *Eve played a cute joke on her dad.* Read the sentence with children, and have a volunteer use green to circle the word that has the CVCe pattern with the long *e* sound. (Eve) Repeat this process with long *o* in *joke* and long *u* sound in *cute*, having volunteers use different colors to circle these words.

Apply

Write the following words in columns on chart paper. Have children blend the sounds and read the words.

cube	home	close
complete	rule	these
awoke	Pete	rude

Ask children to use green to circle words with the CVCe pattern long *e*, blue for words with the CVCe pattern long *o*, and red for words that have the CVCe pattern long *u*.

Objectives

- listen to and blend phonemes
- say the long vowel sound for *o, u,* and *e* in CVCe patterns
- read and write words with the long vowels *o,u,e* in the CVCe pattern

Materials

- Sound/Spelling Cards *ocean, unicorn*
- red, blue, and green markers or crayons
- Phonics Library: *Mike and Dave Sleep Outside*

Two Sounds for *g*

Teach

Tell children to listen to these words: *gumdrop, goat, garlic.* Ask children what sound they hear at the beginning of each word. /g/ Follow the same procedure with *gymnastics, germ, giant.* /j/

Write *pig, gate,* and *gold* on the board, read the words, and have children repeat them. Ask children what sound these words have in common. /g/ Explain that each of these words has the /g/ sound spelled with the letter *g.* Display the Sound/Spelling Card *goose.* Point to the *g* spelling, say /g/, and have children repeat it. Underline the letter *g* in the words on the board, and blend the sounds to read them.

Follow a simular procedure with *gym, gem,* and *badge* and the Sound/Spelling Card *jumping Jill.* Remind children that *g* often has the soft sound /j/ when followed by *i, e,* or *y.*

Practice

Write *gate* and *gem* on the board in a two-column chart. Display *gum,* and have a child read the word and copy it onto the board in the correct column. Repeat this procedure with words *stage, giant, gate, germ, gold, giraffe, dodge,* and *tug.*

Apply

Have each child write a silly sentence using at least one word in which the letter *g* has the /g/ sound, and one word in which the letter g has the /j/ sound. Example: *The giant golden goose was larger than a giraffe.*

Objectives

- listen to and blend phonemes
- identify the two sounds of *g*
- read and write words in which g has the /g/ sound and those in which *g* has the /j/ sound

Materials

- Sound/Spelling Cards *goose, jumping Jill*
- Phonics Library: *Mike and Dave Sleep Outside*

Preview *Mike and Dave Sleep Outside*

Walk children through *Mike and Dave Sleep Outside.* Have them read the first page of the story to name the story characters. Then have them use picture clues to tell how Mike and Dave are alike and how they are different.

Day 5

Objectives
- identify similarities and differences among events and characters
- use a Venn diagram to compare story characters

Materials
- Anthology: *Henry and Mudge and the Starry Night*
- Phonics Library: *Mike and Dave Sleep Outside, Miss Pig's Garden*

Compare and Contrast

Teach

Begin a discussion with children about dogs and cats. Ask, *What is similar about the two animals?* (they are both pets, both like to play) Record children's suggestions in the center section of a Venn diagram.

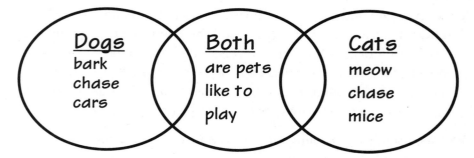

Ask children to tell how dogs and cats are different and record their suggestions under the headings *Dogs* and *Cats* on the Venn diagram. When finished, explain to children that when they tell how things are similar, they are comparing. Explain, too, that when they tell how things are different, they are contrasting.

Practice

Review the story events on pages 151–155 of *Henry and Mudge and the Starry Night.*

Use a Venn diagram to record what Henry does, what Mudge does, and what they both do. Ask children to use this information to compare and contrast what Henry and Mudge do on the camping trip.

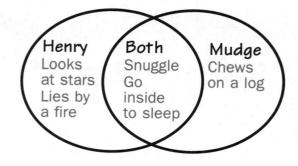

Apply

Have children work in pairs to use a Venn diagram to compare and contrast two other characters in the story, for example, Henry's parents or Henry and his father.

LITERATURE FOCUS: 10–15 MINUTES

Revisit *Henry and Mudge and the Starry Night, Mike and Dave Sleep Outside,* **and** *Miss Pig's Garden*

Page through all the stories with children and ask them to compare and contrast *Henry and Mudge and the Starry Night, Mike and Dave Sleep Outside* and *Miss Pig's Garden*.

Have children look for High-Frequency Words *beautiful, even, quiet, straight,* and *year* in *Henry and Mudge and the Starry Night* and *Miss Pig's Garden*.

Tell children to look through *Henry and Mudge and the Starry Night, Mike and Dave Sleep Outside* and *Miss Pig's Garden* for words with two sounds for *g* and words with long vowel patterns *o*-consonant-*e*, *u*-consonant-*e*, and *e*-consonant-*e*.

Day 1

Objectives
- say words with consonant clusters *r, l, s*
- read and write words with consonant clusters *r, l, s*

Materials
- Teaching Master ES2–3
- Letter Cards: *d, o, p, r,*
- Phonics Library: *A Trip to Central Park*

Get Set for Reading
CD-ROM
Exploring Parks with Ranger Dockett

Education Place
www.eduplace.com
Exploring Parks with Ranger Dockett

Audio CD
Exploring Parks with Ranger Dockett
Audio CD for **Nature Walk**

Lexia Phonics
CD-ROM
Primary Intervention

Consonant Clusters *r, l, s*

Teach

Recite the chant. Repeat it, inviting children to join in.

> **CHANT**
> Fresh fruit, fresh fruit
> Smells so sweet.
> Please help yourself
> to a fresh fruit treat.

Say *fresh* and *fruit*, emphasizing the two initial consonant sounds but blending them smoothly, /fr/. Have children similarly emphasize the consonant cluster as they repeat *fresh fruit.* Write *fresh* and *fruit* and underline the consonant cluster *fr* in each. Point out that the sound for each letter is heard: /f/ and /r/, but they are blended together: /fr/.

Say *smells, sweet, please,* and *treat.* Emphasize each initial consonant cluster as you write *smells, sweet, please,* and *treat,* and have children tell you the two consonant letters that begin each word. (sm, sw, pl, tr)

Say *help* and *yourself,* emphasizing the final consonant sounds but blending them smoothly, /lp/ and /lf/. Have children similarly repeat *help yourself.* Write *help* and *yourself,* and have children tell you the two consonant letters that end each word. (lp, lf)

Blend

Display the letters *p, l, u, m.* Have children name the letters and note the consonant cluster *pl.* Use Blending Routine 1 to model blending the sounds to make /pl/ /ŭ/ /m/. Have children blend the sounds.

Give four volunteers the Letter Cards *d, r, o, p.* Point to a card, and have that child say the sound for the letter. Then have the first two children move close together and blend the consonant cluster *dr.* The other volunteers say /ŏ/ and /p/. Then have children say the whole word.

Guided Practice

Display or **distribute** Teaching Master ES2-3. Point out words with consonant clusters, help children say them, underline the initial or final cluster, and list the words in one of the columns.

Check children's ability with clusters by having them read the listed words.

SKILL FOCUS: PHONICS   10–15 MINUTES

Two Sounds for c

Objectives
- identify the two sounds for c
- read and write words with c

Materials
- Practice Master ES2–3
- Letter Cards: c, e, n, t

Teach

Recite the chant. Repeat, inviting children to join in.

> **CHANT**
> The cat left the country
> to find mice in the city.

Say *cat* and *country*, emphasizing /k/. Have children repeat the words. Write *cat* and *country*, underlining each *c* and repeating /k/. Tell children that /k/ is called the hard *c* sound. Follow the same procedure with *mice* and *city*, emphasizing /s/. Tell children that /s/ is called the soft *c* sound.

Blend

Display the letters *c, e, n, t*. Have children name the letters and say these sounds: /s/ /ĕ/ /nt/. Use Blending Routine 1 to have them blend the sounds to say *cent*. Continue with: *cave, nice, cold, icy, place, pencil*. Ask children to point out the words with hard *c* (cave, cold) and the words with soft *c* (nice, icy, place, pencil).

Practice/Apply

Distribute Practice Master ES2–3, and read both sets of directions with children. Have them independently complete the Practice Master.

Check children's ability to associate the letter *c* with two sounds by having them read their word lists aloud.

LITERATURE FOCUS: 10–15 MINUTES

Preview *A Trip to Central Park*

Walk children through *A Trip to Central Park*. Discuss the illustrations. Help children to identify the soft *c* in *Central* and the consonant cluster *tr* in both *trip* and *central*.

Teaching Master ES 2–3

Consonant Clusters
r, l, s

"Help!" cried Fred. "This bug is a pest."
Fred shook his fist at the bug. "Stop flying here!"
Fred clapped to try to get rid of the bug.
The bug came to rest on Fred's chest.
Fred gave himself a slap.
The bug flew off.
"At last, it is gone!" said Fred.

l clusters	r clusters	s clusters
Help	cried	pest
flying	Fred	fist
clapped	try	Stop
himself		rest
slap		chest
flew		slap
		last

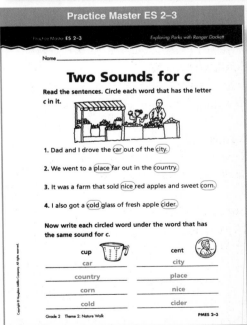

Practice Master ES 2–3

Two Sounds for c

Read the sentences. Circle each word that has the letter c in it.

1. Dad and I drove the (car) out of the (city).
2. We went to a (place) far out in the (country).
3. It was a farm that sold (nice) red apples and sweet (corn).
4. I also got a (cold) glass of fresh apple (cider).

Now write each circled word under the word that has the same sound for c.

cup	cent
car	city
country	place
corn	nice
cold	cider

Day 2

Objective
• distinguish fact and opinion

Materials
• Teaching Master ES2–4
• Practice Master ES2–4
• Anthology: *Exploring Parks with Ranger Dockett*

Fact and Opinion

Teach

Lead a discussion about the lunch routine in your school. Ask questions that elicit facts and opinions.

Record selected suggestions in a two-column chart, as in this example:

Facts	Opinions
Lunch costs $1.90.	The tacos are the best lunch.
You can buy a weekly ticket.	The lunchroom is too noisy.
You can bring your own lunch.	The lunch line is slow.

Say: *Facts are statements that can be proved true or false.* Have children reread the Facts list and tell how they could prove each statement. (Examples: Check the price in the lunchroom, ask about weekly tickets, just watch to see kids with their own lunches.)

Say: *Opinions are people's thoughts and feelings about something. Opinions cannot be proved true or false.* Have children reread the Opinions list and tell why people might agree or disagree with the statements.

Guided Practice

Display or **distribute** Teaching Master ES2–4. Discuss the illustrations with children.

Read the first pair of sentences. Remind children that a fact is a statement that can be proved true. Ask them to identify the fact and tell how it could be proved. ("Birds have feathers." Look in a science book. Ask a bird scientist.) Have children tell why "Birds are the best pets" is an opinion. (People with dogs or cats or other pets might disagree. There's no way to prove who's right.)

Continue with the remaining sentences, writing F or O before each.

Check children's understanding by asking them to state an additional fact and an additional opinion for each set of sentences.

Practice/Apply

Distribute Practice Master ES2–4 . Read aloud the directions

Ask children what they can tell about hermit crabs from the picture and what they know from their own experience.

Have them read the story and complete the page independently.

Check children's ability to distinguish fact and opinion by having them tell why they identified some statements as facts and others as opinions.

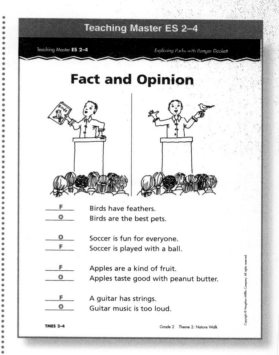

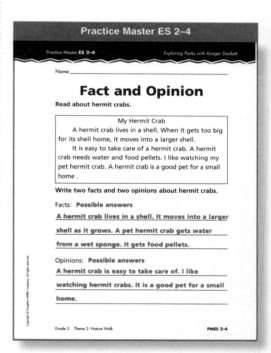

LITERATURE FOCUS: 20–30 MINUTES

Preview *Exploring Parks with Ranger Dockett*

Segment 1

Refer to the bottom of page T129 in the Teacher's Edition and preview with children Segment 1 of *Exploring Parks with Ranger Dockett* (pages 169–175).

Note the suggestions in the Extra Support boxes on the Teacher's Edition pages T130 and T131.

Segment 2

Refer to the bottom of page T129 in the Teacher's Edition and preview with children Segment 2 of *Exploring Parks with Ranger Dockett* (pages 176–183).

Note the suggestions in the Extra Support boxes on the Teacher's Edition pages T134 and T136.

Day 3

High-Frequency Words

Objective
• read and write new High-Frequency Words: *busy, important, later, touch, young*

Teach

Write *busy, important, later, touch,* and *young* on the board and read each word.

Display this poem:

There is a busy little bee,

Who makes delicious honey tea.

This important job he does,

With a busy little buzz.

Later, this bee will make,

A little lemon honey cake.

"Come young, come old," says little bee,

Touch and eat the cake and sip the honey tea.

Read the poem with children. Invite volunteers to circle and read the High-Frequency Words.

Practice

Write the following sentence frames on the board and have children read them to you.

The bee is _____.

He has an _____ job.

The bee will make the cake_____.

Old and _____ bees will come.

They can _____ and eat the cake.

Have children copy the sentences and fill in a High-Frequency Word to complete each sentence.

Apply

Have children show and read their sentences to a partner.

Direct children to draw a picture to go with the sentences.

Commands

Teach

Ask children to tell what parents say when they want children to do something. Record children's responses on the chalkboard.

> Put on a sweater.
> Take the dog out.

Point out that all of the sentences on the chalkboard give orders or tell someone what to do. Explain that a sentence that gives an order is called a command.

Practice

Brainstorm with children a list of commands Ranger Dockett might use on a tour. Examples might include:

Come this way.

Follow me.

Take children on a guided tour of the classroom, to model commands. Ask children to raise hands to signal when a command is used.

Apply

Have children take turns giving a partner a tour of the classroom. Remind children to use commands to tell their partner what to do.

Ask children to write down some of the commands they used.

Review *Exploring Parks with Ranger Dockett*

Ask children to review and retell *Exploring Parks with Ranger Dockett*. After the retelling, ask partners to state one fact and one opinion about the story.

Objectives
• recognize commands
• form sentences that give orders

Materials
• Anthology: *Exploring Parks with Ranger Dockett*

Day 4

Objectives

- identify words with consonant clusters *r,l,s*
- listen for consonant clusters *r,l,s*
- read and write words with consonant clusters *r,l,s*

RETEACH

SKILL FOCUS: PHONICS 10–15 MINUTES

Consonant Clusters *r, l, s*

Teach

Tell children to listen to and blend these sounds:/tr/ /ā/ /n/. Have children repeat the sounds and say the word. (train)

Repeat the procedure with *glad* and *sleep*.

Draw a picture of a tree on the board. Ask children to name the object. Write *tree* on the board and underline the *tr*. Have children read the word with you, listening for the beginning sounds /tr/. Explain that when *r* appears after another consonant, the two sounds are blended together.

Follow the same procedure with the words *clock* for *l* clusters, and *star* for *s* clusters.

Point out that consonant clusters do not always come at the beginning of a word. Write the words *best*, *afraid*, and *complete* on the board. Have volunteers underline the consonant clusters *st*, *fr*, and *pl*.

Use Blending Routine 2 to help children blend the sounds to read each word. For the two-syllable words, label the vowels and consonants, and help children divide the words into syllables. Then cover up parts of the words as needed to help children sound them out. Point out that the letters in a consonant cluster often stay together in the same syllable.

Practice

Draw a three-column chart on the board with the headings *r, l,* and *s*. Have children name words that have consonant clusters with *r, l,* and *s*. Point out that some words can fit under more than one heading.

Apply

Ask children to write sentences using one word from each section of the chart. Ask them to underline the words with *r, l,* and *s* consonant clusters.

Have children pair up and read their sentences to each other. Then as one member of the pair reads a sentence aloud to the whole group, the other can point to the words on the chart that are used in the sentence.

SKILL FOCUS: PHONICS | 10–15 MINUTES

Two Sounds for c

Teach

Tell children to listen closely to these words: *camp, coast, color*. Ask children what sound they hear at the beginning of each word. (/k/) Write *can, cave,* and *cup* on the board, read the words, and have children repeat them with you. Ask children what sound these words have in common. (/k/, spelled with the letter c) Display the large Sound/Spelling Card *cat*. Review the /k/ sound, and point out the *c* spelling of the sound. Underline the letter *c* in each word on the board.

Ask children to listen to these words: *city, ice, cymbal*. Ask what same sound children hear in each word. (/s/) Write *city, ice,* and *cymbal* on the board. Read the words, and have children repeat them with you. Explain that in these words the letter *c* spells the /s/ sound. Display the Sound/Spelling Card *seal*, and point out the *c* spelling of /s/. Tell children that the letter *c* often has the soft sound, /s/ when followed by *i, e,* or *y*. Underline the *ci* in *city*, the *ce* in *ice*, and the *cy* in *cymbal*.

Practice

Ask children to write two sentences using words from the board. Each sentence should contain at least one word with the /k/ sound for *c* and one word with the /s/ sound for *c*. Example: *What color paint would you like on your fence?*

Apply

Tell children to underline the words from their sentences that have the /k/ sound and to circle words that have the /s/ sound.

Invite children to read their sentences to the class. As one child reads a sentence, another child can point to each *c* word that appears on the chart. The class can then read each *c* word together.

LITERATURE FOCUS: | 10–15 MINUTES

Preview *Zeke and Pete Rule!*

Walk children through *Zeke and Pete Rule!* Ask them if they can name a fact about Zeke, and one about Pete, from looking at the pictures.

Objectives
- recognize that there are two sounds for *c*
- listen to words and identify two sounds for *c*
- independently read and write words with two different sounds for *c*

Materials
- Sound/Spelling Cards *cat, seal*
- Phonics Library: *Zeke and Pete Rule!*

Day 5

Objectives
- distinguish between fact and opinion
- identify fact and opinion in the story

Materials
- Anthology: *Exploring Parks with Ranger Dockett*
- Phonics Library: *A Trip to Central Park, Zeke and Pete Rule!*

Fact and Opinion

Teach

Hold up a classroom object for children and ask them to describe it.

Record suggestions in a two-column chart, noting facts in one column and opinions in the other. The chart might be similar to the following:

Facts	Opinions
The ball is yellow.	The ball is fun to play with.
The ball is 8 inches high.	The ball is too small.

Explain that the first column lists facts about the object that can be proven true or false, and that the second column lists opinions, or children's thoughts, beliefs, or feelings about the object. Tell children that, unlike facts, opinions cannot be proven right or wrong and that we can only agree or disagree with them.

Practice

Write the following sentences on the chalkboard:

Have children decide which sentences are facts and which ones are opinions. As you point to each sentence ask:

> Spiders are beautiful. (Opinion)
> Spiders have eight legs. (Fact)
> Oranges grow on trees. (Fact)
> Oranges are my favorite fruit. (Opinion)

- *Does the sentence tell what someone thinks, feels, or believes?*

- *Can the statement be proven right or wrong?*

Apply

Read the following sentences from Exploring Parks with Ranger Docket:

"Ranger Docket was a Boy Scout when he was a little boy."

"The Park is his exciting classroom."

Have children decide which sentence is a fact and which one is an opinion. Then ask children to work independently to write three facts and three opinions about the story.

LITERATURE FOCUS: 10–15 MINUTES

Revisit *Exploring Parks with Ranger Dockett, A Trip to Central Park,* and *Zeke and Pete Rule!*

Page through all the stories with children and review the illustrations and text in each story to recall the facts and opinions.

Have children look through *Exploring Parks with Ranger Dockett, A Trip to Central Park,* and *Zeke and Pete Rule!* for High-Frequency words *busy, important, later, touch* and *young,* and for telling sentences and questions.

Ask children to look for and say words with consonant clusters *r, l,* and *s.*

Day 1

Objectives

- say one sound for a double consonant or *ck* at the end of a word
- read and write words with final double consonants and *ck*

Materials

- Teaching Master ES2–5
- Letter Cards: *c, e, f, f, i, k, l, l, m, o, p, s, s, t, u*

Get Set for Reading CD-ROM

Around the Pond: Who's Been Here?

Education Place

www.eduplace.com
Around the Pond: Who's Been Here?

Audio CD

Around the Pond: Who's Been Here?
Audio CD for **Nature Walk**

Lexia Phonics CD-ROM

Primary Intervention

PRETEACH

SKILL FOCUS: PHONICS   10–15 MINUTES

Double Final Consonants

Teach

Recite the chant. Repeat it, inviting children to join in.

> CHANT
> Huff and puff
> Run up the hill.
> Lie back in the grass
> Stay very still.

Repeat the word *huff*. Then say its final consonant sound: /f/. Have children say *huff* and repeat the final sound. Write *huff* and *puff* on the board, and underline the *double f*. Tell children that when they see double consonants at the end of a word, they should say only one sound. Follow the same procedure with these words from the *chant*: *hill*, *grass*, *still*. Write *back* on the board, and underline the letters *ck*. Tell children that *ck* spells just one sound: /k/.

Blend

Display the letters *m, e, s, s*. Have children name the letters. Use Blending Routine 1 to model how to blend the three sounds /m/ /ĕ/ /s/ to say *mess*. Then have children blend the sounds. Give four children the letter cards. Have the first two children say their letter sounds in order and the second two say their sounds together. Follow a similar procedure using letter cards for these words: *miss*, *lock*, *spell*, *stuff*.

Guided Practice

Display or **distribute** Teaching Master ES2-5. Have children tell about each picture.

Point to the first pair of words. Call on volunteers to blend the letters and read the words.

Have a child read the sentence. Ask: *Which word from the box makes sense with this sentence and picture?* Write *kick* to complete the sentence.

Repeat with the other three sentences.

Check children's understanding by having them read the unused word in each box and use it in an oral sentence.

SKILL FOCUS: PHONICS   10–15 MINUTES

VCCV Pattern: Double Consonants

Teach

Recite the chant. Repeat it, inviting children to join in.

> CHANT
> Yellow buttons
> On the collar
> Of my jacket.

Say *yellow*, clapping each syllable beat. Have children tell how many syllables they hear (2). Write *yellow* on the board. Draw a slash between the syllables, and say each syllable separately: *yell/ow*.

Tell children that if they see a long word with double consonants in the middle, they should break the word apart after the consonants and say each syllable separately. Remind them that a double consonant stands for just one sound. Model by blending the syllables of *yellow, buttons,* and *collar*. Write the word *jacket*. Remind children that *ck* together spell one sound /k/, so they are usually the same in syllable. Have children help you say each syllable, and then the whole word.

Blend

Display *rabbit*. Ask children where to break the word into syllables (between the b's). Draw a slash: *rab/bit*. Use Blending Routine 1 to blend each syllable and the syllables together. Continue with: *pillow, attic, gallon, lesson, traffic, lesson, bucket*.

Practice/Apply

Distribute Practice Master ES2–5. Go over the directions, and have children work independently to complete the Practice Master.

Check children's ability to separate syllables.

LITERATURE FOCUS: 10–15 MINUTES

Preview *In the Woods*

Walk children through *In the Woods*, and discuss the illustrations.

Objectives
- divide words into syllables between double consonants
- keep the letters *ck* together when dividing a word between consonants

Materials
- Practice Master ES2–5
- Phonics Library: *In the Woods*

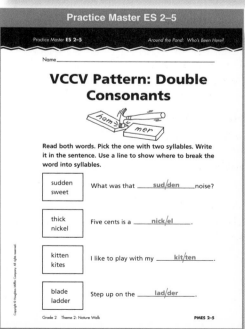

Day 2

SKILL FOCUS: COMPREHENSION   25–30 MINUTES

Categorize and Classify

Teach

Say: *Listen to this list of things packed in a big bag: a beach ball, a towel, skin lotion, a plastic pail and shovel, and a pair of woolen mittens.*

Ask children whether any of the listed things seems not to belong in the bag, and why. (A pair of woolen mittens doesn't belong. Mittens are for cold weather. The other items are for the beach.)

Tell children to think about the reasons that things may belong together in a group.

Guided Practice

Display or **distribute** Transparency Master ES2–6. Have children identify each object shown.

Read aloud the following story accompanying the illustrations. Repeat it so that children can recall the items named.

Objectives
- categorize and classify objects in a story
- categorize and classify objects in lists

Materials
- Teaching Master ES2–6
- Practice Master ES2–6
- Anthology: *Around the Pond: Who's Been Here?*

> **Read Aloud**
>
> *This is a sunny afternoon. I am lying on my back to watch the sky. I see puffy clouds floating slowly. I see a big yellow sun. I see a pale half moon. I see silver airplanes glinting in the sunlight. I see a kite flapping gently. Geese are flying in the shape of a V. A hawk is circling high. A butterfly flutters by. A squirrel leaps from one tall tree branch to another. There is so much to see on this beautiful day.*

Have children guide you in deciding where in the chart to put each of the items depicted in the art and named in the story.

Review by hiding the category names in the chart and having children tell what the listed items in each group have in common.

Practice/Apply

Distribute Practice Master ES2–6 . Read the directions at the top of the page and review the example. Then review the directions accompanying the framed picture art in the bottom of the page. Have children name each animal and decide on a category label.

Direct children to complete the Practice Master independently.

Check children's understanding by having them add another item to each of the five lists and to the frame of farm animals. (Possible responses: 1. pear; 2. tea; 3. puddle; 4. wasp; 5. office building; another farm animal, such as goat or bull.)

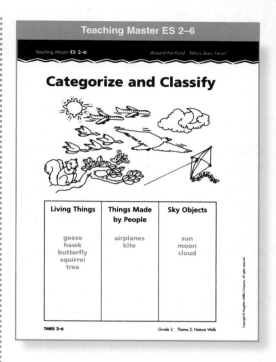

LITERATURE FOCUS:　　　　　20–30 MINUTES

Preview *Around the Pond: Who's Been Here?*

Segment 1

Refer to the bottom of page T195 in the Teacher's Edition and preview with children Segment 1 of *Around the Pond: Who's Been Here?* (pages 191–201).

Note the suggestions in the Extra Support boxes on the Teacher's Edition pages T198 and T199.

Segment 2

Refer to the bottom of page T195 in the Teacher's Edition and preview with children Segment 2 of *Around the Pond: Who's Been Here?* (pages 202–213).

Note the suggestions in the Extra Support boxes on the Teacher's Edition pages T201 and T206.

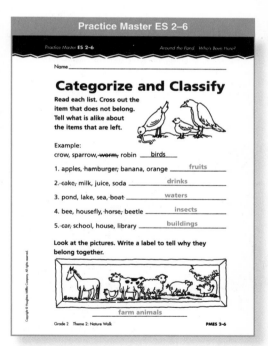

Day 3

Objective

- read and write new High-Frequency Words: *across, brother, great, stand.*

High-Frequency Words

Teach

Write *across, brother, great,* and *stand* on the board and read each word. Point out that each word has a consonant cluster. Ask volunteers to underline the consonant clusters (*cr, br, gr, st*) in the words. Remind students that these consonant clusters have two sounds that are blended together.

Write the following sentence starters on the board, underline the High Frequency word in each, and read the sentence starters aloud.

Tell children that they are going to fill in each blank using a word or words that have the same first consonant cluster as the High-Frequency Word in that sentence. Refer to the High-Frequency Words with underlined consonant clusters you wrote on the board earlier. Have children take turns reading the sentences and orally filling in the blanks.

I walked <u>across</u> the _____. (creek, cracks, crater, craft store)

I <u>heard</u> my brother _____. (Brian, break a glass, breathing, baking bread)

I <u>saw</u> some great _____. (grapes, grades, grizzly bears, groceries)

Please <u>stand</u> by the _____.(stairs, store, stones, stop sign)

Practice

Ask children to copy and then complete the sentence starters by filling in any word that makes sense.

Apply

Invite children one at a time to write two of their sentences on the board or an overhead transparency. Ask children to read their sentences to the class.

Allow each child to be the teacher and lead the class in a group reading of his or her sentences.

SKILL FOCUS: GRAMMAR   10–15 MINUTES

Exclamations

Teach

Read the following sets of sentences to children, using a more excited tone of voice for the second sentence in each pair. Invite children to suggest how they are different. (The second sentence in each set demonstrates excitement or more feeling.)

The game was really fun. The game was <u>really</u> fun!

I don't want to go. I <u>don't</u> want to go!

Write the second sentence of each set on the chalkboard and read them with children. Explain that sentences that show strong feeling are called exclamations and are typically said with greater expression.

The game was really fun!

I don't want to go!

Practice

Draw children's attention to exclamations on pages 210–213 in *Around the Pond: Who's Been Here?* Read the pages aloud with children to model intonation for exclamations.

Ask children to read the passage a second time and raise their hand when they hear an exclamation.

Apply

Have children work independently to write a paragraph about something fun they did with a family member. Remind children to use exclamations only to show strong feelings about something.

LITERATURE FOCUS: 10–15 MINUTES

Review *Around the Pond: Who's Been Here?*

Ask children to review and retell *Around the Pond: Who's Been Here?* After the retelling, ask partners to categorize and classify the story animals by listing them in a chart.

Objectives
- recognize exclamations when listening and reading
- read exclamations with proper intonation
- use exclamations appropriately in writing

Materials
- Anthology: *Around the Pond: Who's Been Here?*

Day 4

SKILL FOCUS: PHONICS   10–15 MINUTES

Double Final Consonants

Objectives

- listen to the sound of a double consonant or *ck* in the middle and at the end of a word
- say the sound of a single letter when they see a double consonant or *ck* at the end or in the middle of a word
- read and write words with final and medial double consonants

Teach

Tell children to listen to and blend these sounds:/b/ /ă/ /l/. Have children repeat the sounds and say the word. (ball) Repeat the procedure with *pass* and *huff*.

Write *ball* on the board and have children read the word with you, listening for the final /l/ sound. Underline the *ll*, and explain that double consonants at the end of the word are said as a single sound.

Point out that double consonants do not always come at the end of a word. Write *tennis* on the board. Underline the double consonants, say *tennis*, and point out that the two consonants also make a single sound in the middle of the word.

Help children mark the VCCV pattern and divide the words into syllables after the first *n*. Then cover up alternative parts of the word to help children sound out each syllable.

Ask children to listen for and identify where they hear /k/ in *sock* and *jacket*. (at the end; in the middle) Write *sock*, underline the *ck*, and say the word. Point out that the *ck* is said as a single sound. Then draw a slash after the *k* to show where the word divides into syllables. Explain that the *ck* is special and stays together at the end of the same syllable. Repeat with *jacket*.

Practice

Have children divide these double final consonants words by drawing a slash between the consonants: *picket, summer, pocket, dinner.*
(pick/et, summ/er, pock/et, dinn/er)

Ask volunteers to pronounce the words and give reasons why they divided the words where they did.

Apply

Have children search the selection *Around the Pond: Who's Been Here?* and the Phonics Library story *In the Woods* for words having double consonants and *ck* in them.

VCV Pattern

Teach

Write *wet* on the board, and ask children to read it and identify the vowel sound (/ĕ/). Point out that when a vowel is closed in by a consonant, it usually has a short sound. Write *we* on the board, and have children read it. Point out the vowel is long when there is no consonant closing it in.

Write *silent* on the chalkboard. Model how to use the VCV pattern to divide the word into syllables by first marking a *V* under each vowel, and then a *C* under the consonant between those vowels. Point to the VCV pattern and explain that when a word follows the vowel-consonant-vowel pattern, children should try dividing the word into syllables between the first vowel and the consonant (V/CV). Draw a slash between the *i* and the *l*. Have children blend the sounds in each syllable and then the syllables to read *silent*.

Practice

Write the following sentence on the board and read it with children:

> There is a <u>spider</u> <u>behind</u> the door.

Have children label the vowels and consonants in the underlined words. Help them to sound out and blend the syllables in each word.

Apply

Write this sentence and have children label the V/CV pattern in each underlined word: *A <u>robot</u> is made to look like a <u>human</u>.* Have them sound out and blend the syllables in each underlined word, and then read the sentence.

Objectives
- use the VCV pattern to divide unfamiliar words into syllables
- blend words with the VCV pattern

Materials
- Phonics Library: *A Snake Sheds Its Skin*

Preview *A Snake Sheds Its Skin*

Walk children through *A Snake Sheds Its Skin.* Point out to children that a snake is an animal with no legs and scales on its skin.

Objectives
- identify similarities among objects
- group objects according to common traits

Materials
- Anthology: *Around the Pond: Who's Been Here?*
- Phonics Library: *In the Woods, A Snake Sheds Its Skin*

SKILL FOCUS: COMPREHENSION   25–30 MINUTES

Categorize and Classify

Teach

Display the following desk supplies where children can see them: pens, pencils, crayons, paper clips, tape, and glue. Help children to see that the objects can be separated into two groups according to what the object is used for.

Point out that some of the objects are used to write and others are used to attach things. Ask children to name the function of each object and identify which group the object belongs in. Record suggestions in a chart similar to the following:

TO WRITE WITH	TO ATTACH THINGS
Pens	Tape
Crayons	Paper Clips

Explain to children that when we categorize and classify, we group objects with similar things.

Recall with children all of the living things they read about in *Around the Pond: Who's Been Here?* Give each child two index cards and instruct children to write *plant* on one card and animal on the other. Read aloud the names of different living things from the story and ask children to raise an index card to tell which category it belongs in.

Practice

Have children help classify animals from the story into three categories on a chart similar to the following:

FOUR LEGS	TWO LEGS	NO LEGS
Raccoon	Ducks	Fish
Turtle	Heron	Snake

Draw a blank chart on the chalkboard. Next, list the categories and ask children to name animals for each category. For example, ask, *What animals have four legs? What animals have two legs?* Then, have children classify a list of animals. Ask, *In which category does a fish belong?* (no legs) **A duck?** (two legs)

Apply

Explain to children that there are many ways to categorize animals, for example, animals that fly and animals that swim. Brainstorm with children other ways to group animals according to similarities. Then ask children to work in groups of three or four to categorize and classify animals from the story in a new chart according to some of the new categories.

LITERATURE FOCUS: 10–15 MINUTES

Revisit *Around the Pond: Who's Been Here? In the Woods,* and *A Snake Sheds Its Skin*

Page through all the stories with children and review the illustrations and text in each story to categorize and classify animals in each story.

Have children look through *Around the Pond: Who's Been Here?* and In the Woods for High-Frequency Words *across, brother, great,* and *stand*.

Ask children to look for and say words with double final consonants or VCCV patterns in the stories from *Around the Pond: Who's Been Here? In the Woods,* and *A Snake Sheds Its Skin*.

Theme 3

THEME 3: **Around Town: Neighborhood and Community**

Around Town: Neighborhood and Community

Selections

Day 1

Objectives

- identify the consonant digraphs *sh* and *ch*
- blend and read words with *sh* and *ch*

Materials

- Teaching Master ES3-1
- Phonics Library: *Sunshine for the Circus*

Get Set for Reading CD-ROM

Chinatown

Education Place

www.eduplace.com
Chinatown

Audio CD

Chinatown
Audio CD for **Around Town**

Lexia Phonics CD-ROM

Primary Intervention

PRETEACH

SKILL FOCUS: PHONICS   10–15 MINUTES

Consonant Digraphs *sh, ch*

Teach

Recite and repeat the chant. Encourage children to join in. Repeat the word shush, stretching the /sh/ sound at the beginning and end of the word. Have children follow your model. Then say chitter-chatter, stretching the /ch/ sound at the beginning of the words.

> **CHANT**
>
> Shush, shush!
>
> No more chitter-chatter
>
> Shhhhh!

Write *shush* and *chatter* on the board. Have children say each word with you as you underline the *sh* and *ch* digraphs.

Have children listen to and repeat some more words with *sh* and *ch*. Use these words: *chair, sheet, dish, teach, shake,* and *cheese.*

Blend

Display *ship*. Use Blending Routine 1 to model how to blend sounds to read the word. Then have children blend sounds to read *ship*. Repeat the modeling step with *gush*. Write these words on the board and have children using blending to read them with you: *shot, smash, wish,* and *flesh*. Continue, using the same steps as above to work with the digraph *ch*. Use *chin* and *rich* for your modeling. Then display *chin, chunk, much,* and *peach* for children to blend and read with you.

Check understanding by having individual children read: *shell, shop, brush, chase, check, cheek,* and *crunch.*

Guided Practice

Display or **distribute** Teaching Master ES3-1. Help children identify the illustration as a treasure chest. Have them read the sentences with you. Then point randomly to words that have the digraph *sh* or *ch*. As each word is read, write it on the side of the treasure chest.

Check children's ability to read *sh* and *ch* words as you review the final list of words with them.

SKILL FOCUS: PHONICS   10–15 MINUTES

Base Words and Endings -er, -est

Teach

Begin by reciting the chant. Then repeat the first line, emphasizing *-er* and *-est*. Have children say the three words with you.

> **CHANT**
> Small, smaller, smallest,
> Rabbit, mouse, and bug.

Write *small*, *smaller*, and *smallest* on the board. Have children compare them and say what is the same and different about them. Underline the endings. Say: *These endings show things are being compared.*

Have children listen to some words and raise their hand each time they hear a word with an ending. Say: *tallest, big, stronger, nice, fastest.*

Blend

Display *thicker*. Have children identify the ending. Underline it, and draw a line between the ending and the base word—*thick/er*. Use Blending Routine 1 to model how to blend sounds to read *thick* and then blend the base word with the ending. Repeat with *tastiest*, noting the change made to the base word before the ending was added. Help children blend these words: *finer, newer, greenest, fresher, hottest.*

Check understanding as children read: *older, wettest, lighter, thickest.*

Practice/Apply

Distribute Practice Master ES3-1 and read the directions with children. Tell them to read and complete the Practice Master independently.

Note children's ability to read base words and endings *-er* and *-est*.

LITERATURE FOCUS: 10–15 MINUTES

Preview *Sunshine for the Circus*

Familiarize children with *Sunshine for the Circus* by walking them through the story. Discuss the illustrations, name the characters, and use words such as *hotter, neatest, bigger, biggest,* and *cutest.*

Objectives

- identify words with the endings *-er* and *-est*
- blend and read words with the endings *-er* and *-est*.

Materials

- Practice Master ES3-1

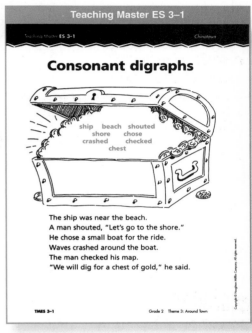

Teaching Master ES 3–1

Consonant digraphs

ship   beach   shouted
shore   chose
crashed   checked
chest

The ship was near the beach.
A man shouted, "Let's go to the shore."
He chose a small boat for the ride.
Waves crashed around the boat.
The man checked his map.
"We will dig for a chest of gold," he said.

TMES 3–1   Grade 2 Theme 3: Around Town

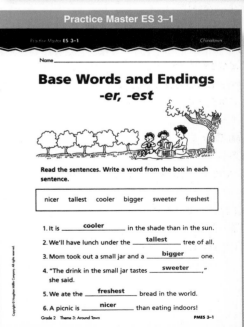

Practice Master ES 3–1

Name _____

Base Words and Endings -er, -est

Read the sentences. Write a word from the box in each sentence.

| nicer | tallest | cooler | bigger | sweeter | freshest |

1. It is _____**cooler**_____ in the shade than in the sun.
2. We'll have lunch under the _____**tallest**_____ tree of all.
3. Mom took out a small jar and a _____**bigger**_____ one.
4. "The drink in the small jar tastes _____**sweeter**_____," she said.
5. We ate the _____**freshest**_____ bread in the world.
6. A picnic is _____**nicer**_____ than eating indoors!

Grade 2 Theme 3: Around Town   PMES 3–1

Day 2

Objective
• make judgments based on the details of a selection

Materials
• Teaching Master ES3-2
• Practice Master ES3-2
• Anthology: *Chinatown*

Making Judgments

Teach

Tell children that reading or listening to stories is a good way to find out about different people and the different kinds of work that they do. In that way children can begin to think about the things they might like to do when they grow up.

Guided Practice

Have children listen to you read the story about people who work at the circus.

Read Aloud

> People who work at the circus live there with their children. Sometimes the children work in the circus with their parents. Sometimes they go to school right there at the circus. Everyone practices circus acts. Each circus act has to wait its turn while other acts perform. Some circus families check on the animals. They may have to get close to lions, tigers, and elephants to feed them and keep them clean.

Display or **distribute** Teaching Master ES3-2 and discuss the illustration.

Help children fill in the chart with information from the story.

Have children say what they like and don't like about the lives of circus workers.

Ask if they would like to be workers in a circus when they grow up.

Practice/Apply

Distribute Practice Master ES3-2 to children. Read the directions with them and discuss the illustration.

Have children read and complete the page independently.

Check children's ability to make judgments as they read as they share their responses.

LITERATURE FOCUS: 20–30 MINUTES

Preview *Chinatown*

Segment 1

Refer to the bottom of page T47 in the Teacher's Edition and preview with children Segment 1 of *Chinatown* (pages 262–271).

Note the suggestions in the Extra Support boxes on the Teacher's Edition pages T49 and T50.

Segment 2

Refer to the bottom of page T47 in the Teacher's Edition and preview with children Segment 2 of *Chinatown* (pages 272–284).

Note the suggestions in the Extra Support boxes on the Teacher's Edition pages T57 and T58.

Teaching Master ES 3–2

Making Judgments

Things People in the Circus Do

Sample answers
Circus families live at the circus.
Circus children work with their parents.
Some circus children go to school right there at the circus.
Everyone practices circus acts.
The acts have to wait their turn to practice.
Circus families check the animals.
They feed the lions.

TMES 3–2   Grade 2 Theme 3: Around Town

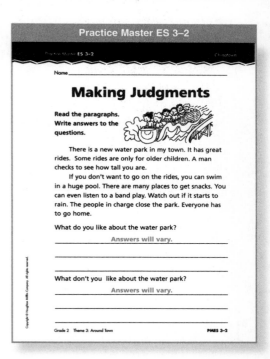

Practice Master ES 3–2

Name _____

Making Judgments

Read the paragraphs.
Write answers to the
questions.

There is a new water park in my town. It has great rides. Some rides are only for older children. A man checks to see how tall you are.

If you don't want to go on the rides, you can swim in a huge pool. There are many places to get snacks. You can even listen to a band play. Watch out if it starts to rain. The people in charge close the park. Everyone has to go home.

What do you like about the water park?
Answers will vary.

What don't you like about the water park?
Answers will vary.

Grade 2 Theme 3: Around Town   PMES 3–2

Day 3

Objective

- read and write new High-Frequency Words: *during, heard, lion, winter*

High-Frequency Words

Teach

Write the following sentence on the board and underline the High-Frequency Words *during, winter, heard,* and *lion*. Read the sentence with children. Point to each High-Frequency Word and ask a volunteer to say it.

During the winter, I heard the lion roar.

Write the word *during* on the board. Read the word with children. Ask youngsters to name things that they do during the school day. Examples: *read, write, eat lunch, play outside.*

Write *winter* on the board. Read the word with children. Ask children to name things they like about winter. Examples: *drinking hot chocolate, playing in the snow, winter holidays.*

Write *heard* on the board. Read the word with children. Ask youngsters to name things they have heard that day. Examples: *alarm clock, cars honking, school bell, teacher talking.*

Write *lion* on the board. Read the word with children. Ask youngsters to tell what they know about lions. Examples: *they live in groups called prides, males have shaggy manes, they roar.*

Practice

Write the following sentence frames on the board.

During the _____ , I _____.

Winter is the season for _____.

I heard _____ , and that made me feel _____.The lion _____.

Read the sentence frames with children. Ask them to complete the sentences on their own paper.

Apply

Invite children to read their sentences to the class. Ask children to pick their favorite sentence out of the four they have written and illustrate it. Have children show their illustrations and read their favorite sentence aloud, explaining why it is their favorite.

Naming Words (Common Nouns)

Teach

Invite children to play a word association game. Begin by naming and pointing to a person, place, or thing, and ask children to respond with the first word that comes to mind. For example, you might say *book* and a child might respond *words*. Record the naming words on a three-column chart with these headings: "Person," "Place," and "Thing." When finished, explain to children that the words in the first three columns are *naming words* that name a person, place, or thing. Ask children to identify which column has words that name a *person*, which column has words that name a *place*, and which column has words that name *things*.

Practice

Give each child two index cards labeled "Naming Word" and "Not a Naming Word." Read to children a list of naming words and words that are not naming words from the story *Chinatown*. The list might include *grandmother, apartment, hold, street, car, park, tell, dancer, most, cobbler, job, graceful, price, chicken,* and *outside*. Ask children to hold up the appropriate card as you read each word. If the word is a naming word, have them identify whether it names a person, place, or thing.

Apply

Have children work with a partner to find naming words in the story. Ask them to write their sentences and circle the naming words.

Objectives
- identify words that name a person, place, or thing
- write sentences with naming words

Materials
- Anthology: *Chinatown*

Review *Chinatown*

Ask children to review and retell *Chinatown*. After the retelling, have small groups discuss what they would like to see or do in Chinatown, providing reasons for their answers.

Day 4

Objectives

- listen for consonant digraphs *th, wh, sh, ch*
- identify consonant digraphs *th, wh, sh, ch (tch)*
- read and write words with consonant digraphs *th, wh, sh, ch (tch)*

Materials

- Sound/Spelling Cards: *sheep, thumb, whale, chick*
- Phonics Library: *Sunshine for the Circus*

Consonant Digraphs *th, wh, sh, ch (tch)*

Teach

Say the word *ship*, and have children repeat it after you. Then tell children to change the /sh/ sound at the beginning of the word to /ch/ Ask what the new word is. (chip) Then say the word *teach* and have children repeat it after you. Tell children to change the /ch/ sound at the end of the word to /th/ Ask what the new word is. (teeth)

Display the Sound/Spelling Card *sheep*. Point out that the letters *s* and *h* work together to make one sound, /sh/ This sound is different than the sound of either letter alone. This is called a digraph. Have children repeat the sound back to you. Then write the word shade on the board, underlining the *sh* digraph. Use Blending Routine 2 to help children sound out the word. For each sound, point to the letter(s), say the sound, and have children repeat it. Have children say the sound for the sh digraph, /sh/ then the long a sound for the *a*-consonant-*e* pattern, /ā/, then blend /sh//ā//ā//ā/. Finally, have them say the sound for d, /d/ and blend /sh//ā//ā//d/ shade.

Repeat this procedure with the other digraph Sound/Spelling Cards *thumb, whale,* and *chick.*

Practice

Write *th, wh, sh, ch /tch* on the board as headings of a four-column chart. Ask children to brainstorm words having the digraph sounds and to identify the column where each word belongs. List the words under the correct headings. Note if a word belongs in more than one column. Finally, have children read each word with you as a volunteer circles the consonant digraph in it.

Apply

Have pairs of children find words with digraphs in *Sunshine for the Circus.* The words they should find are: *sunshine, teach, children, they, cheerful, catch, show, choose, short, shell, shop, beach, fish, splash, much, shake, others, checks, baths, brushed, fresh, dashed, flash,* and *thunder.*

SKILL FOCUS: PHONICS   10–15 MINUTES

Base Words and Endings *-er, -est*

Teach

Write the following sentences on the board and read them with children.

Carlos is tall.
Megan is taller than Carlos.
Jim is the tallest boy in his class.

Underline *tall*, *taller*, and *tallest*. Point to *tall* and explain that it describes Carlos. Point to *taller* and explain that *-er* is added to *tall* to compare two people, Megan and Carlos. Point to *tallest* and explain that *-est* is added to *tall* to compare three people, Carlos, Megan, and Jim.

Tell children that sometimes the spelling of the base word changes when *-er* or *-est* is added. Write on the board the following spelling changes.

- ending consonant is doubled, as in bigger
- ending y is changed to i, as in busiest
- final silent e is dropped, as in larger

Practice

Write the examples on a chart. Help children underline *-er* and *-est*.

Julie's pencil is longer than Tom's. Angela's pencil is the longest.
Adam's book is wider than Paul's. Bridget's book is the widest.
Kim's shirt is redder than Nathan's. Min's skirt is the reddest.

Apply

Have children find words with *-er* and *-est* endings in *Sunshine for the Circus*, write them on the board, and circle the endings.

LITERATURE FOCUS: 10–15 MINUTES

Preview *Mother's Day Parade on Park Street*

Walk children through the story and discuss the illustrations. Name the characters and use words such as *shouted*, *march*, and *leash*.

Objectives

- identify words with the comparative endings *–er* and *–est*
- identify spelling changes to some base words when *–er* and *–est* are added
- read and write words with *–er* and *–est* endings

Materials

- Phonics Library: *Mother's Day Parade on Park Street*

RETEACH

SKILL FOCUS: COMPREHENSION   25–30 MINUTES

Making Judgments

Teach

Have children consider a character in a story that everyone is familiar with, such as *Little Red Riding Hood*. Review the events of the story and ask children to recall the wolf's actions. *The wolf tells lies to Little Red Riding Hood, tricks her, and tries to eat her.* Ask children to form an opinion about the wolf and tell why they think of the wolf that way. Children might say that *the wolf is mean and can't be trusted because he plays tricks on and lies to people and tries to hurt them.* Invite children to tell how they think we should treat one another.

Explain to children that when we read, we use facts from the story and our beliefs to form opinions about the characters or situations. Remind children that no single opinion is correct and that we must use facts from the story to support our opinions.

Practice

Invite children to form an opinion about the boy in *Chinatown* by William Low. Reread the following parts of the story with children:

Page 264 *"Every morning Grandma and I go for a walk through Chinatown. We hold hands before we cross the street. 'Watch out for cars, Grandma,' I tell her."*

Page 284 *"I turn to Grandma, take her hand, and say, 'Gung hay fat choy, Grandma.' She smiles at me. 'And a happy new year to you, too.'"*

Ask children to talk about how the boy treats his grandmother. Tell children to form an opinion about the boy based on what he does and says and on their own beliefs about how people should treat one another. Ask, *Are the things the boy says and does good and fair?* Have children share their opinions with the class and support them with facts from the story. Children might say *I think the boy is a nice person because he spends time with his grandma and is very kind and caring toward her.*

Help children to see that when we read, we use facts from the story and our beliefs to form opinions about characters or situations in a story.

Objectives

- evaluate the characters and events of the story
- form opinions based on the story facts and your own beliefs and values

Materials

- Anthology: *Chinatown*
- Phonics Library: *Mother's Day Parade on Park Street* and *Sunshine for the Circus*

Apply

Invite children to work with a partner to form an opinion about Grandma in the story. Have children refer to the following parts of the story and then write their opinions of Grandma.

Page 273 *"When it gets cold outside and Grandma needs to make medicinal soup, we visit the herbal shop… 'Winter is here,' says Grandma. 'We must get our strength up.'"*

Page 280 *"During the celebrations the streets of Chinatown are always crowded. 'Be sure to stay close by,' Grandma says."*

LITERATURE FOCUS: 10–15 MINUTES

Revisit *Chinatown, Mother's Day Parade on Park Street,* and *Sunshine for the Circus.*

Page through all the stories with children, reviewing the illustrations and text in each story to make judgments.

Have children look through the stories for High-Frequency Words *during, heard, lion,* and *winter,* and for base words with endings *-er* and *-est.*

Ask children to look for words with consonant digraphs *th, wh, sh, ch (tch),* and *ck* in the stories.

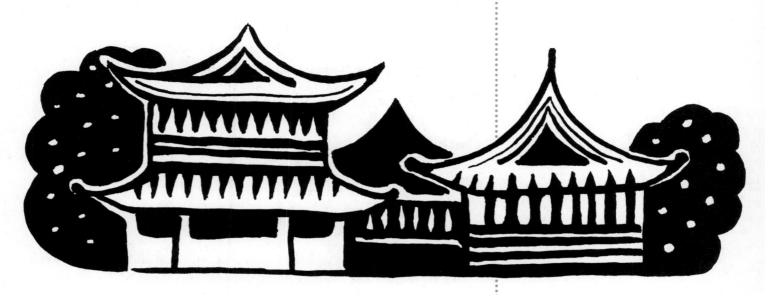

A Trip to the Firehouse

Vowel pairs *ai, ay*

Teach

Use the chant to focus attention on the long *a* sound. Repeat it a couple of times, inviting children to join in. Repeat the words *rain* and *day* with them, stretching the long *a* vowel sound. Remind children that the vowel sound is called long *a*.

> CHANT
>
> Rain, rain.
>
> What a day!
>
> Guess I'll stay
>
> Indoors to play.

Write *rain* and *play* on the board. Underline the letters that stand for the vowel sound.

Tell children they will listen to some words. Have them wave their hand each time they hear a word that has the long *a* vowel sound. Use these words: *plant, train, gray, paint, sadness, gasp, players.*

Blend

Display *chain*. Use Blending Routine 1 to model how to blend sounds to read the word. Then have children blend sounds to read *chain* with you. Repeat the modeling step with *sway*.

Write these words on the board, and have children using blending to read them with you: *trailer, raisin, tray, hay, clay, pain.*

Check children's ability to blend and read words with long *a*.

Guided Practice

Display or **distribute** Teaching Master ES3-3. Call attention to the four rows of word boxes.

Help children read the words in each box with you and circle the words that have the long a sound. Point to the Bonus Word box. Ask children to look back at the boxes and find a word that has two long *a* sounds.

Objectives

- associate the /ā/ sound with *ai* and *ay*
- blend and read words with *ai* and *ay*

Materials

- Teaching Master ES3-3

**Get Set for Reading
CD-ROM**

A Trip to the Firehouse

Education Place

www.eduplace.com
A Trip to the Firehouse

Audio CD

A Trip to the Firehouse
Audio CD for **Around Town**

**Lexia Phonics
CD-ROM**
Primary Intervention

SKILL FOCUS: PHONICS   10–15 MINUTES

Compound Words

Teach

> CHANT
> Our dog, dog, dog
> Needs a house, house, house.
> So let's get together
> And build a DOGHOUSE!

Recite and repeat the chant. Have children echo the second reading and shout out DOGHOUSE! Write *dog*, *house*, and *doghouse* one below the other on the chalkboard. Have children notice how *dog* and *house* have been combined to form the compound *doghouse*.

Blend

Write *snow* and *flake* on the chalkboard. Use Blending Routine 1 to model how to blend the sounds in each separate word as you move your hand under the letters and say the word. Then blend the two words together and say *snowflake*.

Tell children they can blend sounds and say the two words together when they read compound words. Have them use blending to read these compounds with you: *pathway, daylight, cupcake, sunset*.

Check for understanding by having children blend *cookbook, Sunday, railroad, handshake,* and *spaceship*.

Practice/Apply

Distribute Practice Master ES3-3, and read the directions with children. Tell them to read and complete the page independently.

Check children's skill with compound words as they share their work.

LITERATURE FOCUS: 10–15 MINUTES

Preview *Jay the Mailman*

Preview *Jay the Mailman* by walking children through the story. Discuss the illustrations, name the characters, and use words from the story such as *mailbox, everything, handshakes,* and *grandchildren*.

Objectives
- recognize compound words
- blend and read words that are compounds

Materials
- Practice Master ES3-3
- Phonics Library: *Jay the Mailman*

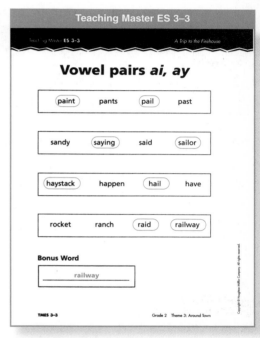

Teaching Master ES 3–3

Teaching Master **ES 3-3**   A Trip to the Firehouse

Vowel pairs *ai, ay*

(paint)	pants	(pail)	past
sandy	(saying)	said	(sailor)
(haystack)	happen	(hail)	have
rocket	ranch	(raid)	(railway)

Bonus Word

railway

TMES 3-3   Grade 2   Theme 3: Around Town

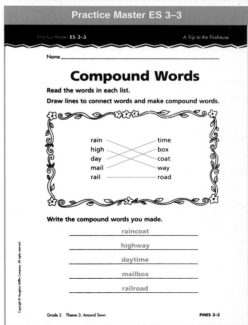

Practice Master ES 3–3

Practice Master **ES 3-3**   A Trip to the Firehouse

Name_____

Compound Words

Read the words in each list.
Draw lines to connect words and make compound words.

rain — time
high — box
day — coat
mail — way
rail — road

Write the compound words you made.

raincoat
highway
daytime
mailbox
railroad

Grade 2   Theme 3: Around Town   PMES 3-3

Day 2

Topic, Main Idea, Details

Objective
- identify the topic, main ideas, and supporting details in a selection

Materials
- Teaching Master ES3-4
- Practice Master ES3-4
- Anthology: *A Trip to the Firehouse*

Teach

Explain that authors have a plan when they write. First, they decide what they will write about. That's the topic. Say: *If an author was going to write about a trip to the library,* the library *would be the topic.*

Continue by saying that authors think about the most important thing they want to say. That's the main idea. Say: *If an author was writing about the library, the main idea could be* The library is a place that gives you new ideas and information.

Tell children that authors give information to help readers understand the main idea. Those are the details. Say: *If an author was writing about how the library is a place of new ideas and information, a detail sentence could be* The latest books, videos, and recordings can be found there.

> My topic is the rainforest.

> I need a good main sentence.

> What details should I include?

Guided Practice

Display or **distribute** Teaching Master ES3-4. Call attention to the headings Topic, Main Idea, and Details. Have children notice that the Details part of the chart is already filled in.

Read and discuss the details with children. Work with children to identify the topic and main idea the details would support.

Practice/Apply

Distribute Practice Master ES3-4 to children and discuss the directions.

Have children complete the Practice Master independently.

Check children's ability to identify topic, main idea, and details as they share their responses with the group.

LITERATURE FOCUS: 20–30 MINUTES

Preview *A Trip to the Firehouse*

Segment 1

Refer to the bottom of page T129 in the Teacher's Edition and preview with children Segment 1 of *A Trip to the Firehouse* (pages 297–305).

Note the suggestions in the Extra Support boxes on the Teacher's Edition pages T131 and T132.

Segment 2

Refer to the bottom of page T129 in the Teacher's Edition and preview with children Segment 2 of *A Trip to the Firehouse* (pages 306–317).

Note the suggestions in the Extra Support boxes on the Teacher's Edition pages T135 and T138.

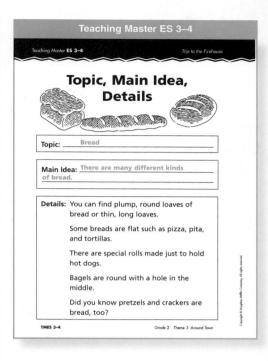

Teaching Master ES 3–4

Teaching Master **ES 3-4**   *Trip to the Firehouse*

Topic, Main Idea, Details

Topic: _____ Bread

Main Idea: There are many different kinds of bread.

Details: You can find plump, round loaves of bread or thin, long loaves.

Some breads are flat such as pizza, pita, and tortillas.

There are special rolls made just to hold hot dogs.

Bagels are round with a hole in the middle.

Did you know pretzels and crackers are bread, too?

TMES 3–4   Grade 2   Theme 3: Around Town

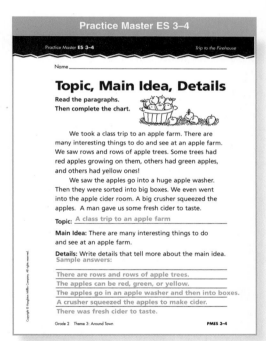

Practice Master ES 3–4

Practice Master **ES 3-4**   *Trip to the Firehouse*

Name _____

Topic, Main Idea, Details

Read the paragraphs. Then complete the chart.

We took a class trip to an apple farm. There are many interesting things to do and see at an apple farm. We saw rows and rows of apple trees. Some trees had red apples growing on them, others had green apples, and others had yellow ones!

We saw the apples go into a huge apple washer. Then they were sorted into big boxes. We even went into the apple cider room. A big crusher squeezed the apples. A man gave us some fresh cider to taste.

Topic: A class trip to an apple farm

Main Idea: There are many interesting things to do and see at an apple farm.

Details: Write details that tell more about the main idea. Sample answers:

There are rows and rows of apple trees.
The apples can be red, green, or yellow.
The apples go in an apple washer and then into boxes.
A crusher squeezed the apples to make cider.
There was fresh cider to taste.

Grade 2   Theme 3: Around Town   PMES 3–4

Day 3

Objective
- read and write new High-Frequency Words: *clothes, guess, order*

SKILL FOCUS: IO–I5 MINUTES

High-Frequency Words

Teach

Prepare by writing these three rhymes on chart paper.

My alarm clock goes beep, beep

To wake me up from deep sleep.

I'm glad it's in working _____ today,

Or I wouldn't get up in time to play!

Shirts, skirts, sweaters, coats, and shoes by the pair.

These are kinds of _____ that many people wear.

How many jellybeans in the jar?

I can only take a _____, I confess.

There are too many to count by far.

Write *clothes, guess, order* on the board and have children read them. Read aloud the rhymes. Have children choose the High-Frequency Word that completes each.

Pair children, then have each pair fold a sheet of paper into thirds and write the words *Clothes, Guess,* and *Order* as column heads. Ask pairs to brainstorm and list or draw pictures of items in each category— kinds of clothes, things people guess about, and things that must be in working order.

Apply

Have children share their lists. Tell them to add to their lists if they hear something new.

SKILL FOCUS: GRAMMAR   IO–I5 MINUTES

Special Nouns (Proper Nouns)

Teach

Begin a discussion with children about places they have visited. Ask them to name one person who went with them. Record children's responses in a chart similar to the one below.

Draw children's attention to the names of people and places on the chart. Explain to children how in this case the names of places and people begin with a capital letter because they name a particular person or place. Provide examples of other special nouns, such as *California* (state), *Chicago* (city), and *Emily* (girl). Continue with the names of buildings, streets, countries, and pets.

Names of Places	Names of People
Orlando, Florida	Maria
Franklin Park	Jeff
Colorado	Michael

Practice

Read to children a list of naming words from the story A Trip to the Firehouse. Have children clap their hands to identify special nouns that name a particular person, place, animal, or thing, such as *David, Spot, Katelyn, Josh,* and *Falmouth*. Continue the activity with additional special nouns, such as the name of your town, school, or principal. Then have children write sentences with some of the special nouns they have identified.

Apply

Have children work in groups of four to six to play the game "I'm Going on a Trip." Instruct the child whose turn it is first to say, "*I am going on a trip to* (name of place) *with* (name of person)." The next player repeats the first player's sentence (changing pronouns) and adds a sentence of his or her own. For example, *"He is going on a trip to Bermuda with Tony. I am going on a trip to Boston with Mary."* Have children write the new sentences each player says and underline the special nouns used. Tell the last player to repeat everyone's sentences and finish the game with an additional sentence.

Review *A Trip to the Firehouse*

Have children review and retell *A Trip to the Firehouse*. Then have children choose a page or section of the story and identify the topic, main idea, and details. You might want children to record this information in a chart.

Objectives
• identify special nouns that begin with a capital letter
• play a game that uses these special nouns

Materials
• Anthology: *A Trip to the Firehouse*

Day 4

Objectives

- listen to and segment phonemes
- say the long *a* vowel sound with words that contain vowel pairs *ai*, *ay*
- independently read and write words with the vowel pairs *ai*, *ay*

Materials

- Sound/Spelling Card *acorn*
- Letter Cards *a(2),h, i, m, p, s, w, y*
- Phonics Library: *Jay the Mailman*

RETEACH

SKILL FOCUS: PHONICS   10–15 MINUTES

Vowel pairs *ai, ay*

Teach

Tell children to blend these sounds, /r/ /ā/ /n/. Ask children what the word is. (rain) Repeat this procedure with the word *clay*.

Display the Sound/Spelling Card *acorn*, say /ā/, and have children repeat it. Remind them that they have learned the *a_e* spelling of /ā/. Point out that *ai* and *ay* are other ways to spell /ā/.

Write the word *wait* on the board and underline the *ai* spelling. Use Blending Routine 2 to help children blend the word. For each sound, point to the letter(s), say the sound, and have children repeat it. Have children say the sound for *w*, /w/ then the sound for *ai*, /ā/, then blend /w//ā//ā//ā/. Finally, have them say the sound for *t*, /t/ and blend /w//ā//ā//ā//t/, *wait*. Repeat with *paint* and *sailing*.

Write *tray* on the board and underline the *ay* spelling. Use Blending Routine 2 to blend the word. Repeat with *spraying* and *playful*. Point out that the *ay* spelling occurs at the end of a word (as in *tray*) or at the end of a syllable (as in *maybe*).

Practice

Have children use their Letter Cards to build words with *ai* and *ay*. Encourage them to make word pairs that begin with the same letter, such as *pay, pail; hay, hail; say, sail; may, mail; way, wail*.

Apply

Have pairs of children find words with *ai* and *ay* in *Jay the Mailman*. Have them say the words aloud, and write the words on the board. Have volunteers come to the board and circle the vowel pairs.

RETEACH

SKILL FOCUS: PHONICS   10–15 MINUTES

Compound Words

Teach

Display the word *fire* and have children read it. Display *house* next to *fire*, and have children read it. Then have them read the whole word, *firehouse.* Tell children *firehouse* is a compound word. Remind them that a compound word is made up of two shorter words that are put together to make a new word. Replace *house* with *fighter.* Have children read the new word. Repeat with *wood* and *place.*

Practice

Write the following words on the chalkboard in two columns, as shown:

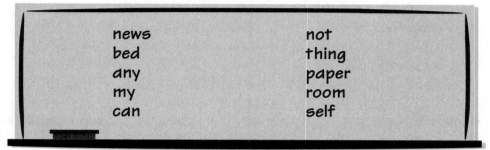

news	not
bed	thing
any	paper
my	room
can	self

Point to *news,* and have children read it. Then ask them to find a word in the second column that can be combined with *news* to make a compound word. Draw a line between *news* and *paper.* Then write *newspaper* on the chalkboard. Have children read the compound word. Repeat with *bedroom, something, myself,* and *cannot.*

Apply

Have children find compound words in *Jay the Mailman* and read them aloud as you write them on the board. Have volunteers come to the board and draw a line between the two smaller words in the compound word.

Objectives
• blend words to make compound words
• independently read and write compound words

Materials
• Blank index cards
• Scissors
• Phonics Library: *Watch Out for Thick Mud!*

LITERATURE FOCUS: 10–15 MINUTES

Preview *Watch Out for Thick Mud!*

Familiarize children with *Watch Out for Thick Mud!* Read the first page to introduce the characters. Discuss the illustrations on succeeding pages. As you talk with children, use words from the story such as *rain, exclaimed, explained,* and *anything.* Ask children to think about what the topic of the story might be.

Day 5

Topic, Main Idea, Details

Teach

Write the following paragraph on the board:

> People who work in our community help us in many ways. A crossing guard helps me cross the street to the school building. At school, I learn new things from my teacher. At the end of the day, the bus driver takes me home. As I walk to my door, I see a postal worker bringing our mail.

Read the paragraph together with children, then ask these questions:

- *How does a crossing guard help the community?*
- *How does a teacher help the community?*
- *How does a bus driver help the community?*
- *How does a postal worker help the community?*

Ask children to tell which sentence gives the main idea of what the paragraph is about. (People who work in our community help us in many ways.) Point out how each of the sentences that follow the first one provide supporting details for the main idea of the paragraph. Finally ask, What is the whole paragraph about? (community helpers/workers) Explain to children that the topic of this paragraph is community helpers or workers because both the main idea and the supporting details are about them.

Practice

Read with children the first page of *A Trip to the Firehouse* by Wendy Cheyette Lewison. Model identifying the topic, main idea, and supporting details with the following Think Aloud:

Think Aloud

> *I read that the fire chief welcomes the children to the firehouse and that everyone tries on a fire helmet. I know that these details tell me about the main idea. David and his class are visiting their neighborhood firehouse today is the main idea because it tells what most of the page is about, and other sentences support the main idea.*

Objective
- identify topic, main idea, and supporting details

Materials
- Anthology: *A Trip to the Firehouse*
- Phonics Library: *Jay the Mailman, Watch Out for Thick Mud!*

Point out that the main idea is often expressed in the first sentence of a paragraph as a main idea sentence. To continue practice with main ideas and supporting details, read the following paragraphs from the story:

Page 9 *"The pole is an important part of the firehouse…"*

Page 14 *"Different kinds of fire trucks do different things…"*

Have children identify details to determine main idea and topic.

Apply

Work together to develop a step-by-step procedure for determining topic and main idea. It might include the following steps:

1. Find the details and ask what they tell about.

2. Ask what the most important idea is and look for a main idea sentence.

3. Ask what the paragraph is about and name the topic.

Use your procedure to determine the topic and main idea of the following paragraph:

Read Aloud

People who work in our community help us in many ways. A crossing guard helps me cross the street to the school building. At school, I learn new things from my teacher. At the end of the day, the bus driver takes me home. As I walk to my door, I see a postal worker bringing our mail.

LITERATURE FOCUS: 10–15 MINUTES

Revisit *A Trip to the Firehouse, Jay the Mailman,* and *Watch Out For Thick Mud!*

Page through all the stories with children, reviewing the illustrations and text in each story for the topics and main ideas.

Have children look through the stories for High-Frequency Words *clothes, guess,* and *order,* and for compound words.

Ask children to look for words with vowel pairs *ai* and *ay* in the stories.

Day 1

Objectives

- associate the /ou/ sound with the vowel pairs *ow* and *ou*
- blend and read words with *ow* and *ou*

Materials

- Teaching Master ES3-5

Get Set for Reading
CD-ROM
Big Bushy Mustache

Education Place
www.eduplace.com
Big Bushy Mustache

Audio CD
Big Bushy Mustache
Audio CD for **Around Town**

Lexia Phonics
CD-ROM
Primary Intervention

PRETEACH

SKILL FOCUS: PHONICS   10–15 MINUTES

Vowel pairs *ow, ou*

Teach

Recite the chant and repeat it, encouraging children to join in. Say the words *town* and *around*, and have children repeat them. Isolate and stretch the /ou/ sound, and have children do the same.

> **CHANT**
> Let's go uptown,
> Let's go downtown,
> Up and down and all around town!

Write *around* and *town* on the board and underline *ou* and *ow*. Have children say some more words with the /ou/ sound: *brown, ground, found, owl, towel, out.*

Have children stand by their seats. Tell them to completely turn around each time they hear a word with the /ou/ sound. Use these words: *snow, power, flower, spoke, bottle, mouse, knot.*

Blend

Display *shout.* Use Blending Routine 1 to model how to blend the sounds, stretching /ou/ and then saying the word. Remind children that the two letters *ou* together stand for /ou/. Then have children blend the word and say it with you. Repeat with *howl, mouth, shower,* and *proud.*

Check understanding as children read *gown, sound, count,* and *power.*

Guided Practice

Display or **distribute** Teaching Master ES3-5, and discuss the illustrations with children.

Help children use what they know about blending sounds to read the sentences and place names. Help them to identify the words that contain /ou/ and write the words in a list.

Check children's skill with /ou/ words as they read the list.

SKILL FOCUS: PHONICS   10–15 MINUTES

Suffix -ly

Teach

Recite the chant and then repeat it. Encourage children to chime in. Repeat *quickly*, emphasizing the /l/ /ē/ sounds the suffix *-ly* stands for. Ask children how the word *quickly* is different from *quick*.

> **CHANT**
>
> Quickly, quickly the ants march on the trail.
>
> Slowly, slowly here comes the snail!

Write *quick* and *quickly* on the board. Have children compare the two words and underline the suffix. Repeat with the word *slowly*.

Blend

Display *loudly* and underline *-ly*. Use Blending Routine 1 to model how to blend the sounds in the base word *loud* and then *-ly*. Say the complete word, emphasizing the /l/ /ē/ sounds at the end. Then have children blend the word with you. Repeat with *safely*.

Display *wildly, gladly, friendly,* and *smoothly*. Call on children to underline the endings. Have children use blending to read the words.

Practice/Apply

Distribute Practice Master ES3-5, and read the directions with children. Tell them to complete the page independently.

Check children's ability to read *-ly* words as they share their answers.

LITERATURE FOCUS: 10–15 MINUTES

Preview *Mouse's Crowded House*

Familiarize children with *Mouse's Crowded House.* Discuss the illustrations, name the characters, and use words such as *bounced, count, thousand, frowning, clowning, exactly,* and *proudly.*

Objectives

- associate the /l/ /ē/ sounds with the suffix *-ly*
- blend and read words with the suffix *-ly*

Materials

- Practice Master ES3-5

Teaching Master ES 3–5

Teaching Master ES 3-5   Big Bushy Mustache

Vowel pairs *ou, ow*

Welcome to New Town!
Here are some of the many places to see!

Magic (Fountain)
(Flower) Park
Fair (Grounds)
High (Tower)
(Downy) Lake
Mile High (Mountain)
(County) Bridge
(Scout) Hiking Trail

TMES 3–5   Grade 2 Theme 3: Around Town

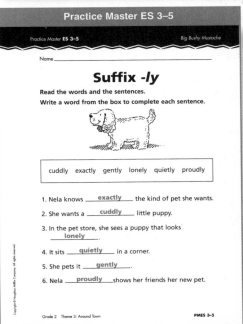

Practice Master ES 3–5

Practice Master ES 3-5   Big Bushy Mustache

Name _____

Suffix *-ly*

Read the words and the sentences.
Write a word from the box to complete each sentence.

| cuddly exactly gently lonely quietly proudly |

1. Nela knows ___exactly___ the kind of pet she wants.

2. She wants a ___cuddly___ little puppy.

3. In the pet store, she sees a puppy that looks ___lonely___

4. It sits ___quietly___ in a corner.

5. She pets it ___gently___.

6. Nela ___proudly___ shows her friends her new pet.

Grade 2 Theme 3: Around Town   PMES 3–5

Day 2

Problem Solving

Teach

Present children with this situation: *Suppose that you and some friends have planned a picnic lunch in the park. Just when the food is all packed and it is time to go, it starts to rain. What can you do to solve the problem?* Encourage children to share their solutions. (Possible answers: Have a picnic dinner, if the weather clears later on; have an indoor picnic lunch; postpone the event until the next day.)

Tell children that characters in stories often have problems to solve and may have to try more than just one way to solve them.

Guided Practice

Read the following to children. To help children recall story information, read the story more than once.

Objectives

- identify story problem and solution

Materials

- Teaching Master ES3-6
- Practice Master ES3-6
- Anthology: *Big Bushy Mustache*

Read Aloud

Ben is upset. He wants to put his a new model airplane together, but can't figure out how. He reads the directions over and over, but they are too confusing. He tries to remember how he put other model planes together, but that doesn't work. Finally, he asks his big brother to help him. Two hours later, he has a new model airplane.

Display or **distribute** Teaching Master ES3-6. Have children notice that it shows a problem/solution chart. Tell children they will help you complete the chart.

Ask children to identify Ben's problem. Then have them recall the three different solutions he tried. Encourage children to say why they think the last solution was successful.

Practice/Apply

Distribute Practice Master ES3-6 and go over the directions with children.

Have them complete the Practice Master independently.

Check children's ability to identify problems and solutions as they share their answers with the group. Be sure to have children say why they think Sara's first two solutions did not work.

LITERATURE FOCUS: 20–30 MINUTES

Preview *Big Bushy Mustache*

Segment 1

Refer to the bottom of page T197 in the Teacher's Edition and preview with children Segment 1 of *Big Bushy Mustache* (pages 326–341).

Note the suggestions in the Extra Support boxes on the Teacher's Edition pages T200 and T203.

Segment 2

Refer to the bottom of page T197 in the Teacher's Edition and preview with children Segment 2 of *Big Bushy Mustache* (pages 342–356).

Note the suggestions in the Extra Support boxes on the Teacher's Edition pages T207 and T212.

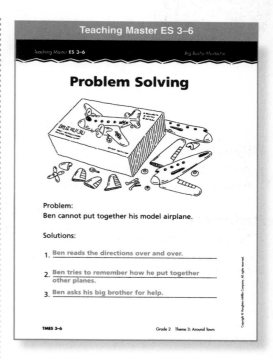

Teaching Master ES 3–6   Big Bushy Mustache

Problem Solving

Problem:
Ben cannot put together his model airplane.

Solutions:

1. Ben reads the directions over and over.

2. Ben tries to remember how he put together other planes.

3. Ben asks his big brother for help.

TMES 3–6   Grade 2 Theme 3: Around Town

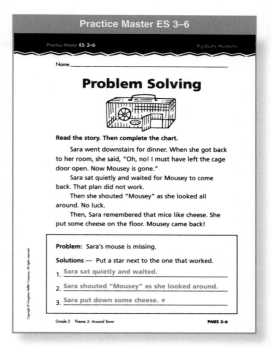

Practice Master ES 3–6   Big Bushy Mustache

Name _____

Problem Solving

Read the story. Then complete the chart.

Sara went downstairs for dinner. When she got back to her room, she said, "Oh, no! I must have left the cage door open. Now Mousey is gone."

Sara sat quietly and waited for Mousey to come back. That plan did not work.

Then she shouted "Mousey" as she looked all around. No luck.

Then, Sara remembered that mice like cheese. She put some cheese on the floor. Mousey came back!

Problem: Sara's mouse is missing.

Solutions — Put a star next to the one that worked.

1. Sara sat quietly and waited.

2. Sara shouted "Mousey" as she looked around.

3. Sara put down some cheese. ★

Grade 2 Theme 3: Around Town   PMES 3–6

Objective
• read and write new High-
  Frequency Words: *behind, soldier,
  story*

RETEACH

SKILL FOCUS: 10–15 MINUTES

High-Frequency Words

Write the following sentences on the board.

I read a <u>story</u> at the library.

Emma sits <u>behind</u> Jordan.

This <u>soldier</u> is in the army.

Read each sentence with children. Ask volunteers to underline *story,*
behind, and *soldier.* Discuss the meaning of each underlined word.

Practice

Assign each child one of the three High-Frequency Words (*behind, soldier, story*). Try to assign each word to about the same number of children. Ask children to write a sentence using the word they were
assigned.

Hang up three pieces of large chart paper at a height children can easily
reach. At the top of each piece of chart paper, write one of the High-
Frequency Words (*behind, soldier, story*) as a heading. Invite children
one at a time to read aloud their sentences. Then have children write
their sentences on the piece of chart paper under the appropriate
High-Frequency Word.

Apply

Invite a group of three or four children to read together the first sentence on each piece of chart paper. Continue by having other groups
of children read one sentence from each piece of chart paper until all
of the sentences have been read.

RETEACH

SKILL FOCUS: GRAMMAR   10–15 MINUTES

One and More than One

Teach

Invite children to help you name parts of the body. Point to an eye or an
arm, and elicit from children the name of the body part. Then ask children to name the parts again, but to name more than one eye or more
than one arm. Record children's responses in a chart on the board.

One	More Than One
eye	eyes
hand	hands
arm	arms
leg	legs
lip	lips
ear	ears
finger	fingers

Objectives
- identify naming words that indicate one or more than one
- form naming words that indicate one or more than one

Materials
- Anthology: *Big Bushy Mustache*

Point out that the words used to name body parts are naming words. Explain to children that adding an *-s* to the end of a naming word changes its meaning from one to more than one. Read aloud words from the chart, and have children raise their hand when you say words that indicate more than one.

Practice

Read aloud sentences from *Big Bushy Mustache*. Ask children to listen for words that indicate one or more than one. Have children raise either one or two hands to identify the words as one or more than one:

"Her eyes settled on Ricky."

"Mi'jo, wash your hands and help me with the apples."

"Ricky jumped up and threw his arms around Papi's neck."

Apply

Use the following sentence starters, asking children to complete each one together:

(Child's name) *has one pencil, but* (child's name) *has two _____.*
(Child's name) *has one cat, but* (child's name) *has two _____.*

As children respond, record their answers. Point out in each instance how the naming word adds an *-s* to show more than one.

LITERATURE FOCUS: 10–15 MINUTES

Review *Big Bushy Mustache*

Ask children to review and retell *Big Bushy Mustache*. Then have children work in small groups. One group member should identify the problem in the story and the other members should identify the three solutions that fail and the one solution that works.

Day 4

Objectives

- listen to and segment phonemes
- blend words with the /ou/ sound spelled *ow* or *ou*
- read and write words with *ow* and *ou*

Materials

- Phonics Library: *Mouse's Crowded House*

SKILL FOCUS: PHONICS   10–15 MINUTES

Vowel Pairs *ow, ou*

Teach

Say the following words, and have children crouch when they hear a word with the same vowel sound as *owl: pit, pout; hound, hand; hill, howl, crow, cow, town, ton, grow, growl.*

Display the Sound/Spelling Card *owl*, say *owl*, and /ou/. Have children repeat /ou/ several times. Remind children that this sound may be spelled with the vowel pairs *ow* or *ou*.

Write the word *loud* on the board, and underline the *ou* spelling. Use Blending Routine 2 to help children blend the word. For each sound, point to the letter(s), say the sound, and have children repeat it. Have children say the sound for *l*, /l/ then the sound for *ou*, /ou/, then blend /l/ /ou/ to say /lou/. Finally have them say the sound for *d*, /d/ and blend the sounds /loud/, *loud*. Repeat with *pout, cloud, town,* and *crowd.*

Practice

Write *loud* and *cow* as headings of a two-column chart on the board. Read the words with children. Point out that both words have the /ou/ sound. Have children name words with the /ou/ sound and write them on the board under the appropriate heading.

<u>loud</u>	<u>cow</u>
found	cowboy
ground	brown
flour	clown

Apply

Have children draw an outline of a large house on their papers, then ask them to find words with the /ou/ sound in *Mouse's Crowded House.* Each time children find an /ou/ word, they can write it inside their houses. When they are done, have partners take turns reading the words.

Suffixes *-ly, -ful*

Teach

Write the word *loud* on the board. Read it with children, then add the suffix *–ly*. Read *loudly* with children, and invite some of them to use it in a sentence.

Follow the same procedure with *play* and add the suffix *-ful*. Point out that the suffix changes *play* to a new word that means "full of play."

Practice

Write *loudly* and *playful* as headings of a two-column chart on the board. Read the words with children. Point out that both words have suffixes.

loudly	playful
sadly	cheerful
quickly	colorful
slowly	helpful

Invite children to name words with *-ly* and *–ful* suffixes. Write the words on the board under the appropriate heading.

Apply

Have pairs of children look for words with suffixes *-ly* and *–ful* in *Mouse's Crowded House*. They should find: *loudly, suddenly, sadly, peaceful, lonely, playful, proudly, sweetly, joyful*. Each time children find a word with a suffix, they should read it aloud while you write the word on the board. Have volunteers come to the board and underline the suffixes.

Preview *Hooray for Main Street*

Preview *Hooray for Main Street*. Read the first page to introduce the main characters. Discuss the illustrations on succeeding pages. As you talk with children, use words from the story such as *rain, exclaimed, explained,* and *anything*.

Objectives

- recognize *-ly* and *-ful* endings in words
- identify base words in words that end with *-ly* and *-ful*
- read and use words that end with *-ly* and *-ful* in sentences

Materials

- Phonics Library: *Hooray for Main Street*

Problem Solving

Objectives
• identify a problem and possible solution
• evaluate solutions to decide which is best

Teach

Ask children if they have ever lost their lunch money or forgotten their lunch. Invite children to share their experiences with the class. Ask children to tell what happened and what they did to solve the problem. Point out to children that having no lunch is the *problem* and what they did to solve the problem is the *solution*. Record the solutions children suggest on the board and have them evaluate the pros and cons of each one. Have children decide on the best solution.

Practice

Review with children events in *Big Bushy Mustache* by Gary Soto. Ask children to identify a problem that arises in the story. (Ricky loses the mustache that he took home from school.) Have children identify the solutions that Ricky tries and invite them to brainstorm other solutions not mentioned in the story. Record children's suggestions in a problem/solution graphic organizer similar to the one that follows:

<u>Problem</u>
• Ricky loses the mustache

<u>Solutions</u>
• Look for the mustache
• Make another mustache from paper.

Instruct children to list the pros and cons of each solution. Have children evaluate the possible solutions and decide which is best.

Apply

Have children develop a step-by-step procedure for problem solving. It might include the following steps:

- Identify the problem.

- Brainstorm possible solutions.

- Examine the solutions.

- Decide which solution is best.

- Carry out the solution.

Brainstorm with children to identify another problem in the story: *Ricky wants to look more like his father.* Have children work with a partner to complete the problem/solution graphic organizer. Encourage children to think about what they would do if they were in Ricky's situation.

LITERATURE FOCUS: 10–15 MINUTES

Revisit *Big Bushy Mustache, Hooray for Main Street,* and *Mouse's Crowded House*

Page through all the stories with children, reviewing the illustrations and text in each story to solve problems.

Have children look through the stories for High-Frequency Words *behind*, *soldier*, and *story*.

Ask children to look for words with vowel pairs *ow* and *ou* in the stories.

Day 1

Objectives

- associate the /ē/ sound with the vowel pairs *ee* and *ea*
- blend and read words with *ee* and *ea*

Materials

- Teaching Master ES 3–7
- Phonics Library: *The Clean Team*

PRETEACH

SKILL FOCUS: PHONICS   10–15 MINUTES

Vowel pairs *ee, ea*

Teach

Recite the chant and then repeat it. Have children echo your second reading. Say the words peep and eat, and have children repeat them with you. Isolate and stretch the long e vowel sound, and have children do the same. Identify the vowel sound as the long e sound.

> **CHANT**
> Little Chick said, "Peep, peep, peep.
> Can't I have something to eat?"

Write *peep* and *eat* on the board, underlining *ee* and *ea*, respectively. Tell children they will say some more words with long *e*: *cheap, seat, meal, feet, peel,* and *leap.*

Tell children to say *peep, peep* each time they hear a word with the long *e* vowel sound. Use these words: *settle, steam, spell, speak, jelly, jeep.*

Blend

Display *green.* Use Blending Routine 1 to model how to blend the sounds, stretching the /ē/ sound and then saying the word. Remind children that the two letters *ee* together stand for one vowel sound. Then have children blend the word and say it with you. Repeat the same steps with the word stream.

Display *cream, feed, teeth, clean,* and *seaweed.* Have children use blending to read them.

Check children's understanding by calling on individuals to read *street, mean, creek, tweed, beast,* and *streak.*

Guided Practice

Display or **distribute** Teaching Master ES3-7. Call attention to the illustration at the top. Read the label *Bean Bag Toss Game* with children. Point out the little bean bags with words printed on them.

Help children use what they know about blending sounds to read the words. Help them find the ones they can toss into the basket.

Check children's ability to blend and read long e words.

SKILL FOCUS: PHONICS   10–15 MINUTES

–*ture* Ending in Two-Syllable Words

Teach

Recite the chant and repeat it. Encourage children to join in. Repeat *mixture*, emphasizing the /chûr/ sounds. Ask children how *mixture* is different from *mix*. Write *mix* and *mixture* on the board, and underline the *-ture* ending in *mixture*. Have children compare the words.

> **CHANT**
> Mix it, mix it, mix it well,
> So the mixture will be swell!

Have children say these words with you and listen for the /chûr/ sounds at the end: *picture, pasture, nature, fixture.*

Blend

Display *future*, and underline *-ture*. Use Blending Routine 1 to model how to blend the sounds in the first syllable and then add the /chûr/ sounds. Have children blend the word with you. Repeat with *fracture*.

Display *capture, culture,* and *nature*. Call on children to underline the ending in each word. Have them use blending to read the words.

Check children's ability to blend and read *fixture, creature,* and *picture*.

Practice/ Apply

Display or **distribute** copies of Practice Master ES3-7. Read the directions with children so they understand that they are circling and writing the words. Tell children to complete the page independently.

Check children's responses to see that they can read *-ture* words.

LITERATURE FOCUS: 10–15 MINUTES

Preview *The Clean Team*

Lead children on a picture walk through *The Clean Team*. Discuss the illustrations throughout the story and use words such as *clean, team, heaps, jeans, neat, pictures,* and *furniture*.

Objectives
- associate the /chûr/ sounds with the ending *-ture*
- blend and read words with *-ture*

Materials
- Practice Master ES3-7
- Phonics Library: *The Clean Team*

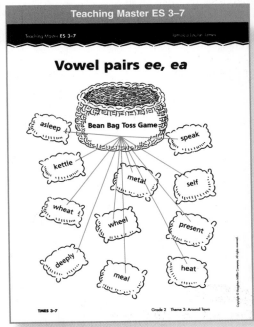

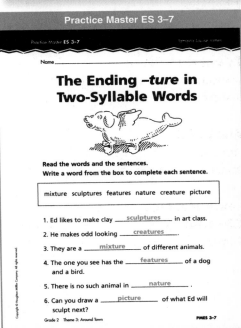

Day 2

Objective
• make inferences about story characters

Materials
• Teaching Master ES3-8
• Practice Master ES3-8
• Anthology: *Jamaica Louise James*

Making Inferences

Teach

Say to children: *Suppose that you see a friend crying. How do you think your friend is feeling? Right. Your friend is sad or upset. Crying and tears are clues. From your own experiences, you know that people who are sad or upset cry.*

Tell children that they can understand more about story characters if they look for clues in what the characters do and say. Children should also think about their own personal experiences. Then they can figure out what a character is like.

Guided Practice

Read the following story to children.

Read Aloud

The teacher is giving back tests. Ray studied very hard for the test. He even missed going to a movie so he could study. He waits quietly as other children get their tests. Then it's his turn. Ray smiles a big smile. He can't wait to show his parents his test!

Display or **distribute** Teaching Master ES3-8 and discuss the illustration with children. Explain to them that the story clues part of the chart is filled in. Help children to identify personal experiences that when combined with these story clues will tell what Ray is like.

Complete the chart with children.

Practice/Apply

Distribute Practice Master ES3-8 and read the directions with children.

Have children work independently to read the paragraphs and answer the questions.

Check children's ability to make inferences as they share their responses with the group.

LITERATURE FOCUS: 20-30 MINUTES

Preview *Jamaica Louise James*

Segment 1

Refer to the bottom of page T271 in the Teacher's Edition and preview with children Segment 1 of *Jamaica Louise James* (pages 367–377).

Note the suggestions in the Extra Support boxes on the Teacher's Edition pages T274 and T275.

Segment 2

Refer to the bottom of page T271 in the Teacher's Edition and preview with children Segment 2 of *Jamaica Louise James* (pages 378–391).

Note the suggestions in the Extra Support boxes on the Teacher's Edition pages T277, T278, and T282.

Teaching Master ES 3–8

Teaching Master **ES 3–8** *Jamaica Louise James*

Making Inferences

What Ray Is Like	Story Clues
Ray is serious about his school work.	Ray studied hard. He missed a movie to study more.
Ray is patient.	Ray waited quietly while other children got their tests back.
Ray is proud of his good grades.	Ray smiled and couldn't wait to show his parents his test.

TMES 3–8   Grade 2   Theme 3: Around Town

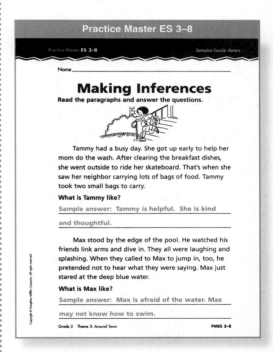

Practice Master ES 3–8

Practice Master **ES 3–8** *Jamaica Louise James*

Name_____

Making Inferences
Read the paragraphs and answer the questions.

Tammy had a busy day. She got up early to help her mom do the wash. After clearing the breakfast dishes, she went outside to ride her skateboard. That's when she saw her neighbor carrying lots of bags of food. Tammy took two small bags to carry.

What is Tammy like?

Sample answer: Tammy is helpful. She is kind and thoughtful.

Max stood by the edge of the pool. He watched his friends link arms and dive in. They all were laughing and splashing. When they called to Max to jump in, too, he pretended not to hear what they were saying. Max just stared at the deep blue water.

What is Max like?

Sample answer: Max is afraid of the water. Max may not know how to swim.

Grade 2   Theme 3: Around Town   PMES 3–8

Day 3

Objective

• read and write new High-Frequency Words: *believe, lady, whole*

RETEACH

SKILL FOCUS: | 10–15 MINUTES

High-Frequency Words

Teach

Write the following sentence on the board.

Can you <u>believe</u> that <u>lady</u> ate the whole <u>thing</u>?

Read the sentence with children. Underline and point out *believe, lady,* and *whole.* Reread the underlined words with children, and discuss the meaning of each. Invite children to say a sentence using each High-Frequency Word *(believe, lady, whole).*

Practice

Write the following sentence starters on the board.

I believe _____.

That lady is my _____.

I'm so hungry I could eat a whole _____.

Read the sentence starters with children. Have children copy them and complete each sentence any way they like. Tell them to use a dictionary or invented spelling for words they do not know how to spell.

Apply

Invite children to share their sentences with the class and illustrate a sentence that was written by someone else. Then have them read the other children's sentences and show the illustrations.

RETEACH

SKILL FOCUS: GRAMMAR | 10–15 MINUTES

Nouns that Change Spelling in Plural

Teach

Read the following sentences aloud, and ask children to complete them:

I make a wish every day. I hope all of my _____ come true.

This watch is very pretty. I see several pretty _____ .

I like this story and that story. I like both _____ .

That woman is strong. There are many strong _____ .

One child is sitting alone. Three _____ are sitting nearby.

Record their responses on a chart next to a column that shows each word's singular form.

One	More Than One
wish	wishes
watch	watches
story	stories
woman	women
child	children

Draw children's attention to the *-es* ending on the words that mean more than one. Explain that when words ending in *s, x, sh, ch,* and the consonant *y* form plurals, they have *-es* endings to indicate more than one. Words ending in the consonant *y,* such as *story,* drop the *y* and add *i* before adding *-es,* such as *stories.* Point out that words like *woman* and *child* also have a change in spelling in the plural.

Practice

Read with children the following sentences in *Jamaica Louise James*:

"*Mama says my stories go on... and on... she tells me,... 'Snap to it, baby!'*"

"*At night, Mama and Granny and I cuddle on the couch while the city quiets down.*"

"*They bought me a real paint set — with eight little tubes of color and two paint brushes.*"

Ask children to record on a chart the story words that take *-es* endings or change spelling to indicate more than one.

Apply

Invite children to write a story, using the words on their charts.

LITERATURE FOCUS: 10-15 MINUTES

Review *Jamaica Louise James*

Ask children to review and retell *Jamaica Louise James.* After the retelling, ask children to tell what one character is like. Have them point out the page(s) that support their thinking.

Day 4

Objectives

- listen to and segment phonemes
- blend words with the long *e* sound spelled *ee* or *ea*
- read and write words with *ee* and *ea*

Materials

- Sound/Spelling Card *eagle*

SKILL FOCUS: PHONICS   10–15 MINUTES

Vowel Pairs *ee, ea*

Teach

Say the following words, and have children raise their hand each time they hear a word with the same vowel sound as *eagle: sheet, shout met, meal drum, dream keep, cape week, went seal, sell.*

Display the Sound/Spelling Card *eagle*, say the long *e* sound, and invite children to repeat it with you several times. Remind children that this sound may be spelled with the vowel pairs *ee* or *ea*.

Write *deep* on the board, underline the *ee* spelling, and use Blending Routine 2 to help children blend the word. For each sound, point to the letter(s), say the sound, and have children repeat it. Start with the sound for *d*, /d/, add the sound for *ee*, /ē/, and have children blend the sounds to say /d/ /ē/. Finally, have children say the sound for *p*, /p/, and blend the sounds /d//ē//ē//p/, *deep*. Repeat with *beet, feed,* and *feet.*

Write *real* on the board, and underline the *ea* spelling. Use Blending Routine 2 to blend the word, and repeat with *seat* and *team.*

Practice

Write *deep* and *real* as headings of a two-column chart. Read the words with children. Point out that both words have the long *e* sound. Invite children to brainstorm *ee* and *ea* words with the long *e* sound. Assist them with spelling the words, and have them write the words under the appropriate heading.

deep	real
street	dream
beet	team
sweet	sneak
week	speak
speed	weak

Encourage children to write three sentences using as many words from the chart as possible. Have children read their sentences to the class.

Apply

Have pairs of children look for long *e* words spelled with the vowel pairs *ee* and *ea* in *The Clean Team*. Each time children find a word with *ee* or *ea*, they should read it aloud while you write it on the board. Have volunteers come to the board and underline the vowel pairs.

Common Syllables *-tion, -ture*

Say the following words, and ask children how many syllables they hear in each one: *action, mention, motion, nation.* (two) Repeat the words, having children listen for the syllable they share. (-tion) Repeat the procedure for *-ture*, using the words *picture, pasture, nature,* and *mixture.*

Write *action,* and say it. Underline *-tion*, say /sh ə n/, and point out that many longer words end with *-tion.* Have children say the syllable. Help them use the VCCV pattern to divide *action* into syllables after the *c.* Help them blend the first syllable sound by sound, and then say *-tion.* Finally, have them blend the syllables together to say *action.* Repeat with *mention.* Follow the same procedure to review the syllable *-ture,* /ch ə r/, using the words *picture* and *pasture.*

Practice

Write *-tion* and *-ture* as headings on the board. Ask children to suggest other words that end with those common syllables. List the words on the board. Finally, read the words with children and discuss their meanings.

-tion	-ture
action	picture
station	furniture
vacation	nature
motion	mixture

Apply

Have pairs of children use the words on the chalkboard to make up a riddle. Ask each pair to take turns reading their riddles to the group.

Preview *Big Hound's Lunch*

Preview *Big Hound's Lunch.* Introduce the characters, discuss the illustrations, and use words such as *please, leash,* and *eat.*

Objectives
- listen to and segment phonemes
- blend words with the syllables *–tion, –ture*
- read and write words with *–tion, –ture*

Materials
- Phonics Library: *Big Hound's Lunch*

Day 5

Objectives
- use clues from the story and their knowledge to make inferences
- complete a chart about story clues and inferences

Materials
- Anthology: *Jamaica Louise James*
- Phonics Library: *Big Hound's Lunch, The Clean Team*

Problem Solving

Teach

Demonstrate for children examples of feelings. After each example, ask children to tell what feeling is expressed and what clues helped them figure it out. You might try the following:

Yawn and say, *I didn't sleep well last night.* (tired)

Hold your stomach and say, *I'm going to go lie down.* (sick)

Put your hands on your hips and say, *Who spilled glue on my jacket?* (angry)

Explain to children that when they use story clues and their knowledge to understand something that isn't directly stated, they are making inferences. Provide children with an opportunity to pantomime different feelings while classmates guess what they are. Explain that they are making inferences.

Practice

Have children make inferences about Jamaica in *Jamaica Louise James* by Amy Hest. Ask children to review the story and tell things that Jamaica does or says. Have children use those clues and what they know from their experiences to make inferences about what Jamaica is like. Record children's observations in a similar chart:

Things Jamaica does or says	What is Jamaica like?
She hangs things for her Grammy's birthday.	thoughtful
She is always drawing and painting.	expressive
She tell stories.	talkative

Apply

Have children work with a partner to make inferences about the character Grammy in the story. Ask children to record on a chart their observations about what kind of a person Grammy is based on what Grammy says and does. Then have children use those clues and what they know from their experiences to tell what Grammy is like.

LITERATURE FOCUS: 10–15 MINUTES

Revisit *Jamaica Louise James, Big Hound's Lunch,* **and** *The Clean Team*

Page through all the stories with children, reviewing the illustrations and text in each story to make inferences.

Have children look through the stories for High-Frequency Words *believe*, *lady*, and *whole*.

Ask children to look for words with vowel pairs *ea* and *ee* in the stories, and for the *–tion* and *–ture* ending in two-syllable words.

Theme 4

THEME 4: **Amazing Animals**

Amazing Animals

Selections

1 Officer Buckle and Gloria

2 Ant

3 The Great Ball Game

Day 1

Objectives

- associate /är/ with *ar*
- blend and read words with *ar*

Materials

- Letter Cards *a, f, k, p, r*
- Teaching Master ES4-1
- Phonics Library: *A Park for Parkdale*

**Get Set For Reading
CD-ROM**

Officer Buckle and Gloria

Education Place

www.eduplace.com
Officer Buckle and Gloria

Audio CD

Officer Buckle and Gloria
Audio CD for **Amazing Animals**

**Lexia Phonics
CD-ROM**

Primary Intervention

PRETEACH

SKILL FOCUS: PHONICS · · · · · 10–15 MINUTES

r-Controlled Vowels *ar*

Teach

Recite the chant to introduce /är/. Repeat it, emphasizing the *ar* words.

> **CHANT**
> Let's go riding in the car.
> It can take us very far!

Say the word *car*, and have children repeat it. Isolate and stretch /är/, and have children repeat it.

Have children stretch /är/ as they say these words: *far, part, smart, bark.*

Have children raise their hand when they hear /är/ as you say these words: *park, take, flat, party, farm, card.*

Blend

Use Blending Routine 1.

Distribute the letter cards *f, a,* and *r* to children. Have children holding the *a* and *r* cards link arms. Then have the child with the *f* card walk towards the other children to form *far.* Have children listen as you blend the sounds, stretching the *ar* sound and then saying the word.

Repeat the same steps with the word *park.* Have children say *park* with you. Then have them blend it on their own.

Guided Practice

Display or **distribute** Teaching Master ES4-1.

Tell children to use what they know about the sound *ar* to read the invitation with you. Randomly point to words and have children read them. Help children to identify any words with the /är/ sound and circle them.

Check children's ability to read *ar* words by having them read aloud all the circled words.

SKILL FOCUS: PHONICS   10-15 MINUTES

r-Controlled Vowels *or, ore*

Teach

Recite the chant with children to introduce /ôr/. Repeat it, emphasizing *corn* and *more*.

> **CHANT**
> More, more, more, please!
> Yellow corn, please!

Say the word *more*, and have children repeat it. Isolate and stretch the /ôr/ sound, and have children repeat it. Have children stretch /ôr/ as they say these words: *snore, chore, short*.

Tell children to stamp a foot on the floor when they hear /ôr/ as you say these words: *born, home, porch, store, stop, born*.

Blend

Display the word *more*. Use Blending Routine 1 to blend the sounds. Note the silent *e*. Then have children blend the word *more*.

Repeat the same steps with *corn*. Have children say *corn* with you. Then have them blend it on their own.

Practice/Apply

Distribute copies of Practice Master ES4-1 and read the directions.

Tell children to use their knowledge of sounds and letters to read the sentences and match them with the correct pictures.

Check children's responses by having them read the /ôr/ words.

LITERATURE FOCUS: 10-15 MINUTES

Preview *A Park for Parkdale*

Preview *A Park for Parkdale* and discuss the illustrations. Use words from the story such as *stores, morning, market*, and *park*.

Ask children to say what the people in the town work together to do. Tell children they will read this story with the rest of the class.

Objectives

- associate /ôr/ with *or* and *ore*
- read words with *or* and *ore*

Materials

- word cards *more, corn*
- Practice Master ES4-1

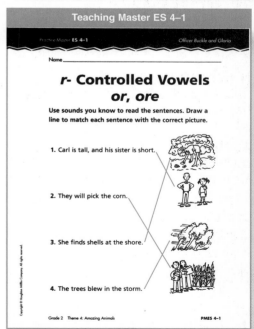

Day 2

Objective
• use story clues to draw conclusions

Materials
• Teaching Master ES4-2
• Practice Master ES4-2
• Anthology: *Officer Buckle and Gloria*

WATCH OUT FOR POWER LINES!

SKILL FOCUS: COMPREHENSION   25–30 MINUTES

Drawing Conclusions

Teach

Tell children you want them to be detectives. Have them listen as you describe a scene: *The wastebasket was turned over. Some papers and an empty cookie box were on the floor. The box had little teeth marks on it. There were paw prints near the basket.* Ask: *What happened to the wastebasket?* (It was knocked over by an animal.)

Ask children to identify clues that help them decide what happened. (teeth marks, paw prints)

Say that good readers are like good detectives. They look for clues in a story that help them understand what is happening.

Guided Practice

Display or **distribute** Teaching Master ES4-2. Have children use details in the pictures to identify the settings.

Tell children to listen as you read about Mort and the choices labeled *What I Think*.

Guide them as they identify the correct conclusion and the clues that helped them draw the conclusion. (paints, pictures, shapes, clay, makes little books)

Practice/Apply

Distribute Practice Master ES4-2, and read the directions with children. Ask volunteers to repeat in their own words what children should do to complete the activity.

Have children read the stories independently and then indicate their responses.

Check children's ability to draw conclusions as they share their responses with the class.

LITERATURE FOCUS: 20–30 MINUTES

Preview *Officer Buckle and Gloria*

Segment 1

Refer to the bottom of page T47 in the Teacher's Edition and preview with children Segment 1 of *Officer Buckle and Gloria* (pages 19-37).

Note the suggestions in the Extra Support boxes on the Teacher's Edition pages T51 and T55.

Segment 2

Refer to the bottom of page T47 in the Teacher's Edition and preview with children Segment 2 of *Officer Buckle and Gloria* (pages 38-51).

Note the suggestions in the Extra Support boxes on the Teacher's Edition pages T59 and T62.

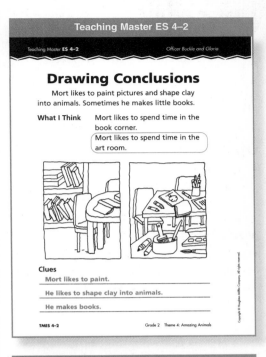

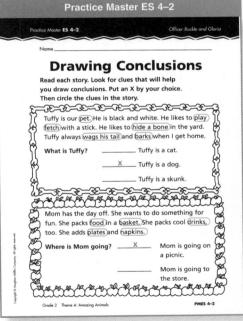

Day 3

Objective
- read and write new High-Frequency Words: *board, listen, told*

Materials
- Anthology: *Officer Buckle and Gloria*

Look both ways before you cross.

Objectives
- replace naming words with pronouns in the story
- write sentences with pronouns

High-Frequency Words

Teach

Write *board, listen,* and *told* on the board. Ask: *Where did I write these words?* (on the board) Ask: *Which of these words is* board? Have children give other examples of what the word *board* can mean.

Ask: *What do I need you to do when I am talking?* (listen) *Which of these words is listen?* Have children give examples of times when they listen.

Write *cold* and *hold* under *told.* Have children read the two new words. Then point out that *told* ends the same way as *cold* and *hold.* Have the students read *told.* Then write the sentence *I told you a story yesterday* on the board.

Practice

Write these sentence frames on the board:

Our teacher _____ us we should _____ when he was talking. Then he wrote on the _____ .

Have volunteers come to the board and complete the sentences using the High-Frequency Words.

Apply

Have children work in pairs to write a sentence for each High-Frequency Word. Then have the pairs trade sentences and read each other's work, circling the High-Frequency Words in the sentences. Have children read the sentences aloud to the class.

Words for Nouns (Pronouns)

Teach

Ask children what they did after school yesterday. Using their names, write sentences on chart paper similar to these:

Jorges played baseball.
Ashley read a book.
Jason and Mia rode bikes.
Natalie rode bikes with Jason and Mia.

Prepare some index cards with these pronouns written on them: *He, She, They, I, We,* and *Them*. Show the index cards, and have the children read the pronouns aloud. Tell children that the names can be replaced with pronouns. Read each sentence substituting pronoun cards for names. Tape the pronoun over the name or names in the sentence. Continue until you have placed a pronoun over each name or pair of names.

Practice

Refer children to *Officer Buckle and Gloria*. Have children replace nouns with pronouns in story sentences. Read each sentence aloud, and have children say the pronoun that belongs in that sentence. Some of the following examples could be used:

Page 25 "Gloria obeys my commands." (She)

Page 26 "The children sat up and stared." (They)

Page 37 "Officer Buckle loved having a buddy." (He)

Apply

Have children find and write sentences that contain pronouns. Have children circle the pronoun. Then have them work with a partner to identify the story character to whom the pronoun refers.

LITERATURE FOCUS: 10–15 MINUTES

Review *Officer Buckle and Gloria*

Ask children to review and retell *Officer Buckle and Gloria*. Then ask partners to take turns drawing conclusions about the story. Remind them to support their ideas with clues from the words and illustrations.

TEST THE WATER BEFORE DIVING IN.

Objectives

- listen to and blend phonemes
- identify the /är/ sound
- independently read and write words with *ar* in them

Materials

- Sound/ Spelling Card *artist*
- Letter Cards a, *c, f, h, m, n, p, r, t, y*

RETEACH

SKILL FOCUS: PHONICS — 25-30 MINUTES

r-Controlled Vowels *ar*

Teach

Tell children to listen closely to these words: *arm, jar, scarf, target, carnival*. Ask what sound these words have in common. /är/ Say words *am, aid, arm; hate, hand, harm; cave, carve, cove.* Have children raise their hand each time they hear a word with the /är/ sound.

Display the Sound/ Spelling Card, *artist,* and have children say the sound /är/ when you point to the *ar* spelling. Write the word *card* on the board. Use Blending Routine 2 to help children blend the word. For each sound, point to the letter(s), say the sound, and have children repeat it. Have children say the sound for *c*,/k/, then the sound for *ar*, /är/, and then blend /kär/. Finally, have them say the sound for *d*,/d/, and blend /kärd/, *card*. Repeat the blending procedure with *hard* and *dark*.

Write *garden*. Help children divide the word into syllables between the *r* and *d*. Help children blend the sounds in each syllable and then blend the syllables to read the word. Repeat with *starting* and *target*.

Practice

Display letter cards *a* and *r* and make words by putting other letter cards before and after the two cards that make the /är/sound. Then have children use their letters to make words such as *arm, art, tar, part, cart, yarn, harm,* and *farm.* Write the words on the board, underline the *ar*, and have children say the word.

Apply

Have children work in pairs as they read *A Park for Parkdale* and write lists of words with *ar* in them that they find in the story. Have children write their lists on the board and compare them.

Objectives

- listen to and blend phonemes
- identify the letters *or* and *ore* as forming the /ör/ sound
- independently read and write words with *or* and *ore* patterns

Materials

- Sound/ Spelling Card *orange*

RETEACH

SKILL FOCUS: PHONICS — 10–15 MINUTES

r-Controlled Vowels *or, ore*

Teach

Say *corn, torch, shore, order,* and ask children what sound these words have in common. (/ôr/)Say these words, and ask children to identify the word with the /ôr/ sound: *cone, corn, torch, touch, pot, port.*

Display the Sound/ Spelling Card *orange* and have children repeat the /ôr/ sound. Point out the *or* spelling of this sound on the card. Next, write the word *fork* on the board and use Blending Routine 2 to help children blend the word. For each sound, point to the letter(s), say the sound, and have children repeat it. Have children say the sound for *f*, /f/, then the sound for *or*, /ôr/, and then blend /fôr/. Finally, have them say the sound for *k*, /k/, and blend /fôrk/, *fork*.

Write *more* on the board and point out the *ore* spelling of the /ôr/ sound. Then follow the same blending procedure as above to blend the sounds in the word *more*.

Practice

Write these sentence on the board:

The waves hit the <u>shore</u> with <u>force</u>.

We used a <u>torch</u> to see until <u>morning</u>.

The <u>horse</u> had a <u>sore</u> leg.

Call children to the board to circle the spelling of the /ôr/ sound for the underlined words. Then have them read the complete sentence.

Have children brainstorm a list of other *or* and *ore* words.

Possible words: *fort, north, formula, forklift, sore, score, chore, before, scoreboard, shoreline.*

Apply

Have children write short stories using words from the board. Tell children to underline words that have the *or* spelling of the /ôr/ sound and to circle words that have the *ore* spelling of the /ôr/ sound.

DON'T GET RATTLED!

LITERATURE FOCUS: 10–15 MINUTES

Preview *Arthur's Book*

Walk children through *Arthur's Book* and discuss the illustrations using words from the story such as *started, hard,* and *story*.

Ask children to use picture clues to conclude where Arthur may get a story idea.

Day 5

Objectives
- draw conclusions about events in a story
- identify feelings based on actions in role plays

Materials
- Anthology: *Officer Buckle and Gloria*
- Phonics Library: *A Park for Parkdale, Arthur's Book*

Drawing Conclusions

Teach

Show children pictures of people in various uniforms, such as a police officer, firefighter, nurse, soldier, or dentist. Or you might simply want to begin with a description of a person in an occupation: *She drives me and all of my schoolmates to school in the morning. She beeps the horn. She turns the wheel. Who is she?* Ask: *What do you think this person's occupation is? What clues do you see (or hear) that help you reach this conclusion?*

Point out that children used the details in the pictures or sentences to draw conclusions. Tell them that they can use their skill in drawing conclusions to understand something that may not be stated directly in a story. Use the following Think Aloud:

> ### Think Aloud
>
> *I am in line at the grocery store. The man in front of me is buying hot dogs, buns, potato chips, sodas, charcoal, and lighter fluid. From the items that I see in his shopping cart, I draw a conclusion that he is going to have a cookout.*

Tell children that you are going to read a list of items. Ask them to draw a conclusion about what they can do with the items.

- flour, sugar, eggs, frosting, candles (make a birthday cake)
- mop, bucket, scrub brush, cleaner (mop the floor)
- lettuce, tomatoes, carrots, cucumber, ranch dressing (make a salad)

Practice

Tell children that they are going to use clues from the text and illustrations in the story *Officer Buckle and Gloria* to figure out some things that happened that the author did not tell them directly.

Direct children to page 22 of the story. Read the text aloud. Ask: *What do you see?* (children are sleeping, someone is throwing airplanes) Ask: *Based on what the story says and what the picture shows, how do you think the students at Napville School were feeling?* (bored) Ask: *Did the author say the students were bored?* (no) Explain that they used the clues in the picture to figure out the children's feelings.

Use other examples in the story, such as the following:

> Page 35 *How does Officer Buckle feel about all the phone calls?* (He looks happy or proud)

> Pages 42–43 *How does Officer Buckle feel when he sees himself on the news?* (surprised) *How does Gloria feel?* (worried, nervous)

Conclude by saying: *Being able to figure things out that are not stated in the story will help you to understand the meaning of the story. This will make you a better reader.*

Apply

Have children take turns acting out different feelings that characters in the story have. Ask the other children to guess the mood or emotion. Some examples of different moods include the following: *bored, happy, proud, friendly, loving, grumpy,* or *unhappy.*

ENJOY THE MILK, NOT THE GLASS.

LITERATURE FOCUS: 10–15 MINUTES

Revisit *Officer Buckle and Gloria, A Park for Parkdale,* and *Arthur's Book*

Page through all the stories with children and review the illustrations and text in each story to recall the conclusions of each story.

Have children look through *Officer Buckle and Gloria* for these high-frequency words: *board, listen,* and *told,* and for words with the /ôr/ sound such as: *more, snoring, morning,* and *enormous.*

Ask children to identify /är/ words from the Phonics Library stories.

Day 1

Objectives

• recognize and say the /nd/, /nk/, and /nt/ sounds
• blend and read words with final *nd, nk,* and *nt*

Materials

• word cards *drank, hand, think, went*
• Teaching Master ES4-3

**Get Set For Reading
CD-ROM**
Ants

Education Place

www.eduplace.com
Ants

Audio CD

Ants
Audio CD for **Amazing Animals**

Lexia Phonics
CD-ROM

Primary Intervention

SKILL FOCUS: PHONICS   10–15 MINUTES

Words with *nd, nk, nt*

Teach

Recite the chant with children. Repeat the words *ground, around,* and *found,* emphasizing the final /nd/.

> CHANT
> Chant, chant, look for an ant.
> Look on the ground, look all around.
> Look in a trunk, look in a sink.
> It's in the Lost and Found, I think!

Tell children to listen to and then repeat some words that end in *nd.* Say: *hand, land, find, kind, bend.* Have children stand when they hear /nd/ in the following words: *band, shake, hand, play, panda.*

Tell children to listen to and then repeat some words that end in *nk.* Say: *thank, trunk, bank, blank.* Have children blink when they hear words that end with /nk/: *bake, sink, skunk, can, shrink.*

Tell children to listen to and repeat words that end in *nt.* Say: *point, print, paint.* Have children point to the child next to them when they hear words that end with /nt/: *plan, plant, ten, tent.*

Blend

Display the word card *think.* Using Blending Routine 1 to model how to blend the sounds, moving your finger under the letters as you read. Blend the sounds softly, and then say the word aloud. Have children repeat the process. Display the word card *drank,* and have children blend it. Repeat with /nd/ and *hand,* and /nt/ and *went.*

Write *plank, send, clink, grand, tent,* and *stunt* on the board, and have children blend the sounds to read them.

Guided Practice

Display or **distribute** Teaching Master ES4-3 and discuss the illustration with children.

Explain to them that they will read the sentences with you and then choose a word from the piggy bank to complete each sentence. As children identify the words, help them write the words in the sentences.

Check children's ability to read and write *nd, nt,* and *nt* words.

SKILL FOCUS: STRUCTURAL ANALYSIS   10–15 MINUTES

Base Words and Endings: -es, -ies (nouns)

Teach

Recite the chant; emphasizing the words *bunches* and *puppies*.

> **CHANT**
> A bunch of puppies here.
> A bunch of puppies there.
> Bunches of puppies everywhere!

Write *bunch* and *bunches*. Underline the *-es* in *bunches* and explain to children that when a naming word ends in *ch*, *-es* is added to show more than one. Write the words *kisses*, *boxes*, and *dishes*, and explain that *es* is also added to words that end in *s, x*, and *sh*.

Write *puppy* and *puppies* and underline the *y* in *puppy* and the *-ies* in *puppies*. Explain to children that when a noun ends in *y*, the *y* is changed to *i* before *-es* is added to make a plural.

Blend

Display the word *babies*. Using Blending Routine 1, move your finger under the letters as you read. Have children repeat the blending process with you. Have children blend *pennies* on their own. Repeat the same steps for plurals ending with *-es*, such as *lunches* and *foxes*.

Practice/Apply

Distribute copies of Practice Master ES4-3 to children and read the directions. Call their attention to *kittens, shells, cars, things*, and *trees*, noting that many words that name more than one thing end with just *-s*.

Check children's ability to identify plural nouns as they read the sentences.

LITERATURE FOCUS: 10–15 MINUTES

Preview *Hank's Pandas*

Preview *Hank's Pandas* by walking children through the story, discussing the illustrations, and plurals such as *pandas, stories,* and *plants*. Ask children to name things Hank does to take care of the panda.

Objectives

- identify *-es* and *-ies* endings
- read words with *-es* and *-ies*

Materials

- Practice Master ES4-3
- word cards *babies, pennies*
- Phonics Library: *Hank's Pandas*

Teaching Master ES 4–3

Teaching Master **ES 4-3**   *Ants*

Final Consonant Clusters *nd, nk, nt*

plenty

blink   drank

grunt   bent   ending

plant   land

1. The girls will _____ **plant** _____ some seeds.
2. What is the _____ **ending** _____ of your story?
3. The plane will _____ **land** _____ soon.
4. He _____ **drank** _____ a glass of cold milk.

TMES 4–3   Grade 2 Theme 4: Amazing Animals

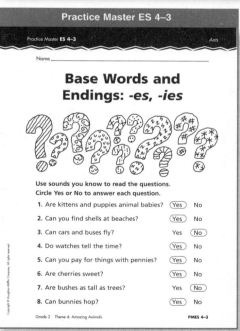

Practice Master ES 4–3

Practice Master **ES 4-3**   *Ants*

Name _____

Base Words and Endings: -es, -ies

Use sounds you know to read the questions.
Circle Yes or No to answer each question.

1. Are kittens and puppies animal babies?   (Yes)   No
2. Can you find shells at beaches?   (Yes)   No
3. Can cars and buses fly?   Yes   (No)
4. Do watches tell the time?   (Yes)   No
5. Can you pay for things with pennies?   (Yes)   No
6. Are cherries sweet?   (Yes)   No
7. Are bushes as tall as trees?   Yes   (No)
8. Can bunnies hop?   (Yes)   No

Grade 2   Theme 4: Amazing Animals   PMES 4–3

Day 2

Objective

• identify and use illustrations, captions, and text to understand main ideas

Materials

• Teaching Master ES4-4
• Practice Master ES4-4
• Anthology: *Ant*

Text Organization

Teach

Write the following on the board:

> Honey bees make honey. They start by taking nectar from flowers. Then, they take the nectar to their beehive. There, they will turn the nectar to honey to eat during the winter.

Read the text aloud and ask children: *What do honeybees make?*

Write *Main Idea* on the board above the sentence *Honeybees make honey,* and ask children to provide you with details from the text that help to support the main idea.

Explain that children can look at pictures, listen for repeated words in stories, and read the text to figure out what the main idea is.

Guided Practice

Display or **distribute** Teaching Master ES4-4 to children, and read aloud the directions. Be certain children are aware of the stated main idea and the final question that relates to the illustration.

Read aloud the text and call on children to underline the details in the text that support the main idea.

Ask children to write a complete sentence to answer the last question on the page.

Practice/Apply

Distribute Practice Master ES4-4. Have children take note of the illustration and the caption below it. Point out the main idea statement.

Tell children to use the picture, caption, and what they read to help them fill in details that support the main idea.

Check children's ability to pick out details that support the main idea by reviewing their responses with them.

LITERATURE FOCUS: 20–30 MINUTES

Preview *Ant*

Segment 1

Refer to the bottom of page T133 in the Teacher's Edition and preview with children Segment 1 of *Ant* (pages 61-69).

Note the suggestions in the Extra Support boxes on the Teacher's Edition page T136.

Segment 2

Refer to the bottom of page T133 in the Teacher's Edition and preview with children Segment 2 of *Ant* (pages 70-83).

Note the suggestions in the Extra Support boxes on the Teacher's Edition pages T142 and T144.

Teaching Master ES 4–4

Teaching Master **ES 4–4**   Ants

Text Organization

Read the information. Then read the main idea. Underline details in the paragraph that tell more about the main idea.

Animals need doctors, too. These doctors check dogs and cats for fleas and ticks. They give animals shots and pills to keep them well. Some can mend birds' broken wings. I would like to help animals some day.

Main Idea: Animal doctors do many things to help animals.

What does the picture tell you an animal doctor can do?

_____Animal doctors can check a dog's teeth._____

TMES 4–4   Grade 2 Theme 4: Amazing Animals

Practice Master ES 4–4

Practice Master **ES 4–4**   Ants

Name _____

Text Organization

Read the information. Then read the main idea. Use the caption for the picture and the details in the selection to tell about the main idea on the lines below.

Birds carry what they need to make nests.

Birds build nests as their homes. Some nests are in trees. Others are on the ground. Most nests are made of grass and twigs. Some nests are large, but others are small.

Main Idea: Birds build nests.

Detail: Birds carry what they need to make nests.

Detail: Some nests are in trees.

Detail: Some nests are on the ground.

Detail: Most nests are made of grass and twigs.

Detail: Some nest are large, but others are small.

Grade 2 Theme 4: Amazing Animals   PMES 4–4

Day 3

Objective

• read and write new High-Frequency Words: *between, care,* and *weigh*

High-Frequency Words

Teach

Write *between* on the board. Then draw a vertical line between the *be* and the *tween*. Cover *tween* and ask children to read *be*. Then cover *be* and ask children to read *tween*. Remind them that a double *e* makes the sound /ē/. Uncover the whole word and have children read it. Have children give examples of sentences with the word *between* in them.

Write *care* on the board and read it. Have students repeat the word. Ask volunteers for examples of sentences with the word *care*.

Write the word *weigh* on the board, read it, and have children repeat it. Tell children that this word has an unusual spelling and have them spell it aloud with you. Ask volunteers for examples of sentences with the word *weigh*.

Practice

Write the following sentence frames on the board:

I wrote _____ on the board.

I care about _____ .

I will weigh the _____ .

Have children copy the sentence frames and complete them. Then have children read their answers aloud. You may wish to make lists of the different words and phrases used to complete each sentence.

Apply

Have children write one sentence for each word. Then have them exchange papers and take turns reading the sentences.

Singular Possessive Nouns

Teach

Write a list of the children's names on the board. Ask each child to name his or her favorite toy. Write the name of the toy next to the child's name, leaving space to add *'s*. Tell children: *When I want to show that an object belongs to someone, I add an apostrophe and an -s to the name.* Go down the list and add *'s* to each child's name.

Have each child write his or her name on an index card and add *'s*. Assemble a small pile of objects such as crayons, pencils, and books. Hand an object to a child and ask: *Whose crayon is this?* Have the child hold up his or her name card. Continue with this process until each child's name has been used as a possessive noun.

Practice

Write the following sentences on the board:

The ant tunnels filled the colony. (ant's tunnels)

An ant antennae are like a nose and fingers. (ant's antennae)

A worker job is to find food. (worker's job)

Read the sentences aloud. Work with children to add the *'s* to show ownership.

Apply

Have children write and complete the following sentences about ants:

An _____ home is called an anthill. (ant's)

The _____ job is to lay eggs. (queen's)

Have children share their completed sentences.

Review *Ant*

Ask children to review and retell *Ant*. After the retelling, have children choose a page or section of the story and identify the main idea and details. You may want children to record this information in a text organization chart.

Objectives

- write names as singular possessive nouns
- identify singular possessive nouns in the story
- form singular possessive nouns in writing

Materials

- Anthology: *Ant*

Day 4

Objective

• independently read and write words with *nd, nt, mp, ng, nk*

Materials

• Letter Cards *a, b, c, d, e, g, i, k, l, m, n, o, p, r, s, t, u, w, y*

Words with *nd, nt, mp, ng, nk*

Teach

Have children listen for and identify the final sound in words ending with a single consonant, such as *cap, light,* and *knob.* (/p/, /t/, /b/) Then have them listen for and repeat the final consonant sounds in each of these words: *sand, lamp, pant, went, hand, dump.* (/nd/, /mp/, /nt/, /nt/, /nd/, /mp/) Finally, challenge children to listen for and repeat the final consonant sounds in *think* and *song.* (/nk/, /ng/)

Remind children that *n* sometimes joins together with another consonant at the end of a word or syllable. Write *sand* on the board, circle the *nd,* and say the word. Have children repeat it and then say the /nd/ sounds several times. Note how the two sounds blend together. Next, write the word *land* on the board and use Blending Routine 2 to help children blend the word. For each sound, point to the letter, say the sound, and have children repeat it. Have children say the sound for *l,* /l/, then the sound for short *a,* /ă/, and then blend the two sounds. Next, have them say the sound for *n,* /n/, and blend the three sounds, /lăn/. Finally, have them say the sound for *d,* /d/, and blend all the sounds to say *land.*

Follow the same procedure, using these words and consonants:

• *pant* for the letters *nt*

• *lamp* for the letters *mp*

• *long* for the letters *ng*

• *pink* for the letters *nk*

Practice

Ask children to place their cards for *n* and *d* together on their desk or workspace. Then ask children to make words by adding to these letters. Have volunteers tell you what words they are making, and write the words on the board. Repeat this procedure with *nt, mp, ng,* and *nk,* asking children to make words with each pair of letters.

Apply

Have children work in pairs as they read *Hank's Pandas.* Have them find words with *nd, nt, mp, ng,* and *nk.* On the board, write a chart with each pair of letters as a column heading. Then ask children to take turns writing their words beneath the appropriate heading.

Base Words and Endings -s, -es, -ies (Nouns)

Teach

Write the words *cat, watch,* and *city* on the board. Point out that each of these nouns names one thing. Explain that to name more than one thing you must make the noun plural by adding *-s, -e,* or *-ies.*

Write *cats* beneath *cat.* Explain that we add *-s* to most nouns to make them plural.

Write *watches* beneath watch. Explain that when nouns end in *ch, ss, x,* or *sh,* you add *-es* to make them plural.

Write *wives* below *wife.* Point out that when nouns end in *f* or *fe,* you change the *f* to *v* and add *-s* or *-es.*

Write *cities* beneath *city.* Explain that when nouns end in a consonant plus *y,* you change the *y* to *i* and add *-es.*

Practice

Recite the following phrases. Have children write the phrases down.

One hand, two hands.

One mix, two mixes.

One fly, two flies.

Have volunteers write the phrases on the board. Review the spellings of the singular and the plural nouns with children.

Apply

Have children write two sentences for each pair of nouns they have written, using the singular noun in the first sentence, and the plural noun in the second sentence.

Objectives

- listen to words to identify endings *-s, -es, -ies* (nouns)
- independently read and write words with *-s, -es, and -ies* endings

Materials

- Phonics Library: *Marta's Larks*

Preview *Marta's Larks*

Walk children through *Marta's Larks* and discuss the illustrations, using words from the story such as *larks, birds, bugs, sing* and *thinks.*

Ask children where Marta lives and what details in the pictures let them know. Then tell them that they will read this story with the group.

Day 5

Objectives
- identify main ideas in text organization
- locate pages in the story with main ideas

Materials
- Anthology: *Ant*
- Phonics Library: *Hank's Pandas, Marta's Larks*

Text Organization

Teach

Write the following story on six sentence strips:

I woke up when my alarm went off.

Next, I put on my red shirt.

I got to school on time.

I ate a banana and cereal.

First, I took a shower.

Then I got on the school bus.

Read the story to children. Ask: *Does my story make sense?* (no) Have children help you organize the story in a way that makes sense by rearranging the sentence strips.

Tell children that when we tell a story, we have to organize it in a way that makes sense. We might organize it by which things happened first, as in the story organization above.

Tell children that authors also have to organize their information in a way that makes sense. Explain that, as readers, we use the author's organization to decide which ideas are the most important and how ideas relate to each other.

Practice

Tell children that they are going to find out how the author organized the story *Ant*. Begin on page 63. Together, read the text aloud. Ask: *What is the main idea?* (you hardly ever see just one ant)

Direct children to pages 64–65 of the story. Read the text aloud. Ask: *What is the main idea of these pages?* (ants live in colonies) Say: *So far, we have seen that the author has a main idea for each set of pages. Did she tell us there would be a main idea?* (no) Ask: *How did we find out what the main idea was?* (read the words, looked at the pictures, listened for repeated words) Explain that they used clues in the text to figure out how the author organized the text.

Use the same procedure, identifying how the text is organized on these pages:

Pages 66–67   ant antennae

Pages 68–69   ants help each other

Repeat that they used main ideas on each set of pages to help them figure out how the story is organized.

Apply

Write the following words on the board: *leafcutter ants, army ants, farmer ants, carpenter ants, weaver ants.* Have children copy the words and tell them that each one is a main idea. Ask them to find the pages on which each main idea is described, and write the page numbers next to it

• *Carpenter ants* (pages 70–71)

• *Leafcutter ants* (pages 72–73)

• *Weaver ants* (pages 74–75)

• *Farmer ants* (pages 76–77)

• *Army ants* (pages 78–79)

LITERATURE FOCUS: 10–15 MINUTES

Preview *Ant, Hank's Pandas,* and *Marta's Larks*

Page through all the stories with children and ask them to recall the main ideas of each story.

Tell children to look through *Ant* for the following High-Frequency Words: *between, care,* and *weigh,* and for words that end in *nd, nk,* and *nt* such as *ant, ground, around, find, kinds, bend, plant,* and *think.*

Ask children to look for and say words with *-s, -es,* and *-ies* endings in each story.

Day 1

Objectives

- associate the /ō/ sound with the vowel pairs *oa* and *ow*
- blend and read words with *oa* and *ow*

Materials

- word cards: *crow, goal, oak, oath, rowboat, toad, throw*
- Teaching Master ES4-5
- Practice Master ES4-5
- Phonics Library: *Crow's Plan*

Get Set for Reading CD-ROM

The Great Ball Game

Education Place

www.eduplace.com
The Great Ball Game

Audio CD

The Great Ball Game
Audio CD for **Amazing Animals**

Lexia Phonics CD-ROM

Primary Intervention

PRETEACH

SKILL FOCUS: PHONICS   25–30 MINUTES

Vowel pairs *oa, ow*

Teach

Recite the chant with children to introduce the /ō/ vowel sound.

Say the word *row* and have children repeat it. Isolate and stretch the long *o* vowel sound and have children repeat it. Do the same with the words *boats, grow, oats, know,* and *goats.*

Have children stretch the long *o* sound as they say these words with you: *road, flow, coat,* and *croak.*

Have children pantomime growing each time they hear a word with the /ō/ sound: *got, goat, blow, slow, not, now, snow.*

> **CHANT**
>
> Row, row, row your boats,
> Grow, grow, grow your oats,
> Know, know, know your goats!

Blend

Use Blending Routine 1.

Display the word card for *crow.* Model how to blend the sounds, stretching the long *o* sound and then saying the word. Explain to children that the two letters *ow* together stand for the long *o* vowel sound. Then have children blend the word and say it with you. Ask a volunteer to use *crow* in a sentence.

Repeat the same steps with the word card for *goal,* saying that the two letters *oa* stand for the long *o* vowel sound.

Display the word cards for *oak, oath, rowboat, toad,* and *throw.* Have children use blending to read them.

Guided Practice

Display or **distribute** Teaching Master ES4-5, and discuss the illustration with children. Write *toaster* below the picture, and ask children to read the word with you. Have children notice the words written on the slices of bread. Tell them to use what they know about blending sounds to read the words with you.

Direct attention to the sentences. Have children read them with you. Explain that they should find words on the slices of bread to complete the sentences. Help children identify the words and write them in the sentences.

Read the completed sentences with children.

Practice/Apply

Distribute Practice Master ES4-5 and discuss the illustrations and directions with children.

Tell children to find the long *o* words in the story and then write them on the lines.

Have children read the story and complete the Practice Master independently .

Check children's ability to read long *o* words by having them read their answers aloud.

LITERATURE FOCUS: 10–15 MINUTES

Preview *Crow's Plan*

Walk children through *Crow's Plan* and discuss the illustrations, naming the characters and using words from the story such as *floats, croaked, hollow, show, goal,* and *throw*.

Ask children what problem Crow solves. (He cleans up Oak Lake with the help of his friends.)

Tell children they will read this story with the rest of the group.

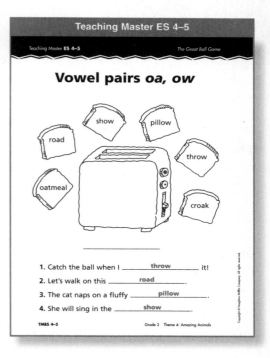

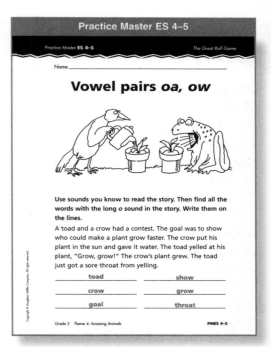

Day 2

Cause and Effect

Teach

Tell children to watch you carefully. Fan your face with your hand or a piece of paper for a moment to convey that you feel warm. Then go and open the window. Discuss your actions with children. Ask: *What did I do first? What did I do next? Why did I open the window?*

Explain that one good way of understanding what is happening around us is to look for reasons why things happen. Explain that this is true when reading stories, too. Paying attention to why things happen helps readers better understand and enjoy stories.

Guided Practice

Display or **distribute** Teaching Master ES4-6 and discuss the illustration with children. Read the story and the questions with them.

Guide children as they answer the *Why* questions.

Objective

- identify cause-and-effect relationships in the story

Materials

- Teaching Master ES4-6
- Practice Master ES4-6
- Anthology: *The Great Ball Game*

Practice/Apply

Distribute Practice Master ES4-6 to children, and read the directions with children.

Have them read the page independently and make their responses.

Check children's comprehension of cause and effect as children share their responses.

LITERATURE FOCUS: 20–30 MINUTES

Preview *The Great Ball Game*

Segment 1

Refer to the bottom of page T203 in the Teacher's Edition and preview with children Segment 1 of *The Great Ball Game* (pages 91–99).

Note the suggestions in the Extra Support boxes on the Teacher's Edition pages T205 and T206.

Segment 2

Refer to the bottom of page T203 in the Teacher's Edition and preview with children Segment 2 of *The Great Ball Game* (pages 100–109).

Note the suggestions in the Extra Support boxes on the Teacher's Edition pages T211 and T212.

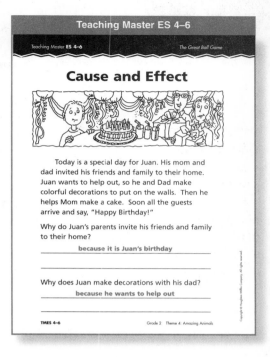

Teaching Master ES 4–6

Teaching Master **ES 4–6** — *The Great Ball Game*

Cause and Effect

Today is a special day for Juan. His mom and dad invited his friends and family to their home. Juan wants to help out, so he and Dad make colorful decorations to put on the walls. Then he helps Mom make a cake. Soon all the guests arrive and say, "Happy Birthday!"

Why do Juan's parents invite his friends and family to their home?

_____ because it is Juan's birthday _____

_____

Why does Juan make decorations with his dad?

_____ because he wants to help out _____

_____

TMES 4–6   Grade 2   Theme 4: Amazing Animals

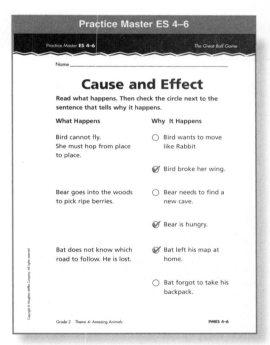

Practice Master ES 4–6

Practice Master **ES 4–6** — *The Great Ball Game*

Name_____

Cause and Effect

Read what happens. Then check the circle next to the sentence that tells why it happens.

What Happens	Why It Happens
Bird cannot fly. She must hop from place to place.	○ Bird wants to move like Rabbit
	● Bird broke her wing.
Bear goes into the woods to pick ripe berries.	○ Bear needs to find a new cave.
	● Bear is hungry.
Bat does not know which road to follow. He is lost.	● Bat left his map at home.
	○ Bat forgot to take his backpack.

Grade 2   Theme 4: Amazing Animals   PMES 4–6

Day 3

Objective
- read and write new High-Frequency Words: *ago, field, half, war*

Materials
- word cards *ago, field, half, war*

SKILL FOCUS: 10–15 MINUTES

High-Frequency Words

Teach

Hold up the word card *war* and read it aloud. Tell children that they are going to play tug-of-war. Next, hold up the *field* card. Read the word and tell children where they are going to play the game. Then, hold up the *half* card. Divide the children into equal teams and line them up. Hold up the *ago* card. Tell children that a short time ago you explained the details of the tug-of-war activity, and now it is time to play.

Take the children and the word cards outside or clear a space inside. Hold up each card and cue children to say the word at the appropriate time as they prepare to play the game. (We are going to play tug-of-… (war). We are going to play on the… (field).)

Practice

Display the High-Frequency Word cards on the chalk ledge. Have children draw pictures of the class playing tug-of-war. Ask them to write descriptions underneath their drawings, using the high-frequency words.

Apply

Have children show their pictures to the class and read aloud their descriptions.

Objectives
- identify plural possessive nouns
- punctuate plural possessive nouns in sentences

Materials
- Anthology: *The Great Ball Game*

SKILL FOCUS: GRAMMAR   10–15 MINUTES

Plural Possessive Nouns

Teach

Write the following sentences with plural nouns on the board:

The boys will bring the hockey sticks.

The boys' hockey sticks are in the gym.

Read the sentences with children. Explain that in the first sentence, the word *boys* is a plural noun; it ends in *-s*, and it tells us that there is more than one boy. Then explain that in the second sentence, the word *boys'* is a plural possessive noun. It has an apostrophe to show that the hockey sticks belong to the all the boys.

Practice

Direct children to page 100 in the story *The Great Ball Game*. Read aloud this sentence:

"On the Animals' side Fox and Deer were swift runners, and Bear cleared the way for them as they played." Ask: *Where do you see an apostrophe in this sentence? Where is the apostrophe in the word* Animals'?

Write the following sentences on the board:

The Birds wings made them better than the Animals.

The Animals teeth made them better than the Birds.

The Birds penalty was to leave the land for a half of each year.

Read the sentences aloud. Tell children that each possessive noun is missing an apostrophe. Ask them to tell you where to place the apostrophe. (Birds' wings, Animals' teeth, Birds' penalty)

Apply

Have children punctuate the possessive nouns in the sentences:

Birds wings help them to fly. (Birds')

Animals teeth help them to eat and catch prey. (Animals')

The Birds penalty was given because they lost the game. (Birds')

Have children copy the sentences and draw pictures to illustrate the concepts. Then have them share what they have drawn and written. Ask children how the meaning of the sentences would change if they were written with, *The Bird's wings, An Animal's teeth*, or *The Bird's penalty*. Help children to see that the *'s* refers to just one bird or animal.

LITERATURE FOCUS: 10–15 MINUTES

Review *The Great Ball Game*

Have children review and retell *The Great Ball Game*. Then have children work in pairs. One partner names something that happened in the story (effect) and the other partner tells why it happened (cause). Children should alternate identifying effects and causes.

Day 4

RETEACH

SKILL FOCUS: PHONICS   25-30 MINUTES

Vowel pairs *oa, ow* (long o)

Teach

Tell children to listen to and blend these sounds: /s/ /ōp/. Have children repeat the sounds and say the word. (soap) Repeat with *glow*.

Display the Sound/Spelling Card *ocean* and review the long *o* sound, /ō/, as heard in the word *ocean*. Have children repeat the long *o* sound back to you, /ō/ /ō/ /ō/. As you point to the various sound/spellings, remind children that you've already talked about the *o_e* spelling of the long *o* vowel sound. Tell children that the long *o* vowel sound can also be spelled with the letters *oa* or *ow*.

Write *boat* on the board. Use Blending Routine 2 to help children blend the word. For each sound, point to the letter(s), say the sound, and have children repeat it. Have children say the sound for *b*, /b/, then the sound for *oa*, /ō/, then blend /bōōō/. Finally, have them say the sound for *t*, /t/, and blend /b ō ō ō t/, *boat*.

Write *row* on the board, and point out the *ow* spelling of the /ō/ sound. Follow the same blending procedure as above.

Provide clues about words spelled with *oa* and *ow* to help children generate a word list. Write the words on the board.

CLUE	WORD
Rest your head on it	pillow
Something stays on top of the water	floats
Used to clean hands, clothes, and dishes	soap
What the wind does	blows

Objectives
- say the long *o* vowel sound with *oa, ow* vowel pairs
- independently read and write words with vowel pairs *oa, ow*

Materials
- Sound/Spelling Card *ocean*
- Phonics Library: *Crow's Plan, Brent Skunk Sings*

Practice

Have children choose one *oa* word from the board to write on a sheet of paper. Have them choose an *ow* word to write on the back of the paper. Next, lay a large sheet on the floor. Tell children it is a boat. Have children take turns holding up their *oa* words and reading them. After each word is read correctly, respond, *Come into the boat.* Tell children to bring their papers with them.

Have them take turns reading their *ow* words. After each word is read correctly, respond, *Now row the boat.* Have children pantomime a rowing motion.

Apply

Have children work in pairs as they read *Crow's Plan.* Have them find words with vowel pairs *oa* and *ow.* Write on the board a chart with each vowel pair as a column heading. Then ask children to take turns writing their words beneath the appropriate vowel pair.

LITERATURE FOCUS: 10–15 MINUTES

Preview *Brent Skunk Sings*

Preview *Brent Skunk Sings.* Discuss the illustrations and name the characters: Brent Skunk, Grandad Frank, and the dentist. Use words from the story such as *dentist, teeth, mouth, closed, clean, count,* and *open.*

Ask children why the dentist wanted Brent to open his mouth. (to count, clean and check his teeth) Then tell them that they will read this story with the rest of the class.

Day 5

SKILL FOCUS: COMPREHENSION   25–30 MINUTES

Cause and Effect

Teach

Write the following sentences on the board:

The flowers grew because we had a lot of rain.

We had a lot of rain, so the flowers grew.

Since we had a lot of rain, the flowers grew.

As a result of the rain, the flowers grew.

Explain that in each of these sentences one event makes another event happen. Tell them when one event causes another event it is called a *cause and effect.*

Ask: *What happened in each of those sentences?* (the flowers grew) Explain that the part of the sentence that tells what happened is the effect. Ask: *Why did the flowers grow?* (because of the rain) **Explain** that the part of the sentence that tells why something happened is the cause.

Read the sentences aloud again. Point out the words *so, since, because,* and *as a result.* Tell children that these are all words that signal a cause and effect relationship.

Practice

Remind children that there are many events in the story *The Great Ball Game.* Identify each of the following events as the cause, and let the children tell the effect.

- The Birds and Animals have an argument, so… (they decided to have a ball game to settle it)

- The Birds are on one team because… (they all have wings; they can fly)

- The Animals are on the other team since… (they all have teeth)

- Bat doesn't know where to go because… (he has teeth and wings)

- As a result of Bat's playing,… (the Animals win)

Tell the children that when they read they can look for the words *so, because, since,* and *as a result* to help them see how the events flow in a story.

Objectives

- identify cause-and-effect key words *because, so, since,* and *as a result*
- make a cause-and-effect chart about the story

Materials

- Anthology: *The Great Ball Game*
- Phonics Library: *Crow's Plan, Brent Skunk Sings*

Apply

Copy the cause and effect chart below on the board. You may want to add sentences from other story details. Have children complete the chart with partners or as a class. Remind them that a *cause* tells why something has happened and an *effect* tells what happened.

CAUSE	EFFECT
The birds are swifter, so	(they keep stealing the ball)
(The birds don't want him, so)	Bat joins the Animal team.
(because he could see better)	Bat flies when it gets dark
(Because the birds lose the game,)	They have to leave for half of every year.

LITERATURE FOCUS: 10–15 MINUTES

Revisit *The Great Ball Game, Crow's Plan,* and *Brent Skunk Sings*

Page through all stories wih children and review what happens and why in each story.

Have children look through *The Great Ball Game* for the following high-frequency words: *ago, field, half* and *war.*

Have children find and say words with the long *o* sound in *Crow's Plan.*

Theme 5

Family Time

Selections

1 Brothers and Sisters

2 Jalapeño Bagels

3 Carousel

4 Thunder Cake

Brothers and Sisters

Day 1

SKILL FOCUS: PHONICS   25–30 MINUTES

The -*er* Ending in Two-Syllable Words

Objectives

- associate /ər/ with *er* in two-syllable words
- blend and read words that end with *er*

Materials

- Teaching Master ES5-1
- Practice Master ES5-1
- Phonics Library: *My Sister Joan*

Teach

Recite the chant. Repeat it, emphasizing /ər/ in the second syllable of *winter*, *summer*, and *better*.

> **CHANT**
> Winter or summer,
> Summer or winter.
> I can't say which one I like better!

Repeat *better*, clapping each syllable beat. Ask children in which syllable they hear /ər/. Repeat with the words *summer* and *winter*.

Have children say these words: *banner*, *monster*, *sister*, and *partner*. Ask them to repeat each word emphasizing /ər/ in the second syllable.

Blend

Use Blending Routine 1.

Display *winter*. Point to the consonant letters *n* and *t* in the middle of the word. Remind children they can break a word into syllables between two consonants (VCCV pattern). Draw a slash between the syllables *win* and *ter*.

Model blending the sounds in each syllable and then blending the syllables together. Run your finger under the final *er* as you say /ər/.

Repeat the same steps for the word *summer*. Have children blend the word with you.

Display *better*, *number*, *slender*, and *supper*. Have children break the words into syllables and then blend the syllables into words on their own.

Technology

Get Set for Reading CD-ROM

Brothers and Sisters

Education Place

www.eduplace.com
Brothers and Sisters

Audio CD

Brothers and Sisters
Audio CD for **Family Time**

Lexia Phonics CD-ROM

Primary Intervention

Guided Practice

Display or **distribute** Teaching Master ES5-1. Have children tell what the illustration shows and use what they know about sounds to read the story with you.

Point out the words that end with *er*, and have children read them. As each word is read correctly, circle it.

Check children's ability to read two-syllable words ending with *er* by having them read aloud the circled words.

Practice/Apply

Distribute copies of Practice Master ES5-1 and complete the directions with children.

Tell them to use what they know about sounds to complete the page independently.

Check children's responses by having them read aloud each word with *er*.

LITERATURE FOCUS: 10–15 MINUTES

Preview *My Sister Joan*

Familiarize children with *My Sister Joan* by walking them through the story. Discuss the illustrations, name the characters, and use words from the story such as *sister*, *summer*, *grasshoppers*, *stingers*, *baby-sitter*, and *brothers*.

Ask children if they would like to take care of a little sister like Joan. Have them tell why or why not.

Tell children they will read this story with the rest of the class.

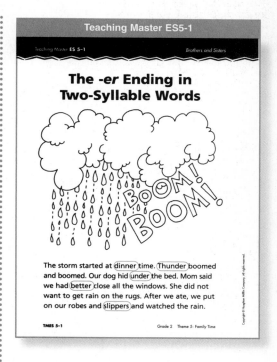

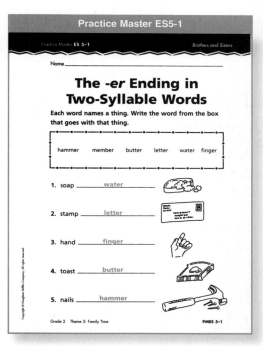

Day 2

Objectives
- make generalizations
- identify information that supports a generalization

Materials
- Teaching Master ES5-2
- Practice Master ES5-2
- Anthology: *Brothers and Sisters*

Making Generalizations

Teach

Tell children that a generalization is a statement about a group. The statement is true for most of the group most of the time.

Say: *Here is a generalization.* The children in my class are talented. *Let me tell you how I can support that generalization.* Mention several children in the class by name, noting a special ability or talent—reading, drawing, making friends, and so on. Tell children that a generalization must have facts to support it.

Explain that stories sometimes include enough pieces of information for listeners or readers to make a generalization.

Guided Practice

Display or **distribute** Teaching Master ES5-2. Discuss the illustration with children.

Point to the generalization, and have children read it with you. Tell them to listen to a story and think about the details in it that support the generalization.

Do this →

Read Aloud

> One day at the playground, the babysitters talked together while the children played. Karen said that once little Mike tried to pour some milk by himself, and he spilled it all over the kitchen. Josh said that little Sara used her mom's lipstick to draw pictures. Jane said little Pete tried to catch a frog and fell into the pond. The sitters all suddenly stopped talking when they saw the children running out of the open gate.

Reread the generalization with children. As children offer support for the generalization, help them write the details in the list.

Practice/Apply

Distribute Practice Master ES5-2, and read the directions with children.

Have children read the paragraphs and incomplete generalizations independently.

Have them write a word to complete each generalization.

Check children's ability to make generalizations by reviewing their responses.

LITERATURE FOCUS: 20–30 MINUTES

Preview *Brothers and Sisters*

Segment 1

Refer to the bottom of page T47 in the Teacher's Edition and preview with children Segment 1 of *Brothers and Sisters* (pages 162–169).

Note the suggestions in the Extra Support box on the Teacher's Edition page T49.

Segment 2

Refer to the bottom of page T47 in the Teacher's Edition and preview with children Segment 2 of *Brothers and Sisters* (pages 170–180).

Note the suggestions in the Extra Support boxes on the Teacher's Edition pages T51, T54, and T56.

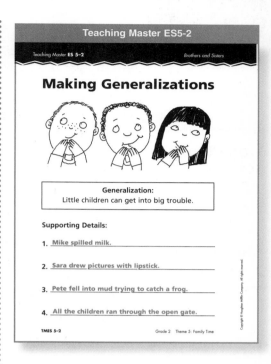

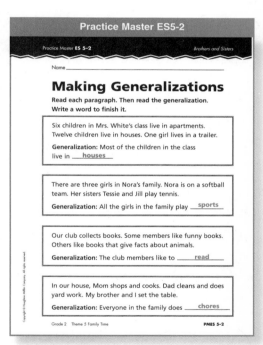

Day 3

RETEACH

SKILL FOCUS: 10–15 MINUTES

High-Frequency Words

Objective
- read and write new High-Frequency Words: *middle, trouble, uncle*

Materials
- Anthology: *Brothers and Sisters*

Teach

Write *middle, trouble,* and *uncle* on the board. Read them with children. Point out that each word has two syllables. Read the words again and clap out the syllable beats as you say them. Then have children clap the syllable beats and reread the words with you. Invite children to say sentences using each word.

Practice

Write the following sentence starters on the board.

I ate the middle of _____.

Once I got in trouble by _____.

I wish I had an uncle who _____.

Read the sentence starters with children. Ask them to copy the sentence starters on their own paper. Then tell them to complete the sentences any way they wish.

Write each sentence starter as a heading on a piece of chart paper. Allow children to write how they completed each sentence under the appropriate heading.

Example:

I ate the middle of a _____.

pie	*cake*
pizza	*donut*
sandwich	*slice of bread*

Apply

Have children read the sentences they created. After children have shared their sentences, invite the class to read the sentences aloud together by inserting each answer written on the chart paper into the sentence starter.

SKILL FOCUS: GRAMMAR · 10–15 MINUTES

Verbs

Teach

Ask children to come to the front of the classroom in pairs to pantomime different actions, such as walk, jump, and clap. Have the class tell what each pair is doing.

Write the responses on the chalkboard and underline each action word.

Sarah and Jim (walk). Maria and Dave (jump)

Explain to children that words that describe what people or animals do are called verbs. Verbs are often called action words.

Practice

Write on the chalkboard and read aloud the following sentence about a character in Brothers and Sisters: Dorrie cuddles the baby all the time. Ask, *What does Dorrie do?* (cuddles) Underline the word in the sentence, and point out to children that it is a verb because it describes what Dorrie does. Ask a volunteer to pantomime the action.

Apply

Have children work in groups of five to write chain stories. Provide a list of verbs to use in sentences, such as *walk, talk, play, go, tell, share, get, help,* and *call.* Instruct each child to write a sentence on the top of the page, using one of the verbs in the list and pass the page to the right. Direct children to underline the verb in the sentence they receive and add a sentence of their own using a different verb from the list. When children get their original paper back, have them read the story aloud to the group.

LITERATURE FOCUS: · 10–15 MINUTES

Review *Brothers and Sisters*

Ask children to review and retell *Brothers and Sisters.* Then ask each child to make a generalization based on the story. Have them support their generalization with an example.

Objectives
• identify words that show action
• write a chain story and underline the verbs

Materials
• Anthology: *Brothers and Sisters*

Day 4

The *-er* Ending in Two-Syllable Words

Objectives

- say the / ər/ sound for the *-er* ending
- read and write two-syllable words ending in *-er*

Materials

- Phonics Library: *The Big Party Plan*

Teach

Ask children to blend these sounds, /t//ō ō ō/s//t/. Ask children what the word is. (toast) Then ask children to add the/ ər/ sound to the end of the word. Ask children what the new word is. (toaster) Tell children to blend these sounds, /rr//ē ē ē//d/ Ask children what the word is. (read) Then ask children to add the /ər/ sound to the end of the word. Ask children what the new word is. (reader)

Write *mother, father, brother,* and *sister* on the board. Read the words with children.

Underline the *-er* in each word. Point out to children that all of these words end with the /ər/ sound. Tell children that all of these words have two syllables. Read the words again, and clap out the syllable beats as you say them. Then have children clap the syllable beats and reread the words with you.

Practice

Have children brainstorm a list of two-syllable words that end with *-er*. Invite them to write the words on the board or on an overhead transparency. Have children write three sentences using a two-syllable *-er* word in each sentence.

Have a few volunteers lead the class in a group reading of the words listed on the board or overhead transparency. Then have children read their sentences to the class. Ask each child to pick one of the three sentences to write on chart paper. After children have written their sentences, display the chart paper. Read the sentences aloud with the whole class or in small groups.

Apply

Have pairs of children find two-syllable words with *-er* in *My Sister Joan*.
The words they should find are: *sister, Buster, matter, summer,
grasshopper, butter, stingers, dinner, better, holler(ed)*, and *younger*.
Each time children find an *-er* word, they should read it aloud while
you write the word on the board. Have volunteers come to the board
and circle the ending.

Preview *The Big Party Plan*

Walk children through *The Big Party Plan* and discuss the illustrations.
Name the characters and use words from the story such as *slippers,
flowers, streamers* and *banners*.

Ask children to identify some details that support this statement:
Everyone in the Chang family works hard to throw the party.

Tell children that they will read this story with the rest of the class.

Day 5

Objectives

- identify words that signal generalizations
- use story facts to make broad statements

Materials

- Anthology: *Brothers and Sisters*
- Phonics Library: *The Big Party Plan, My Sister Joan*

RETEACH
SKILL FOCUS: COMPREHENSION   25–30 MINUTES

Making Generalizations

Teach

Begin a discussion about children's shoes. Ask, *How many children are wearing tie shoes? How many children are wearing shoes with straps? How many children are wearing slip-on shoes?* Record in a chart the number of children with each type of shoe. Make generalizations from the information in the chart. For example, you might say, *Most of you have shoes that tie.*

Tell children that the statements are *generalizations* made from facts in the chart. Explain that generalizations are broad statements that are true for most things in a group most of the time. Tell children that words like *most, all, always, generally, often, many, usually, few,* and *never* can signal statements that are generalizations.

Practice

Have children read aloud pages 163–166 in *Brothers and Sisters*. Ask children to tell what the characters in the story say about having a new baby in the family. In a chart, record children's responses and the number of characters for whom the statement is true.

What children say about the new baby:	How many agree?
The new baby is fun.	1
I like to hold the new baby.	3
Mom is so busy with the baby	1
I'm tired of everyone talking about the baby.	1

Ask the class to help make generalizations about what the children say about a new baby in the family. (Most children like to hold the new baby.) Remind children that they must base their generalizations on facts that they read.

Apply

Have children work with a partner to write generalizations about grown-ups who are brothers and sisters. Have children read about grown-up brothers and sisters on pages 178–180 in the story. Encourage children to use facts from the story and what they know about grown-up brothers and sisters in their own families to make generalizations.

Revisit *Brothers and Sisters, The Big Party Plan,* and *My Sister Joan*

Page through all the stories with children, and ask them what generalizations they can make.

Ask children to look through *Brothers and Sisters* for the High Frequency Words *middle, trouble,* and *uncle.*

Have children look for words with *-er* in the second syllable in *The Big Party Plan* and *My Sister Joan.*

Day 1

Objective
• blend and read contractions

Materials
• Teaching Master ES5-3

**Get Set for Reading
CD-ROM**
Jalapeño Bagels

Education Place
www.eduplace.com
Jalapeño Bagels

Audio CD
Jalapeño Bagels
Audio CD for **Family Time**

**Lexia Phonics
CD-ROM**
Primary Intervention

PRETEACH

SKILL FOCUS: STRUCTURAL ANALYSIS   10–15 MINUTES

Contractions

Teach

Recite and repeat the chant, emphasizing the contractions. Encourage children to echo your second reading.

> CHANT
>
> I'm your friend
>
> And you're my friend.
>
> We're the best of friends!

Print *I am* and *I'm* on the board. Help children compare them. Point out the letter *a* in *I am* and the apostrophe that replaces it in *I'm*. Explain that a contraction is a shorter way of saying two words.

Have children read *I am* and then *I'm* with you.

Continue with *you're* and *you are*, and *we're* and *we are*.

Blend

Print *she's* on the chalkboard. Use Blending Routine 1 to model how to blend the sounds, and print *she is* above the contraction. Circle the apostrophe and tell children it takes the place of a letter. Have children name that letter.

Continue with the contractions *can't* and *they'll*, having children blend the sounds to say each contraction. Write *cannot* and *they will* to show how this time two letters are replaced by an apostrophe.

Guided Practice

Display or **distribute** Teaching Master ES5-3. Read the words in the bag with children and help them to answer the question.

Help children read the first incomplete sentence, choose a contraction to complete it, write it in the sentence, and read the completed sentence aloud. Follow the same procedure with the remaining sentences.

Check children's ability to read contractions by pointing to contractions randomly and having children read them and tell what two words have been put together to form each one.

SKILL FOCUS: PHONICS   10–15 MINUTES

The -*le* Ending in Two-Syllable Words

Teach

Recite the chant and repeat it, encouraging children to join in.

Say *giggle*, clapping the syllables. Ask children how many syllables they hear. (two) Say it again, emphasizing /gəl/. Have children repeat it.

> CHANT
>
> Giggle, giggle, wiggle.
>
> Jiggle, jiggle, laugh.

Have children say these words: *wiggle, jiggle, little, table, paddle*. For each word have them say the separate syllables and the complete word.

Blend

Display the word *fiddle*. Point to the consonant letters *d* and *d* in the middle. Remind children that they can break a word into syllables between two consonants. Draw a line between the syllables.

Use Blending Routine 1 to model blending the sounds in the first syllable. Point to *dle* as you blend the sounds in the second syllable. Have children blend the word. Repeat the steps for the word *candle*. Display *puddle, middle, tumble, thimble*, and have children blend them.

Practice/Apply

Distribute copies of Practice Master ES5-3 and read the directions with children. Have them read the page independently and complete the sentences.

Note children who need more support with consonant *le* words.

LITERATURE FOCUS: 10–15 MINUTES

Preview *Lost and Found*

Familiarize children with *Lost and Found* by walking them through the story. Discuss the illustrations, name the characters, and use words from the story such as *apple, mumbled, chuckle, fumbled,* and *stumbled*.

Objectives

* identify a consonant followed by *le* at the end of a word
* blend and read two-syllable words ending with *le*

Materials

* Practice Master ES5-3
* Phonics Library: *Lost and Found*

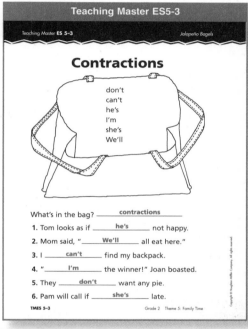

Teaching Master ES5-3

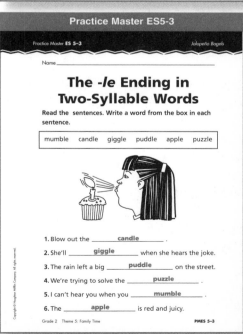

Practice Master ES5-3

Day 2

Following Directions

Teach

Tell children that when people make something, they should follow the steps in the correct order.

Say: *When I cook, I follow a recipe. A recipe tells me what to do step by step and in what order. Many recipes use the words* first, next, then, *and* last.

Guided Practice

Display or **distribute** Teaching Master ES5-4. Tell children that they will read with you a recipe for making a snack. They should note what ingredients are needed and the order of what to do.

Write the following on the chalkboard.

> Celery stuffers are tasty and simple. You will need stalks of celery, cream cheese, raisins, honey, and a butter knife. Rinse the celery under cold water and dry it. Next, spread cream cheese on each stalk. Put some raisins on top. Last, drizzle on a little honey.

Read the recipe outline on Teaching Master ES5-4 with children. Then have them help you fill in the information. Review the finished recipe.

Objective
• use order words to describe the steps in a recipe

Materials
• Teaching Master ES5-4
• Practice Master ES5-4
• Anthology: *Jalapeño Bagels*

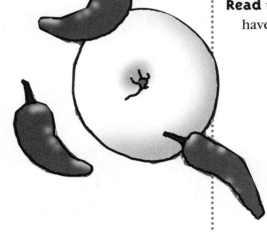

Practice/Apply

Distribute Practice Master ES5-4, and read the directions with children.

Discuss the steps for making a fruit smoothie.

Have children write their directions independently.

Check children's ability to follow directions as they share their responses.

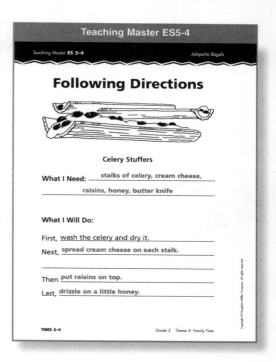

LITERATURE FOCUS: **20–30 MINUTES**

Preview *Jalapeño Bagels*

Segment 1

Refer to the bottom of page T127 in the Teacher's Edition and preview with children Segment 1 of *Jalapeño Bagels* (pages 193–203).

Note the suggestions in the Extra Support boxes on the Teacher's Edition pages T129 and T131.

Segment 2

Refer to the bottom of page T127 in the Teacher's Edition and preview with children Segment 2 of *Jalapeño Bagels* (pages 204–213).

Note the suggestions in the Extra Support boxes on the Teacher's Edition pages T135 and T136.

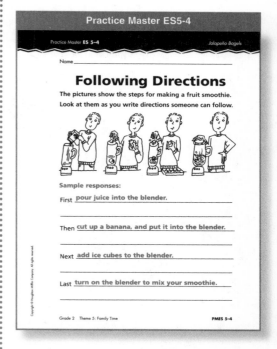

Day 3

Objective
- read and write new High-Frequency Words: *early*, *hair*, *instead*

Materials
- several dictionaries
- small strips of paper
- a container for paper strips
- three sheets of chart paper or butcher paper
- Anthology: *Jalapeño Bagels*

RE**TEACH**

SKILL FOCUS: 10–15 MINUTES

High-Frequency Words

Teach

Write *early*, *hair*, and *instead* on the board. Read the words with children.

Put children in small groups and give each group a dictionary. Have groups use the dictionaries to look up the definitions of the High-Frequency Words. Choose a child to read each definition to the class. Next to each High-Frequency Word on the board, write its definition. Review the words and definitions with children.

Practice

Write the following sentence starters on the board:

I like to be early for _____.

My hair color is _____.

I want to_____.

Instead of _____.

Read the sentence starters with children. Have them write the sentence starters on their own paper. Then have them fill in the blanks in any way they wish.

Apply

Have children read their sentences aloud, then ask them to exchange papers. Tell children to read aloud the sentences they have, replacing I with the name of the student who wrote the sentences.

RE**TEACH**

SKILL FOCUS: GRAMMAR   10–15 MINUTES

Verbs That Tell About Now

Teach

The girls run.   *The girl runs.*

The people laugh.   *He laughs.*

Ask children to identify the verbs in the sentences from the chart. Explain to children that the verbs tell about an action that happens *now*. Help children to understand that the girls run right now and the people laugh right now. Then explain that verbs that tell about now must agree with the subject, or person doing the action. Have children look at the first two sentences in the chart. Point out that in the sentence *The girl runs*, the verb has an *-s* ending. Tell children that a present-time verb will have an *-s* or *-es* ending when the subject is a singular noun, or a naming word that indicates one.

Objectives
- identify verbs that tell about now
- write a paragraph with verbs that tell about now

Practice

Read with children the following sentence from *Jalapeño Bagels*:

"Early Sunday morning, when it is still dark, my mother wakes me up."

Help children to identify the verb in the sentence. (wakes) Point out to children that the verb tells what happens now. Draw children's attention to the *-s* ending on the verb wakes. Rewrite the sentence, replacing mother with parents, and ask children to tell what the verb should be. Remind children that present-time verbs must agree with the subject.

Apply

Have children write a paragraph, using verbs that tell about now. Children should begin the paragraph with the sentence starter, *Every day _____* . If necessary, provide this list of verbs as suggestions: *wake, eat, go, walk, brush, read, work*, and *play.*

LITERATURE FOCUS: 10–15 MINUTES

Review *Jalapeño Bagels*

Ask children to review and retell *Jalapeño Bagels*. After the retelling, have small groups choose a food from the story and name the steps for making it.

Day 4

Objectives
- identify words that contractions stand for
- combine words into contractions
- read and write contractions

Materials
- 3 x 5-inch index cards

RETEACH

SKILL FOCUS: PHONICS   10–15 MINUTES

Contractions

Teach

Say a sentence that uses the words *I am*, similar to the following: *I am going to ask you a question.* Ask children how to say *I am* in a shorter way. (I'm) Repeat the sentence, using *I'm* to replace *I am*: *I'm going to ask you a question.* Repeat this procedure using sets of words and contractions such as *I will* and *I'll*; *he is* and *he's*; *is not* and *isn't*.

Write *I + will = I'll, he + is = he's, and is + not = isn't* on the board. Read the words and contractions with children. Explain that a contraction is a short way of writing two words. Point out that one or more letters is left out of each contraction, and an apostrophe is put in place of the letter or letters.

Write *I'm, I've, you're,* and *let's* on the board. Read the contractions with children. Ask which two words are used to make these contractions. Lead children to conclude that *I'm* is the contraction for *I am, I've* is the contraction for *I have, you're* is the contraction for *you are,* and *let's* is the contraction for *let us.*

Practice

Write *will, is,* and *not* as headings on a three-column chart. Have children brainstorm a list of contractions that use *will, is,* and *not.*

will	is	not
he'll	he's	aren't
I'll	it's	can't
she'll	she's	couldn't
they'll	what's	don't
we'll	where's	isn't
you'll	who's	shouldn't

Have children write three sentences using one contraction from each column of the chart.

Apply

Have children share their sentences with the class. Have each child pick one of his or her sentences to write on the board.

The -*le* Ending in Two-Syllable Words

Teach

Say *maple* and have children repeat it, clapping the syllables as they say them. Repeat this procedure with *candle* and *turtle*.

Write *maple,* and help children divide it into syllables. Remind them that a consonant plus *le* makes up the last syllable, so the word divides after the *a*. Draw a slash mark, and cover the second syllable. Point out how *ma* is an open syllable, meaning it has a long vowel sound. Help children say *ma*. Uncover *ple* and have children say /əl/. Have them read the word.

Write *candle*; underline the *dle*. Say that a consonant plus *le* makes up the last syllable, so the word should be divided after the *n*. Cover the *dle*, and point out that *can* is a closed syllable, meaning the vowel sound is short. Have children sound out the first syllable. Uncover the *dle*, have children blend the sounds, and then blend the syllables to read the word. Point out the *r*-controlled vowel sound in *turtle*.

Practice

Use *maple*, *candle*, and *turtle* as headings for a three-column chart. Have children suggest other words ending with -*le* that belong in each column. For each word, ask a child to underline the consonant plus *le*.

maple	candle	turtle
cradle	simple	marble
fable	mumble	circle
needle	cattle	purple

Apply

Have children pick four words from the list on the board and write a sentence for each one. Have them circle the consonant -*le* in each word.

Preview *What Will Lester Be?*

Walk through the story with children and discuss the illustrations, using words from the story as you go.

Objectives

- identify the consonant plus -*le* ending in two-syllable words
- read and write two-syllable words ending in -*le*

Materials

- Sound/Spelling Card lion
- drawing paper
- crayons or markers
- Phonics Library: *What Will Lester Be?*

Day 5

RETEACH

SKILL FOCUS: COMPREHENSION   25–30 MINUTES

Following Directions

Objectives

- recognize order words (first, next, then and finally)
- list recipe directions in order

Materials

- Anthology: *Jalapeño Bagels*
- Phonics Library: *Lost and Found, What Will Lester Be?*

Teach

Review with children the steps to follow in a school fire drill. Write the directions on the chalkboard. Draw children's attention to order words you use in the directions, such as *first*, *next*, and *finally*. Explain to children how important it is that they follow directions carefully and complete each step in order.

Practice

Write the following steps for making chango bars on chart paper and then divide the steps into sentence strips.

First melt the butter and margarine.

While this is melting, cream brown sugar and eggs.

Then add melted butter and margarine.

Combine flour, baking powder. and salt and stir into sugar mixture.

Fold chocolate chips and nuts into the finished batter.

Pour mixture into greased 9 x 13-inch baking pan.

Finally, bake 45 to 50 minutes at 350 degrees.

Display the sentence strips in order on the chalk tray for the class to read aloud together. Draw children's attention to other words, *first*, *then*, *finally* that indicate the order of the steps. Then rearrange the sentence strips. Invite children to tell how the chango bars would be different if the directions were not followed step-by-step. Ask children to put the steps back in the correct order.

Apply

Have children read pages 202 and 205 with a partner and list in order the things Pablo and his father do to make bagels. Remind children to look for order words to help them understand the sequence of the steps. Ask children to write about what would happen if they did not follow directions carefully. For example, what would happen if they put the bagels in the oven and then boiled them? (They would be soggy bagels.) What would happen if they tried to roll the dough into circles after the dough was cooked? (It would break apart.)

Revisit *Jalapeño Bagels, Lost and Found,* and *What Will Lester Be?*

Page through *Jalapeño Bagels* with children, and ask them what directions Pablo follows with his mother and father in their bakery.

Ask children to find contractions in *Jalapeño Bagels, Lost and Found,* and *What Will Lester Be?*

Have children find the High-Frequency Words *early, hair,* and *instead* in *Lost and Found.*

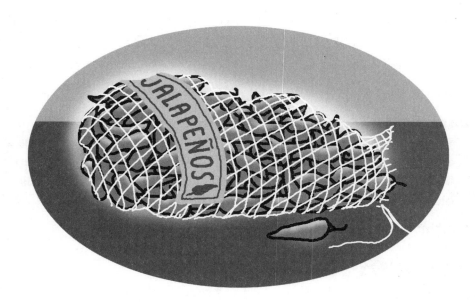

Day 1

SKILL FOCUS: PHONICS · 10–15 MINUTES

Sound of *y* at the End of Longer Words

Teach

Read the chant twice, asking children to echo your second reading.

> **CHANT**
> Funny, fuzzy,
> Fuzzy, funny,
> Little caterpillar.

Repeat the word *funny*, and have children name the number of syllables they hear. (two) Ask children to say the word with you and to listen for the long *e* sound in the second syllable.

Tell children to repeat these words that end with /ē/: *fuzzy*, *sorry*, *hurry*, *scratchy*, and *family*. Encourage them to stretch the long *e* sound at the end of each word.

Blending

Display *muddy*. Remind children that they can try breaking a long word into syllables before they blend sounds. Point out the two consonants *d* and *d*, and draw a line between them. Then use Blending Routine 1 to blend the sounds in each syllable, emphasizing /ē/ in the second syllable. Have children blend the word with you.

Continue with *salty*, *muddy*, *happy*, *floppy*, *sadly*, and *bunny*.

Guided Practice

Display or **distribute** Teaching Master ES5-5. Ask children to use what they know about sounds to read the story with you.

Help children find the words that end with *y* and circle them.

Check children's ability to read words ending with *y* by having them read aloud all the circled words.

Objectives

- associate /ē/ with final y in multisyllable words
- blend and read words that end with y

Materials

- Teaching Master ES5-5
- Phonics Library: *Aunt Lizzy Finds Her Cake*

Get Set for Reading
CD-ROM
Carousel

Education Place
www.eduplace.com
Carousel

Audio CD
Carousel
Audio CD for **Family Time**

Lexia Phonics
CD-ROM
Primary Intervention

SKILL FOCUS: PHONICS | 10–15 MINUTES

The Prefix *un-*

Teach

Recite the chant and then repeat. Encourage children to chime in.

> CHANT
>
> Is that an unhappy you?
>
> Tell me that it is untrue!

Repeat *unhappy*, emphasizing the prefix, and ask children how *unhappy* is different from *happy*. (unhappy is not happy.)

Write *unhappy* and *happy* on the board, and underline the prefix. Tell children that *un-* often adds the meaning "not" to a word.

Have children say these words: *untrue, unkind, unfair*. Ask them to use "not" to tell what each one means. (not true, not kind, not fair)

Blend

Display *unbeaten*. Break the word into three syllables, *un/beat/en*, before using Blending Routine 1 to blend the sounds in each syllable and then blend the syllables. Repeat the word, emphasizing *un-*. Point out meaning by saying, *An* unbeaten *team has not been beaten.* Then have children blend the word with you. Repeat with *unhealthy, unlucky,* and *unwilling*.

Practice/Apply

Distribute copies of Practice Master ES5-5, and read the directions with children. Tell them to read the page independently.

Check children's ability to read words with the prefix *un-*.

LITERATURE FOCUS: | 10–15 MINUTES

Preview *Aunt Lizzy Finds Her Cake*

Familiarize children with *Aunt Lizzy Finds Her Cake* by walking them through the story, discussing the illustrations, naming the characters, and using words from the story.

Objectives

- recognize words with *un-*
- blend and read words with *un-*

Materials

- Practice Master ES5-5

Teaching Master ES5-5

Teaching Master **ES 5–5** — Carousel

Sound of *y* at the End of Longer Words

Vera was tired of the rainy weather. The yard was all muddy. She couldn't go outside. Vera's mom had an idea. "Let's make berry ice cream," she said. "It is tasty." Vera smiled. Vera helped her mom.
Later the whole family had ice cream. They ate every last bit of it. It was very good!

TMES 5–5 — Grade 2 Theme 5: Family Time

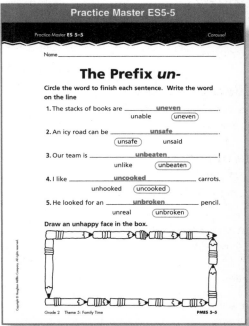

Practice Master ES5-5

Practice Master **ES 5–5** — Carousel

Name _____

The Prefix *un-*

Circle the word to finish each sentence. Write the word on the line

1. The stacks of books are _____ **uneven** _____ .
   unable (uneven)

2. An icy road can be _____ **unsafe** _____ .
   (unsafe) unsaid

3. Our team is _____ **unbeaten** _____ !
   unlike (unbeaten)

4. I like _____ **uncooked** _____ carrots.
   unhooked (uncooked)

5. He looked for an _____ **unbroken** _____ pencil.
   unreal (unbroken)

Draw an unhappy face in the box.

Grade 2 Theme 5: Family Time — PMES 5–5

Day 2

Objective
• make judgments about story characters

Materials
• Teaching Master ES5-6
• Practice Master ES5-6
• Anthology: *Carousel*

Making Judgments

Teach

Explain that sometimes story characters do things that seem right, and sometimes they do things that seem wrong.

Remind children of a familiar folktale character, such as Goldilocks, and state an opinion about the character.

Say, for example: *My opinion is that Goldilocks was selfish and foolish to go into the bears' house. She should have asked their permission first.*

Tell children to think about their own beliefs when they read about story characters. Explain that they can form opinions and make judgments about characters by paying attention to what the characters do and say.

Guided Practice

Display or **distribute** Teaching Master ES5-6. Have children tell what they notice in the two illustrations. Tell them that the boy in both pictures is a story character named Reggie.

Tell children to listen to a story about Reggie. Read the following story.

Read Aloud

One afternoon, Reggie was playing at Marcus's house. "Would you like to join us for dinner?" Marcus's mother asked Reggie. "Thank you," said Reggie. "May I call my mom to get permission?"

Reggie called his mother. She said, "You can stay. Please remember your manners." Reggie sat down to dinner. When he saw the lima beans on his plate, he made a face. "I hate lima beans!" he said. "I won't eat them!"

Repeat it if necessary, so that children can recall the details:

Ask children what Reggie is doing in the first picture (getting permission to stay at his friend's house for dinner) and in the second picture (making a face about the food).

Encourage discussion, and then help children record their judgments about Reggie's actions.

Practice/Apply

Distribute Practice Master ES5-6 and read the directions with children.

Discuss the pictures with them.

Have children read the stories independently.

Check children's responses after they complete the Practice Master to be sure they can make judgments about characters.

LITERATURE FOCUS: 20–30 MINUTES

Preview *Carousel*

Segment 1

Refer to the bottom of page T195 in the Teacher's Edition and preview with children Segment 1 of *Carousel* (pages 221–235).

Note the suggestions in the Extra Support boxes on the Teacher's Edition pages T199 and T201.

Segment 2

Refer to the bottom of page T195 in the Teacher's Edition and preview with children Segment 2 of *Carousel* (pages 236–251).

Note the suggestions in the Extra Support boxes on the Teacher's Edition pages T206 and T210.

Teaching Master ES5–6

Making Judgments

Sample responses:
Opinion of Reggie: He seems polite. He has good manners.

Reasons: He says thank you. He remembers to call his mother for permission to stay for dinner.

Opinion of Reggie: Reggie is rude.

Reasons: Reggie shouldn't say he hates the food. He shouldn't make a face.

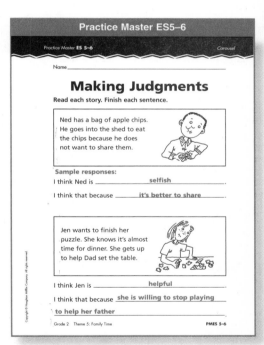

Practice Master ES5–6

Name

Making Judgments
Read each story. Finish each sentence.

Ned has a bag of apple chips. He goes into the shed to eat the chips because he does not want to share them.

Sample responses:
I think Ned is selfish
I think that because it's better to share

Jen wants to finish her puzzle. She knows it's almost time for dinner. She gets up to help Dad set the table.

I think Jen is helpful
I think that because she is willing to stop playing to help her father

Day 3

Objective

• read and write new High-Frequency Words: *aunt, million, pair*

High-Frequency Words

Teach

Write the word *aunt* on the board. Read it aloud. Ask if anyone has an aunt. Then draw a family tree on the board. Draw a mother and father with one child at the bottom. Then draw the mother's sister. Explain that this is the child's aunt.

Write the word *million* on the board. Read it aloud. Then write the numeral for a million on the board. Explain that a million is a very large amount. Ask children to name what they might find a million of in the world. Examples might be grains of sand on the beach, pages in a library, and teaspoons of water in a lake.

Write the word *pair* on the board. Under *pair* write *fair*, *hair*, and *chair*. Explain that these words rhyme. Have children read the words aloud. Ask them to name things that come in pairs such as mittens and socks.

Practice

Write the following sentence frames on the board:

My aunt has a _____.

My aunt wants a _____.

Have children copy the sentence starters onto a sheet of paper. Have them finish the sentences using the words *million* and *pair*. Children may choose to illustrate their sentences.

Apply

Have children show and read their sentences to the class. Then ask children to exchange and read one another's sentences.

SKILL FOCUS: GRAMMAR — 10–15 MINUTES

Verbs That Tell About the Past

Teach

Write the following sentence starters, and ask children to complete:

Last week, I missed one day of school.

When I was little, I lived in a different town.

Draw children's attention to the verbs in the chart. Explain that verbs ending in *-ed* tell about what people or animals did in the past.

Practice

Write the following excerpt from page 188 of Carousel on the board:

"Alex pushed peas from side to side on her plate. She stabbed a potato chunk with her fork, dragged it through the gravy, and ate it like an ice-cream cone."

Ask children to help identify verbs in the sentences as you read them aloud. Underline the verbs, and use guided questions to elicit from children that the verbs all tell about the past. Ask, *What endings do the verbs have?*

Apply

Invite children to play a game. Direct the first player to perform an action, such as clapping. Instruct the next player to tell what just happened and add an action of his or her own. For example,

Player 1, Jill: *(claps hands)*

Player 2, Ben: Jill clapped her hands. *(stamps foot)*

Player 3, ___: Jill clapped her hands. Ben stamped his foot. *(does a jumping jack)*

LITERATURE FOCUS: — 10–15 MINUTES

Review *Carousel*

Ask children to review and retell *Carousel*. After the retelling, have partners discuss what they thought of Alex's behavior.

Objectives
- identify verbs that tell about the past
- play a game that emphasizes action in the past

Materials
- Anthology: *Carousel*

Day 4

Objectives
- listen to and blend phonemes
- identify the long e sound in longer words that end with *y*
- independently read and write words that end in *y*

Materials
- Sound/Spelling Card *eagle*

RETEACH

SKILL FOCUS: PHONICS　　　　10–15 MINUTES

Sound of *y* at the End of Longer Words

Teach

Tell children to listen carefully to these words: *hungry, dusty, city, carry, study*. Ask children how many syllables are in each word. (two) Then repeat the words, and ask children to name the sound heard at the end of each word /ē/.

Write the word *funny* on the board. Have children read the word aloud. Ask: *What sound does the y make?* (/ē/) Then write the words *happy, sorry,* and *heavy* on the board. Have children read the words, listening for the long *e* sound at the end of each word.

Explain that often, when the letter *y* comes at the end of a longer word, it stands for the long *e* sound.

Display the Sound/Spelling Card *eagle*, say the long e sound, /ē/, and have children repeat it. Remind children that they have already learned several spellings of the long e sound. Point out the *y* spelling of the long e sound, explaining that the line before the letter *y* is to remind children that the letter *y* has the long e sound when it comes at the end of a word.

Practice

Write these sentences on the board:

Jenny ate crunchy candy at the county fair.

Twenty people and a puppy came to the party.

Have children copy the sentences, circling the words with the y spellings of the long e sound. Then have them take turns reading the sentences to a partner. Finally, call children to the board to read each sentence and circle the words ending in *y*.

Apply

Have pairs of children find longer words that end with *-y* in *Aunt Lizzy Finds Her Cake*. The words they should find are: *Lizzy, messy, funny, fuzzy, hurry, Willy,* and *Benny*. Ask one of each pair to write the words on the board and the other to divide the words into syllables, drawing a line between them.

SKILL FOCUS: PHONICS   10–15 MINUTES

The Prefix *un-*

Teach

Write *able* on the board, and have children read it. Then write *unable*.

Cover *un-* and have children read the word. Cover *able* and have children sound out the short *u* and the *n*. Then uncover the whole word and have children read it. Explain that *un-* is a prefix that means "not," or "the opposite of." Ask: *What does unable mean?* (not able) Continue with *unhurt, uneven, unfair,* and *unripe*.

Practice

Write "not" and "the opposite of" as two columns on a chart. Have children take turns suggesting words that begin with *un-* and that match the meaning at the top of the column.

not	opposite of
unhappy	unlock
unable	undo
unbroken	unpack
unsure	untie
untrue	unhook

Apply

Have children fold drawing paper into four squares. Ask them to pick a word from each column on the board and write it on a square. Then have them write each word without the prefix *un-* on another square. Ask children to illustrate the meanings of the words they wrote.

LITERATURE FOCUS: 10–15 MINUTES

Preview *My Brother*

Preview *My Brother* by discussing the illustrations. Name the characters, and use words from the story such as *brother, hurry, walk,* and *story*.

Objectives

- identify and pronounce the prefix *un-* in words
- identify the meaning of the prefix *un-*
- independently read and write words with the prefix *un-*

Materials

- Phonics Library: *My Brother*

Day 5

Objectives

- use facts from a story and their beliefs to form opinions about characters and situations
- use guided questions to help them form opinions

Materials

- Anthology: *Carousel*
- Phonics Library: *Aunt Lizzy Finds Her Cake*

SKILL FOCUS: COMPREHENSION   25–30 MINUTES

Making Judgments

Teach

Invite three volunteers to the front of the class to role-play the following situation:

> A child wants to color. The child approaches two different children and asks, "May I color with you?" One child is happy to have a coloring partner and to share markers. Another child refuses to have anyone join him or her.

Discuss with children the different ways the children reacted to the situation. Explain that we use details about children's actions and our beliefs to form opinions about them. Remind children that no single opinion is correct and that they should base their opinions on facts. Tell children that we do the same thing with characters and situations in stories.

Practice

Read with children pages 226–230 in *Carousel*. Ask children to consider Alex's situation and actions. Use the following guided questions, such as those that follow, to help children assess Alex's behavior and form an opinion about the situation.

How is Alex behaving?

Is her behavior fair to her aunts?

Why is Alex upset?

Does that make it okay for Alex to act the way she is acting?

Ask children to identify facts from the story to support the opinions they form.

Apply

Have children work with a partner to talk about what happened with Alex's dad. Encourage children to reread page 246 in the story. Ask them to consider the following questions: *Why did Alex's dad miss her birthday? Did Alex's dad mean to upset her? What did Alex's dad do when he talked with her the next morning?* Have children write opinions of what happened with Alex's dad, based on facts in the story and their own beliefs.

Revisit *Carousel, Aunt Lizzy Finds Her Cake,* and *My Brother*

Page through all the stories with children, and ask for their judgments about characters.

Ask children to look through *Carousel* for the High Frequency Words *aunt*, *million*, and *pair*.

Have children look for words with the prefix *un-* and multisyllabic words that end with *y* in all of the stories.

Day 1

Objectives
- recognize *-ed* and *-ing* as endings on base words
- blend and read words with *-ed* and *-ing* endings

Materials
- Teaching Master ES5-7
- Phonics Library: *Eight Daughters!*

Technology

Get Set for Reading CD-ROM
Thunder Cake

Education Place
www.eduplace.com
Thunder Cake

Audio CD
Thunder Cake
Audio CD for **Family Time**

Lexia Phonics CD-ROM
Primary Intervention

PRETEACH

SKILL FOCUS: STRUCTURAL ANALYSIS 10–15 MINUTES

Base Words and *-ed*, *-ing* Endings

Teach

Recite the chant and then repeat it. Encourage children to chime in.

> CHANT
> Pop, pop, popping,
> POPPING popcorn.
> I popped popcorn.
> Pop, pop, pop.

Repeat *popping*, emphasizing the *-ing* ending. Ask children how the word *popping* is different from *pop*.

Write *pop* and *popping* on the board, and underline the ending. Have children compare the two words and note the double *p* in *popping*. Tell them that a consonant may double before an *-ing* or *-ed* ending.

Repeat *popped*, write it on the board, and underline the ending *-ed*. Have children note the doubled *p*.

Have children say these words with you and listen for ending sounds: *humming, getting, clapping, clapped, spotted, hummed*.

Blend

Display *stopping* and underline the *-ing* ending. Use Blending Routine 1 to model blending sounds, emphasizing *-ing*. Then have children blend the word with you. Repeat the steps for the words *drumming, cutting*, and *shopping*.

Repeat the blending routine for words with *-ed*. Use *drummed, patted, tapped, pinned, nodded*, and *hopped*.

Guided Practice

Display or **distribute** copies of Teaching Master ES5-7. Help children identify the illustration and complete the phrase.

Help children read the list of words and complete the sentences.

SKILLS FOCUS: PHONICS | 10–15 MINUTES

Silent Consonants *gh, k* in *kn,* and *b* in *mb*

Teach

Recite the chant twice. Repeat *knock*. Ask children what sound they hear at the beginning of *knock*. (/n/)

> CHANT
> Knock, knock, knock!
> Neighbors at the door.
> Knots, knots, knots!
> Comb my hair some more.

Write *knock* and *knots* on the board, and point to the initial *kn*. Tell children that in words beginning with *kn*, only /n/ is heard. The *k* is silent.

Have children say the word *neighbors*. Help them break *neighbors* into syllables and then write it on the board. Point to *gh*, explaining that the two letters are silent in some words.

Write *comb* on the board, and point to the final *mb*. Tell children that in words ending with *mb*, only the *m* is heard. The *b* is silent.

Blend

Display *knife*. Use Blending Routine 1 to model how to blend the sounds. Cover the letter *k* with your hand while you blend. Then repeat the whole word. Ask children to blend the word with you.

Practice/ Apply

Distribute copies of Practice Master ES5-7, and read the directions with children. Have them complete the Practice Master independently.

Check children's ability to identify words with silent consonants.

LITERATURE FOCUS: | 10–15 MINUTES

Preview *Eight Daughters!*

Familiarize children with *Eight Daughters!*. Discuss the illustrations, name the characters, and use words from the story.

Objective
• blend and read words with silent letters

Materials
• Practice Master ES5-7

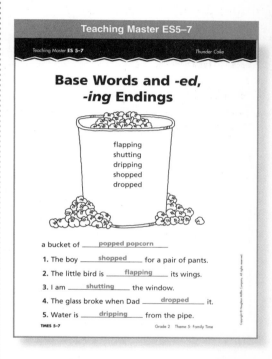

Teaching Master ES5–7

Teaching Master **ES 5–7** — *Thunder Cake*

Base Words and -ed, -ing Endings

flapping
shutting
dripping
shopped
dropped

a bucket of ___popped popcorn___
1. The boy ___shopped___ for a pair of pants.
2. The little bird is ___flapping___ its wings.
3. I am ___shutting___ the window.
4. The glass broke when Dad ___dropped___ it.
5. Water is ___dripping___ from the pipe.

TMES 5-7 — Grade 2 Theme 5: Family Time

Practice Master ES5–7

Practice Master **ES 5–7** — *Thunder Cake*

Name_____

Silent Consonants *gh, k* in *kn,* and *b* in *mb*

Read the sentences. Draw a line to match each sentence with a picture.

1. The kitten climbs the ladder.

2. He slipped and hurt his knee.

3. Mom is cutting with a small knife.

4. She taught her dog a trick.

5. There is a big knot in the rope.

Grade 2 Theme 5: Family Time — PMES 5-7

Day 2

Objective

- identify sequence of events in a story

Materials

- Teaching Master ES5-8
- Practice Master ES5-8
- Anthology: *Thunder Cake*

Sequence of Events

Teach

Explain that a story has a beginning, a middle, and an end. Events happen in a certain order—first, next, after that, and at last.

Tell children that if they pay attention to the order of events, they will understand and remember a story.

Guided Practice

Write the following on the chalkboard and then read it with children:

> Henry's Day
> Henry woke up. He ate breakfast and got dressed.
> When he arrived at work, Henry put on a costume,
> an orange wig, white makeup, and a bright red nose.
> Show time began! Henry rode a tiny bike around
> the circus ring.
> Everyone clapped for Henry the clown.

Display or **distribute** Teaching Master ES5-8.

Help children recall the order of events in Henry's Day, and have them assist you in filling out the chart.

Practice/Apply

Distribute Practice Master ES5-8, and discuss the illustration with children.

Read the directions with them, and suggest that they first number the sentences in the box to show time order and then copy the sentences.

Check children's responses to be sure they know the order in which events happened.

LITERATURE FOCUS: 20–30 MINUTES

Preview *Thunder Cake*

Segment 1

Refer to the bottom of page T269 in the Teacher's Edition and preview with children Segment 1 of *Thunder Cake* (pages 261-279).

Note the suggestions in the Extra Support boxes on the Teacher's Edition pages T276 and T277.

Segment 2

Refer to the bottom of page T269 in the Teacher's Edition and preview with children Segment 2 of *Thunder Cake* (pages 280-291).

Note the suggestions in the Extra Support boxes on the Teacher's Edition pages T280 and T284.

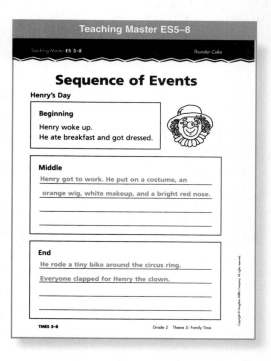

Day 3

Objective
- read and write new High-Frequency Words: air, *child*, *heavy*, *hour*

Materials
- 3 x 5-inch index cards

SKILL FOCUS: 10–15 MINUTES

High-Frequency Words

Teach

Write *air*, *child*, *heavy*, and *hour* on the board and read each word.

Write the following words under *air*: *fair*, *stair*, *chair*. Ask a child to read each of these words. Ask what the four words have in common. (They rhyme.) Then point out that the rhyming sound is spelled the same in all the words: air.

Underline the *ch* in child. Ask, *What sound does ch make?* Have students name other words that begin with *ch*. Then underline the *ld* in child. Point out that this is a blend; the two letters blend together to make one sound. Finally, point out that the *i* in child is a long *i*.

Point to the word *heavy*. Say it and then have children repeat the word. Point out that the *ea* vowel pair makes the short *e* sound in this word. Then explain that when *y* comes at the end of the word and follows a consonant, it makes a long *e* sound. Write the following words under *heavy* as examples: *ready*, *lady*, *somebody*. Have children read the words aloud, noticing the sound the y makes. Then ask, *Which word also has the short e sound spelled ea?*

Cover the *h* in hour and ask children to read the word that remains. Then uncover the *h* and ask them to read the word. Point out that the *h* in hour is silent.

Practice

Write the words *air*, *child*, *heavy*, and *hour* on separate 3 x 5 cards. Give a card to a child and have that child use the word in a sentence. Repeat until all children have had a chance to make a sentence.

Apply

Have children write one sentence using each of the four High-Frequency Words. Have them leave blanks where the High-Frequency Words should go. Then have children exchange sentences and fill in the blanks.

Verbs *is/are, was/were*

Teach

Write the following sentences:

Jen is my sister.

The puppies are cute.

The box was empty.

The windows were open.

Explain to children that not all verbs are action words. Tell them that the words *is, are, was,* and *were* are called linking verbs because they join the naming part of a sentence with the rest of the sentence. Explain that the words *is* and *are* tell about now and tell about one, whereas the words *was* and *were* tell about the past and tell about more than one.

Practice

Write the following sentences from *Thunder Cake* on the chalkboard:

"The air was hot, heavy, and damp." (linking verb)

"I climbed up high on the trellis." (action verb)

"I was scared." (linking verb)

"The lightning flashed again." (action verb)

Give children two index cards to label linking verb and action verb. As you read the sentences have children raise the correct index card.

Apply

Instruct children to write four questions, using a different linking verb in each sentence. Then have children exchange papers with a partner and answer the questions, using the same linking verbs. For example, *What is your favorite game?* (My favorite game is kickball.)

Objectives

- identify linking verbs that tell about now or the past, and one or more than one;
- write linking verbs in sentences.

Materials

- Anthology: *Thunder Cake*

Review *Thunder Cake*

Ask children to review *Thunder Cake*. Then have them retell the story, using the correct sequence of events. You might want children to complete a sequence of events chart before they retell the story.

Day 4

Objectives

- listen to words to identify the *-ed*, *-ing* endings
- independently read and write words with *-ed*, *-ing* endings, doubling the final consonants when necessary

Base Words and Endings *-ed*, *-ing*

Teach

Say several words such as *jumped*, *pals*, *lunch*, *hugged*, and *patted*. Have children raise their hands each time they hear a word ending in *-ed*. Repeat the procedure, substituting words with *-ing* endings.

Write these sentences on the board:

She hopped.   *She is hopping.*

Point to the first sentence and ask, *When did she hop?* (For example, She hopped yesterday.) Remind children that *-ed* added to a verb that the action happened in the past.

Remind children that the *-ed* ending can be pronounced three ways: /t/ /d/, or /ed/. Point out that the *-ed* ending is pronounced /t/ in the word *hopped*. Say the word and have children listen for the final /t/ .

Point to the second sentence and ask, *When is she hopping?* (She is hopping now.) Remind children that *-ing* added to a verb can show that the action is happening right now.

Ask children to name the base word of *hopped* and *hopping*. Write *hop*. Ask what happens to the *p* when *-ed* or *-ing* is added to the word. (It's doubled.) Explain that when *-ed* or *-ing* is added to a word ending with a short vowel and a consonant, the final consonant usually doubles.

Practice

Write the following words on the board: *drop, bat, hug, fan,* and *pin*. Choose children to come forward one at a time and add *-ed* endings to the words. As they do so, point out that the final consonants double. Have children circle the consonant they added.

Repeat the procedure with the following words and *-ing*: *shop, tan, skip, drip, clap,* and *stop*.

Apply

Have children find words with double final consonants and endings *-ed*, and *-ing* in *Eight Daughters!*.

Silent Consonants *gh*, *k* in *kn*, and *b* in *mb*

Teach

Ask children to blend these sounds: /nnn//ĭ ĭ ĭ//t/. Ask children what the word is. (knit) Repeat this procedure with the words *tight* and *thumb*.

Write *knee* on the board and read it. Ask children to name the sounds in the word. (/n//ē/) Then point out that the letter *k* is silent in *knee*; it doesn't stand for any sound. Follow the same procedure with *knife* and *knock*.

Write *high* on the board and read it. Ask children to name the sounds in the word. (/h//ī/) Then point out that the letters *gh* are silent in *high*; they don't stand for any sound. Follow the same procedure with *light* and *taught*.

Write *limb* on the board and read it. Ask children to say the sounds in the word. (/l//ĭ//m/) Then point out that the letter *b* is silent in *limb*; it doesn't stand for any sound. Follow the same procedure with *climb*, *crumb*, and *dumb*.

Practice

Write the following words on the board: *kneel, known, knock, numb, plumber, through,* and *fight*. Have children come to the board and put a line through the silent letter or letters in each word.

Apply

Have children find words with silent consonants *gh*, *kn*, and *b* in *Eight Daughters!*.

Preview *The Family Garden*

Preview *The Family Garden* by discussing the illustrations. As you do, name the characters and use words from the story such as *garden, plows, topped, weeds, bloom,* and *harvest*. Ask children to say what happens at the end of the story.

Objectives

- identify words with silent consonants *gh*, *kn*, *b*
- independently read and write words with silent consonants *gh*, *kn*, *b*

Materials

- Phonics Library : *The Family Garden*

Day 5

Objectives

- identify the order in which events happen and the order words *first*, *then*, *next*, and *finally*
- arrange story events in the correct sequence

Materials

- Anthology: *Thunder Cake*
- Phonics Library: *Eight Daughters!*, *Family Garden*

SKILL FOCUS: COMPREHENSION   25–30 MINUTES

Sequence of Events

Teach

Write on separate strips of paper the following lines from the song *Five Little Monkeys:*

Five little monkeys jumping on the bed,

One fell off and bumped his head,

Mama called the doctor and the doctor said,

No more monkeys jumping on the bed.

Sing the song with children, using the sentence strips as cues. Then draw children's attention to the order in which things happen in the song. Explain to them that this order is the *sequence of events*.

Display the sentence strips in random order on the chalk tray. Ask children to help you put them in the correct order. Help children to understand that authors who write stories also put story events in a certain sequence.

Practice

Work with children to make a timeline of the sequence of events in *Thunder Cake* by Patricia Polacco. Read aloud pages 270–278. As you read, have children identify events to record in the timeline. Point out the order words in the sentences as you read.

When finished, name one or two of the story's events and have children refer to the timeline to tell what happens before, after, or between the events. Explain to children that knowing the sequence of events helps us understand what we read.

Apply

Divide the children into small groups. Have children write events from the story on index cards and then work together to put the events in order. Encourage children to refer to the timeline and the story if they need help.

Revisit *Thunder Cake, Eight Daughters!,* and *The Family Garden*

Page through *Thunder Cake, Eight Daughters!,* and *The Family Garden,* and have children recount events in sequence.

Help children find and read words with the endings *-ed* and *-ing,* and words with *gh, kn,* and *mb.*

Have children read aloud sentences containing the High Frequency Words *air, child, heavy,* and *hour.*

Theme 6

Talent Show

Selections

1 The Art Lesson

2 Moses Goes to a Concert

3 The School Mural

Day 1

Objectives

- associate the /oo/ sound with the vowel pairs *oo* and *ew*
- blend and read words with *oo* and *ew*

Materials

- Teaching Master ES6-1
- Practice Master ES6-1
- Phonics Library: *Our Classroom Zoo Book*

**Get Set for Reading
CD-ROM**
The Art Lesson

Education Place
www.eduplace.com
The Art Lesson

Audio CD
The Art Lesson
Audio CD for **Talent Show**

**Lexia Phonics
CD-ROM**
Primary Intervention

PRETEACH

SKILL FOCUS: PHONICS   25–20 MINUTES

Vowel pairs *oo, ew*

Teach

Use the chant to introduce the /oo/ vowel sound. Recite the chant and then repeat it. Encourage children to echo your second reading.

> CHANT
>
> I like *oodles* and *OOdles*
>
> Of *noodles* in my soup!

Repeat *noodles*, stretching out the vowel sound with children. Then isolate and say the /oo/ sound with them.

Tell children they will say some more words with the /oo/ sound. Use *spoon, grew, moon, flew,* and *balloon*.

Have children say /oo/ each time they hear a word that contains that vowel sound. Say: *goat, goose, stop, stoop, room,* and *roam*.

Blend

Use Blending Routine 1.

Display *tools*. Model how to blend the sounds, stretching the vowel sound and then saying the word. Explain to children that the two letters *oo* together stand for the /oo/ vowel sound. Then have children blend the word and say it with you.

Repeat the same steps with the word *grew*, saying that the two letters *ew* stand for the /oo/ vowel sound.

Display *pool, shoot, smooth, chew,* and *threw*. Have children blend them.

Guided Practice

Display or **distribute** Teaching Master ES6-1. Point out the school bus and the street signs. Tell children that the bus only stops at streets that have the /ōō/ sound.

Have children use what they know about blending sounds to read the street signs with you. After each one is read, ask if the bus should stop there. Mark the street signs that have the /ōō/ sound with an X.

Review the names of all the streets at which the school bus will stop.

Practice / Apply

Distribute Practice Master ES6-1 to children, and read the directions with them. Direct their attention to the pictures and the words in the box, and have children identify them.

Have children read the riddles independently and then answer them with words from the box.

Check children's ability to read /ōō/ words as you review their answers.

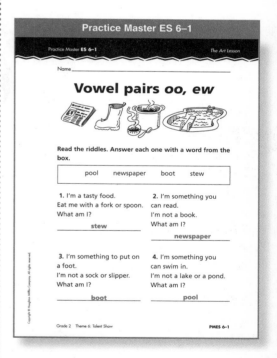

LITERATURE FOCUS: 10–15 MINUTES

Preview *Our Classroom Zoo Book*

Familiarize children with *Our Classroom Zoo Book*. Walk them through the story and discuss the illustrations, naming the characters and using words from the story such as *zoo, cool, tools, drew, moose, goose,* and *flew*.

Have children identify the animals drawn for the zoo book. Then tell them they will read this story with the rest of the class.

Day 2

Objective
- use story details to identify an author's viewpoint

Materials
- Teaching Master ES6-2
- Practice Master ES6-2
- Anthology: *The Art Lesson*

Author's Viewpoint

Teach

Tell children that authors sometimes let readers know how they feel about something by the things their story characters do and say. Give examples such as: If a character in a story is always collecting things like rocks, baseball cards, and new state coins to make collections, the author probably likes collecting things, too; If a character says he or she loves a snowy winter day by the fire, the author probably loves that kind of day, too.

Guided Practice

Display or **distribute** Teaching Master ES6-2 and discuss the picture with children. Explain that you will read a story to them and that they should listen carefully for details that will help decide how the author of the story feels about something.

Read Aloud

> Nina's birthday was coming soon. She knew just what she wanted. And so did everyone else. Nina talked about cats all the time. She said they made good pets. She read books about cats. She had pictures of cats all over her room. She even had a backpack shaped like a cat's head!

Read the words in the first box of the chart with children. Help them recall details from the story to complete the first part of the chart.

Read the completed box and the words in the second box with children.

Ask them how the author probably feels about cats, and record their responses in the second box of the chart.

Practice/Apply

Distribute Practice Master ES6-2 to children and read the directions with them. Have children read the page independently and circle their answer.

Check children's ability to identify the author's viewpoint as they discuss their answers.

Preview *The Art Lesson*

Segment 1

Refer to the bottom of page T47 in the Teacher's Edition and preview with children Segment 1 of *The Art Lesson* (pages 352–365).

Note the suggestions in the Extra Support boxes on the Teacher's Edition pages T50 and T52.

Segment 2

Refer to the bottom of page T47 in the Teacher's Edition and preview with children Segment 2 of *The Art Lesson* (pages 366–378).

Note the suggestions in the Extra Support boxes on the Teacher's Edition pages T58 and T60.

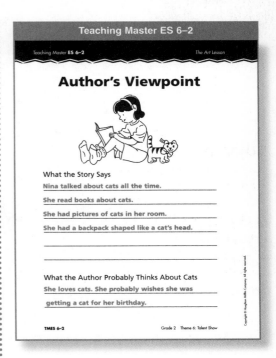

Teaching Master ES 6–2

Author's Viewpoint

What the Story Says
Nina talked about cats all the time.
She read books about cats.
She had pictures of cats in her room.
She had a backpack shaped like a cat's head.

What the Author Probably Thinks About Cats
She loves cats. She probably wishes she was
getting a cat for her birthday.

TMES 6–2   Grade 2   Theme 6: Talent Show

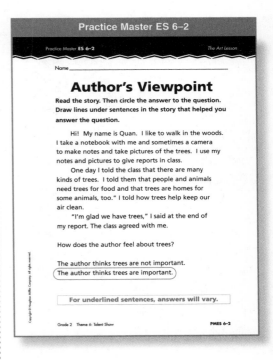

Practice Master ES 6–2

Name

Author's Viewpoint

Read the story. Then circle the answer to the question. Draw lines under sentences in the story that helped you answer the question.

Hi! My name is Quan. I like to walk in the woods. I take a notebook with me and sometimes a camera to make notes and take pictures of the trees. I use my notes and pictures to give reports in class.
One day I told the class that there are many kinds of trees. I told them that people and animals need trees for food and that trees are homes for some animals, too." I told how trees help keep our air clean.
"I'm glad we have trees," I said at the end of my report. The class agreed with me.

How does the author feel about trees?

The author thinks trees are not important.
The author thinks trees are important.

For underlined sentences, answers will vary.

Grade 2   Theme 6: Talent Show   PMES 6–2

Day 3

Objective

- read and write new High-Frequency Words: *fair, gold, woman*

Materials

- Sets of cards with the following words: *fair, gold, woman*

RETEACH

SKILL FOCUS   10–15 MINUTES

High-Frequency Words

Teach

Display word cards *fair, gold, woman*. Read the words and ask children to use each one in a sentence. Then write this sentence on the board:

The _____ (woman) divided the _____ (gold) beads in a way that was _____ (fair) to all the children.

Have children tell you which high-frequency word should go on which write-on line.

Pass out a set of word cards to pairs of children. Write the sentences below on the board:

The _____ (woman) paid a _____ (fair) price for the _____ (gold) watch.

Is it _____ (fair) for the _____ (woman) to win the _____ (gold) prize?

"The team in the _____ (gold) uniforms played a _____ (fair) game," the _____ (woman) said.

It is _____ (fair) to share the _____ (gold) paint," said the _____ (woman) .

Have the pairs work together to complete the sentences using their word cards. Ask volunteers to read the completed sentences aloud.

Practice

Have children make up their own sentences that have all three high-frequency words in them. Invite them to illustrate their sentences.

Apply

Have children exchange pictures and sentences with their partner. Have them show their partner's picture and read their partner's sentence to the whole group.

Irregular Forms of Verbs

Teach

Explain to children that some verbs that show actions in the past do not end in *-ed*. These *irregular verbs* change in other ways—by changing a vowel, adding a consonant, or sometimes by not changing at all. Write the following examples on the chalkboard and discuss them with children:

Present	Past
grow	grew
run	ran
come	came

Practice

Write the following sentences from *The Art Lesson* on the board, and have children draw a line under each irregular verb.

"Tommy <u>knew</u> he wanted to be an artist when he grew up."

"He <u>drew</u> pictures everywhere he went."

"Herbie <u>made</u> huge cities in his sandbox."

Apply

Write the following sentences on the chalkboard. Have children complete each sentence with the irregular form of the verb in parentheses.

Tommy _____ he wanted to be an artist. (know, knew)

He _____ pictures all the time. (draw, drew)

Tommy _____ to art school. (go, went)

Objectives
- identify irregular forms of verbs *(do, come, know, want, grow, draw, go, make, tell)*
- complete a chart and write sentences, using forms of irregular verbs

Materials
- Anthology: *The Art Lesson*

Review *The Art Lesson*

Have children review and retell *The Art Lesson*. After the retelling, have children discuss how the author feels about an event in the story. Ask them to find reasons for their ideas in the text.

Day 4

Objectives

- identify that vowel pairs *oo, ew, ue, ou* can stand for /ōō/
- independently read and write words with vowel pairs *oo, ew, ue, ou* that stand for /ōō/

Materials

- Sound/Spelling Card *moon*
- self-stick notes
- Phonics Library: *Jade's Drumming*

Vowel pairs *oo, ew, ue, ou*

Teach

Have children blend the following sounds: /m/ /ōō/ /n/. Ask what the word is. (moon) Repeat this procedure with *glue* and *chew*. Ask children what sounds these three words have in common. (/ōō/) Say the /ōō/ sound, and invite the children to repeat it. Then name several words such as *moon, pet, spoon, cry, chew, helmet*, and *blue*, having children raise their hand each time they hear the /ōō/ sound.

Display the Sound/Spelling Card *moon*, and remind children that there are several ways to spell the /ōō/ sound. Use self-stick notes to cover all but the *oo* spelling of the sound. Write *moon* and *soon* on the board, underlining the *oo*. Use Blending Routine 2 to help children sound out each word. For example, as you point to the letters in *moon*, have children say the sound for m, /m/, then the sound for oo, /ōō/, then blend /m //ōō//ōō//ōō/. Finally, point to the letter *n*, have children say /n/, and blend /mmm //ōō//ōō// nnn/, *moon*. Next, have children come to the board and underline the *oo* in each word.

Repeat this procedure with other words and sound/spellings for the /ōō/ sound. Examples include *dew* and *flew* for the vowel pair *ew*; *blue* and *glue* for the vowel pair *ue*; and *group* and *soup* for the vowel pair *ou*.

Practice

Label four columns with the headings *moon, dew, blue,* and *soup*. Have children think of additional words such as *broom, cool, crew, screw, clue, true,* and *youth* to add to the chart under the word with the same spelling of /ōō/. Assist children with spelling the words if needed by pointing to the appropriate spelling on the Sound/Spelling Card. Finally, give clues such as "the opposite of false" (true) or "you sweep the floor with this" (broom), and have children point to the answer as they read it from the board.

Apply

Have children find words with vowel pairs *oo, ew, ue, ou* that stand for the /o͞o/ sound in *Our Classroom Zoo Book*. The words they should find are: *classroom, zoo, Moon's, room, cool, tools, drew, hue, glue, droopy, Lou, glue, Mansoor, broom,* and *food*. Each time a child finds an /o͞o/ word, he or she should read it aloud while you write the word on the board. Have volunteers come to the board and circle the vowel pairs.

LITERATURE FOCUS: 10–15 MINUTES

Preview *Jade's Drumming*

Preview *Jade's Drumming* by discussing the illustrations, naming the characters, and using words from the story such as *drumming, drumsticks, drummer, too, grew,* and *bragged.*

Ask children what the author probably thinks about playing the drums. Tell children they will read this story with the rest of the class.

Day 5

Objectives

- demonstrate their understanding of the word viewpoint
- identify how the author feels based on the information in the story

Materials

- Anthology: *The Art Lesson*
- Phonics Library: *Jade's Drumming, Our Classroom Zoo Book*

Author's Viewpoint

Teach

Ask children if they have ever played a game with a friend and found that their friend had different beliefs about how the game should be played. For example, in basketball, one child might believe that you get to shoot again if you make a basket while the other child believes that the ball is turned over to the next player. Explain to children that players in the example had different viewpoints. Say, *A person's viewpoint is what he or she understands or knows about something, including beliefs and attitudes. Your viewpoint depends on what you know and believe and on your experience.*

Explain that authors have viewpoints when they write stories and that we, as readers, figure out an author's viewpoint by finding evidence in the story.

Practice

Remind children that the story *The Art Lesson* is about the author/illustrator's experience growing up, and that through the story, we are able to tell how he feels about art. Ask children the following questions:

- *Does Tommy have fun at school making pictures?* Have children find evidence in the story. (pages 362, 369, 373)

- *How do you think the author Tomie dePaola feels about the teacher allowing little Tommy to have more than one piece of art paper to draw pictures on?* The author feels favorably about the teacher's decision. (pages 375–378)

Help children to see that the author's viewpoint comes through the feelings of little Tommy since the author is writing about his own life. Ask them to find evidence that the author is writing about himself. (pages 377–379)

Apply

Assign pairs of children one of the stories in Theme 5, *Family Time*. Have them find evidence that shows the author's viewpoint about the family. Guide children with questions such as the following:

How does the author show family members acting toward each other?

What do the family members feel good about?

Have children share their findings. Help children to see how the story provides evidence of the author's viewpoint.

LITERATURE FOCUS: 10–15 MINUTES

Revisit *The Art Lesson, Jade's Drumming,* and *Our Classroom Zoo Book*

Page through all the stories with children, reviewing the illustrations and text in each story to find out the authors' viewpoint.

Have children look through the stories for High-Frequency Words *fair, gold,* and *woman,* and for irregular forms of verbs such as *do, come, know, want, grow, draw, go, make,* and *tell.*

Ask children to look for words with vowel pairs *ew, oo, ou,* and *ue* in the stories.

Day 1

SKILL FOCUS: PHONICS   25–30 MINUTES

Long *i* (*igh*)

Teach

Recite the chant twice to introduce the long *i* vowel sound. Then repeat the chant, and have children echo your reading.

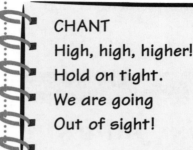

> CHANT
> High, high, higher!
> Hold on tight.
> We are going
> Out of sight!

Say *high*, stretching the vowel sound. Invite children to do the same. Then isolate and say the /ī/ sound with children.

Tell children they will repeat some more words with the /ī/ sound. Say these words one at a time and have children repeat them: *tight, thigh, flight, sigh, fight.*

Read aloud the following words. Have children point to their eyes every time they hear a word with the long *i* vowel sound: *sit, sight, bright, brink, light, lit.*

Blend

Use Blending Routine 1.

Display *sight.* Model how to blend the sounds, stretching the vowel sound and then saying the word. Explain to children that the letters *igh* stand for the /ī/ vowel sound. Recall that children have learned that the letters *gh* can be silent in some words. Then have children blend the word and say it with you. Use *sight* in a sentence.

Repeat the same steps with the word *thigh*.

Display *mighty, knight, lightning,* and *higher.* Have children blend them.

Objectives

- associate the /ī/ sound with *igh*
- blend and read words with *igh*

Materials

- Teaching Master ES6-3
- Practice Master ES6-3
- Phonics Library: *Dwight the Knight*

**Get Set for Reading
CD-ROM**

Moses Goes to a Concert

Education Place

www.eduplace.com
Moses Goes to a Concert

Audio CD

Moses Goes to a Concert
Audio CD for **Talent Show**

**Lexia Phonics
CD-ROM**

Primary Intervention

Guided Practice

Display or **distribute** Teaching Master ES6-3 and discuss the illustration. Tell children they will read a story about a stormy night.

Have children use what they know about blending sounds to read the story with you.

Point randomly to long *i* vowel words, and help children read them.

Practice / Apply

Distribute Practice Master ES6-3 to children, and read the directions with them.

Have children read the clues and write the answers independently.

Check children's ability to read long *i* (*igh*) words as they share their responses with the group.

Preview *Dwight the Knight*

Introduce children to *Dwight the Knight.* Discuss the illustrations, name the characters, and use words from the story such as *knight, fight, night, delight,* and *fright.*

Ask: *What are knights supposed to do? Why do you think Dwight doesn't want to fight?* Then tell children they will read this story with the rest of the class.

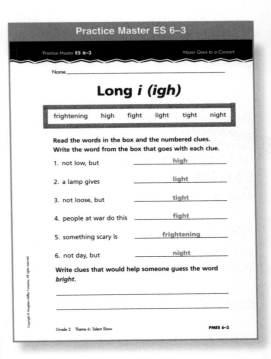

Day 2

Objective
- note story details

Materials
- Teaching Master ES6-4
- Practice Master ES6-4
- Anthology: *Moses Goes to a Conert*

Noting Details

Teach

Write this sentence on the chalkboard: *Andy is a boy in second grade.* Read the sentence with children, and ask them what they know about Andy. Then write this sentence: *Andy is a boy in second grade who has won prizes for his drawings and clay animals.*

Ask children what new information they have about Andy. Make the point that the new information, or details, in the second sentence helps children better understand what Andy is like.

Guided Practice

Explain that you will read a story. Children should listen carefully for details that will help them understand more about a character named Tonya.

Read Aloud

Tonya wants to be voted the best second-grader. She thinks she has a good chance. Tonya knows that she is a whiz at math. She can add and subtract in her head. She is the best in gym class. She can do tumbles and make goals in soccer games. Tonya's teacher is proud of her because she helps in the community. Tonya helps to keep the park in the neighborhood clean.

Display or **distribute** Teaching Master ES6-4 and read the statements about Tonya on the details chart. Help children recall information from the story and write details that support each statement.

Read the completed chart with children.

Practice / Apply

Distribute Practice Master ES6-4 to children, and read the directions with them.

Have children read the story independently and write answers to the questions.

Check children's ability to note details as you review their answers with the group.

LITERATURE FOCUS: 20–30 MINUTES

Preview *Moses Goes to a Concert*

Segment 1

Refer to the bottom of page T131 in the Teacher's Edition and preview with children Segment 1 of *Moses Goes to a Concert* (pages 391–405).

Note the suggestions in the Extra Support boxes on the Teacher's Edition pages T134 and T137.

Segment 2

Refer to the bottom of page T131 in the Teacher's Edition and preview with children Segment 2 of *Moses Goes to a Concert* (pages 406–423).

Note the suggestions in the Extra Support boxes on the Teacher's Edition pages T145 and T146.

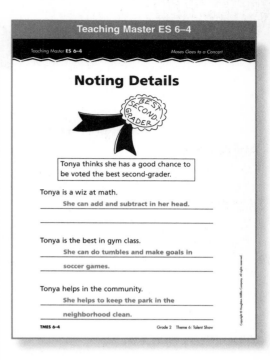

Teaching Master ES 6–4

Noting Details

Tonya thinks she has a good chance to be voted the best second-grader.

Tonya is a wiz at math.
    She can add and subtract in her head.

Tonya is the best in gym class.
    She can do tumbles and make goals in
    soccer games.

Tonya helps in the community.
    She helps to keep the park in the
    neighborhood clean.

TMES 6–4   Grade 2 Theme 6: Talent Show

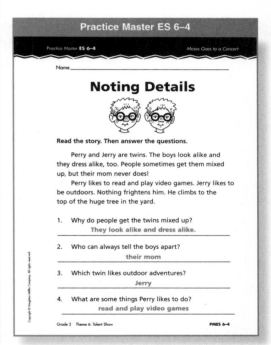

Practice Master ES 6–4

Name _____

Noting Details

Read the story. Then answer the questions.

    Perry and Jerry are twins. The boys look alike and they dress alike, too. People sometimes get them mixed up, but their mom never does!
    Perry likes to read and play video games. Jerry likes to be outdoors. Nothing frightens him. He climbs to the top of the huge tree in the yard.

1.   Why do people get the twins mixed up?
     They look alike and dress alike.

2.   Who can always tell the boys apart?
     their mom

3.   Which twin likes outdoor adventures?
     Jerry

4.   What are some things Perry likes to do?
     read and play video games

Grade 2 Theme 6: Talent Show   PMES 6–4

Day 3

Objective

- read and write new High-Frequency Words: *mind, alphabet, heart*

High-Frequency Words

Teach

Write *mind, alphabet,* and *heart* on the board. Read the words with children. Discuss the meaning of each word. Invite volunteers to come up to the board and copy the words.

Ask youngsters to find *mind, alphabet,* and *heart* in the story. With the class, read the sentences in which these words appear in the story. Then have children make up their own sentences using *mind, alphabet,* and *heart.*

Practice

Write the following sentence starters on the board:

I changed my mind about _____ because _____.

I use the alphabet to _____.

Once I had my heart set on _____.

Ask children to copy the sentence starters on their own paper. Tell them to complete the sentences any way they wish.

Apply

Encourage children to read their sentences to the class. You may wish to have children pick one of their three sentences to write on the board or on an overhead transparency.

Adjectives, including *a, an,* and *the*

Teach

Write the following sentences on the chalkboard:

I like shopping at the big market.

I ate a sweet peach.

The market has many purple flowers.

It is an outdoor market.

Have children read the sentences aloud. Stop after each one and ask, *What kind of market? What kind of peach?* As children respond, explain that words that describe nouns are called adjectives. Explain that an adjective can tell *what kind* or *how many*. Then point out a third type of adjective. The words *a, an,* and *the* are special adjectives. They tell more about nouns too.

Practice

Write the following sentences or phrases from *Moses Goes to a Concert* on the chalkboard. Ask children to identify the adjective or adjectives in each.

Moses plays on his <u>new</u> drum.

a <u>loud musical</u> sound

<u>eleven beautiful</u> balloons

Apply

Work with children to identify adjectives related to sounds. Begin by asking them to think about words that describe sounds and record their ideas on a word web. Have them write a sentence with each word.

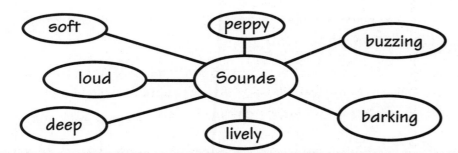

LITERATURE FOCUS: 10–15 MINUTES

Review *Moses Goes to a Concert*

Ask children to review and retell *Moses Goes to a Concert*. Then have children work in small groups. Each group member should identify one story detail.

Objectives
- define an adjective
- identify adjectives in the story
- use adjectives to describe sounds in sentences

Materials
- Anthology: *Moses Goes to a Concert*

Day 4

Objectives

- say the long *i* sound for the *igh* and *ie* spellings
- read and write long *i* words with the *igh* and *ie* patterns

Materials

- Sound/Spelling Card *ice cream*
- Phonics Library: *Who Drew the Cartoon?*

RETEACH

SKILL FOCUS: PHONICS   25–30 MINUTES

Long *i* (*igh, ie*)

Teach

Say the words *high, night,* and *tie.* Ask children what sounds the words have in common. (long i)

Display the Sound/Spelling Card *ice cream*, and remind children that the long *i* sound can be spelled in different ways. Then write *high* on the board and underline the *igh*. Point out the *igh* spelling on the Sound/Spelling Card. Then use Blending Routine 2 to help children sound out *high*. For example, blend the word *high* by having children say the *h* sound, /h/, then the long i sound /ī/ and finally blend the sounds to say the word *high*. Repeat the procedure, using *tie* for the *ie* spelling of long *i*.

Continue this process with other words such as *knight, high, pie, right,* and *night*. Write each word on the board and have children sound it out. Then ask children what sounds all the words have in common. /ī/ Invite children to circle the letter combinations *igh* or *ie* that appear in each word on the board.

Practice

Write these and other sentence starters on the board.

> When I grow up, I might _____.
> I sigh when I have to _____.
> My favorite kind of pie is _____.
> Some of the best summer sights are _____.

Read the sentence starters with children. Have children copy the sentence starters on their own paper. Tell them to complete the sentences. Then have children read their completed sentences to partners.

Apply

Have pairs of children find long *i* words spelled with *igh* and *ie* in *Dwight the Knight*. The words they should find are: *Dwight, knight, Mighty, right, pie, brightly, night, delight, fright, sights, delightful, lightning,* and *flight*. Each time children find a long *i* word spelled with *igh* or *ie*, they should read it aloud while you write the word on the board. Have children read the words as volunteers come to the board and circle the *igh* and *ie* spellings.

LITERATURE FOCUS: 10–15 MINUTES

Preview *Who Drew the Cartoon?*

Familiarize children with *Who Drew the Cartoon?* Discuss the illustrations, naming the characters and using words from the story such as *cartoon, artist, talent, sketches, bright,* and *comic*.

Ask: *What are some things an artist must be able to do to create a cartoon strip?* Then tell children they will read this story with the rest of the class.

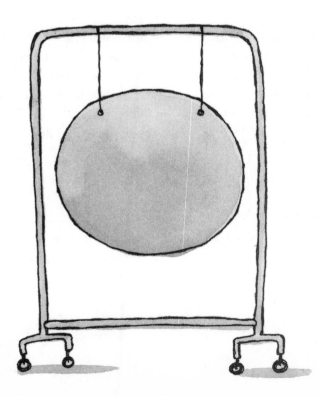

Day 5

Objectives

- identify details in stories to understand characters and events
- complete a word web with details from the story

Materials

- Anthology: *Moses Goes to a Concert*
- Phonics Library: *Dwight the Knight, Who Drew the Cartoon?*

Noting Details

Teach

Ask children to describe a small area of the classroom. Guide children to give details that include colors, shapes, and sizes of objects. Make a word web like the one below on the board. Explain that you can use a word web to help write and think about details.

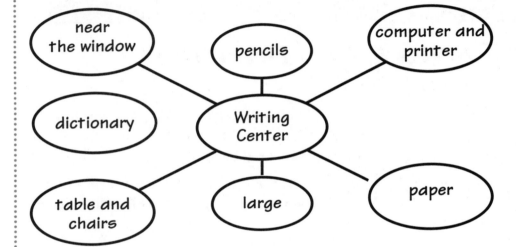

Practice

Work with children to identify details in the story *Moses Goes to a Concert* by Isaac Millman. Tell children that you will work together to identify details about the character Moses. Use a word web to record children's suggestions of the details the author uses to describe the character. (he is deaf, he signs, he likes drums, he asks questions, and so on) Have children use both the text and the illustrations.

Apply

Have children work in pairs to find details about other characters and things in the story *Moses Goes to a Concert*, for example, the concert hall, the percussionist, and the instruments. Tell students to use both the text and the pictures to find details. Have children record their details in a word web.

Revisit *Moses Goes to a Concert, Dwight the Knight,* and *Who Drew the Cartoon?*

Page through all the stories with children and review the illustrations and text in each story to note the details of each story.

Have children look through *Moses Goes to a Concert, Dwight the Knight,* and *Who Drew the Cartoon?* for High Frequency Words *alphabet, heart,* and *mind,* and for adjectives *a, an,* and *the.*

Ask children to look for words with the long *i* sound such as *knight, fight, delight, fine,* and *idea* in the Phonics Library stories.

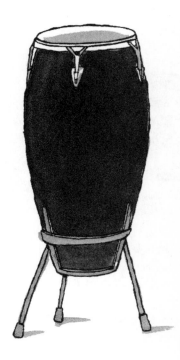

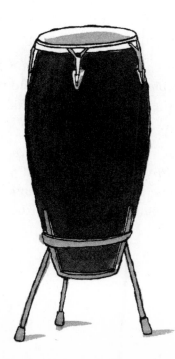

Day 1

Objectives

- recognize *–ed* and *–ing* as endings
- associate /d/ and /t/ with the *–ed* ending; /ing/ with the *–ing* ending
- blend and read words with *–ed* and *–ing* endings

Materials

- Practice Master ES6-5
- Teaching Master ES6-5
- Phonics Library: *Will Holly Sing?*

Get Set for Reading CD-ROM

The School Mural

Education Place

www.eduplace.com
The School Mural

Audio CD

The School Mural
Audio CD for **Talent Show**

Lexia Phonics CD-ROM

Primary Intervention

PRETEACH

SKILL FOCUS

25–30 MINUTES

More Words with *-ed* or *-ing*

Teach

Recite the chant and then repeat it. Encourage children to chime in.

> **CHANT**
>
> The dog is chasing, chasing, chasing,
>
> The cat who's racing, racing, racing.
>
> The dog chased, but the cat raced.

Repeat *chasing*, emphasizing the *-ing* ending. Ask children how the word *chasing* is different from *chase*. Write *chase* and *chasing* on the board and underline the ending. Have children compare the two words and note that the final *e* in chase was dropped when the ending was added. Tell children that when *-ing* is added to words with the *vowel-consonant-e* pattern, the final *e* is dropped before the *-ing* ending is added. Follow the same procedure for *racing*.

Repeat the chant again, now focusing on *chased* and *raced*.

Blend

Use Blending Routine 1.

Display *skating* and underline the *-ing* ending. Ask children what the base word is. (skate) Model how to blend the base word and the ending. Emphasize the /ing/ sounds in the ending. Then have children blend the word with you. Follow the same procedure with *skated*, emphasizing the /d/ ending sound.

Display the words *hiking, taking, hiding, joked, hoped,* and *smiled* one at a time. Call on children to underline the ending and identify the base word in each. Have children use blending to read the words.

Guided Practice

Distribute or **display** copies of Teaching Master ES6-5. Have children identify the picture at the top of the page.

Have children read the sentences and the word choices with you.

Help them to identify the correct word and circle it.

Reread all the completed sentences with children.

Practice / Apply

Distribute Practice Master ES6-5 to children. Discuss the pictures and the directions.

Tell children to use what they know about blending to read the sentences independently.

Check children's ability to read words with *-ed* and *-ing* as you go over their responses. Point randomly to *-ed* and *-ing* words, and have children read them.

LITERATURE FOCUS: 10–15 MINUTES

Preview *Will Holly Sing?*

Preview *Will Holly Sing?* Discuss the illustrations, name the characters and use words from the story such as *whined, placing, stroked, baked,* and *smiling.*

Ask children to say why Holly is worried. Then tell them they will read this story with the rest of the class.

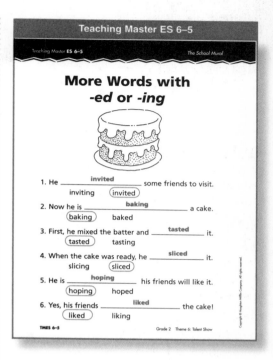

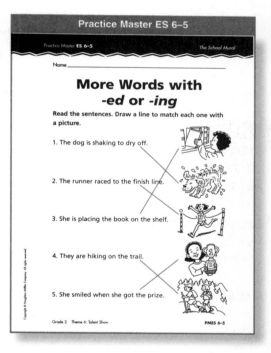

Day 2

Objective
- identify a problem and a solution in a story

Materials
- Teaching Master ES6-6
- Practice Master ES6-6
- Phonics Library: *Fright Night*

Problem Solving

Teach

Say: *If you are writing in your notebook and your pencil point breaks, that is a problem, right? What could you do to solve the problem?* List children's suggestions on the chalkboard: sharpen the pencil, borrow a pencil from a classmate, look for another pencil in their backpack, and so on. Say that people have problems they need to solve and so do characters in stories.

Guided Practice

Display or **distribute** Teaching Master ES6-6. Explain that you will read a story in two parts. Children should listen carefully for the problem the character has and how she solves it in each part. Read the first paragraph and then stop to have children identify the problem and its solution. Then read the second paragraph and follow the same procedure.

Read Aloud

> Nell wants a pet, but her whole family says, "No." They say that everyone will sneeze because of the animal's hair. Nell has an idea. She goes to the pet store and gets a turtle. A turtle does not have hair.
>
> Nell looked at her new turtle. It looked sad. It didn't move much or eat. Nell read a book about turtles. It said turtles need company. She went to get another turtle at the pet store.

Read labels on the chart with children and help them to identify the problem and solution in each paragraph.

Help children write the problems and solutions in the boxes.

Practice / Apply

Distribute Practice Master ES6-6 to children and read aloud the directions. Have children read the paragraphs independently and make their responses.

Check children's responses to be sure they can identify problems and solutions as they read.

LITERATURE FOCUS:

20–30 MINUTES

Preview *The School Mural*

Segment 1

Refer to the bottom of page T205 in the Teacher's Edition and preview with children Segment 1 of *The School Mural* (pages 432–443).

Note the suggestions in the Extra Support boxes on the Teacher's Edition pages T208 and T209.

Segment 2

Refer to the bottom of page T205 in the Teacher's Edition and preview with children Segment 2 of *The School Mural* (pages 444–452).

Note the suggestions in the Extra Support boxes on the Teacher's Edition pages T211 and T214.

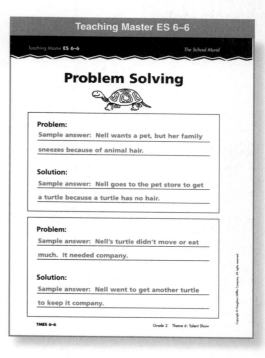

Teaching Master ES 6–6

Teaching Master ES 6–6 — The School Mural

Problem Solving

Problem:
Sample answer: Nell wants a pet, but her family sneezes because of animal hair.

Solution:
Sample answer: Nell goes to the pet store to get a turtle because a turtle has no hair.

Problem:
Sample answer: Nell's turtle didn't move or eat much. It needed company.

Solution:
Sample answer: Nell went to get another turtle to keep it company.

TMES 6–6   Grade 2 Theme 6: Talent Show

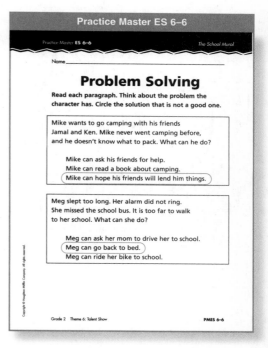

Practice Master ES 6–6

Practice Master ES 6–6 — The School Mural

Name

Problem Solving

Read each paragraph. Think about the problem the character has. Circle the solution that is not a good one.

Mike wants to go camping with his friends Jamal and Ken. Mike never went camping before, and he doesn't know what to pack. What can he do?

Mike can ask his friends for help.
Mike can read a book about camping.
(Mike can hope his friends will lend him things.)

Meg slept too long. Her alarm did not ring. She missed the school bus. It is too far to walk to her school. What can she do?

Meg can ask her mom to drive her to school.
(Meg can go back to bed.)
Meg can ride her bike to school.

Grade 2 Theme 6: Talent Show   PMES 6–6

Day 3

Objective
- read and write new High-Frequency Words: *below, neighbor, should*

SKILL FOCUS: 10–15 MINUTES

High-Frequency Words

Teach

Write the High-Frequency Words *below, neighbor,* and *should* on the board. Read them with children.

Discuss the meaning of each word.

   below (under, beneath)

   neighbor (someone who lives nearby)

   should (must, ought to)

Have children say sentences that include *below, neighbor,* and *should.* You may wish to write their sentences on the board or on an overhead transparency.

Practice

Write the following sentence frames on the board:

> The _____ is below the _____.
> _____ is my neighbor in our classroom.
> You should always _____.

Read the sentence frames with children. Ask children to copy the sentence frames on their own paper. Tell them to complete the sentences any way they wish.

Apply

Assign partners and have children read their sentences to one another. Then allow time for students to read their sentences to the class.

Hang three large pieces of chart paper on the wall or a bulletin board. Write one High-Frequency Word *(below, neighbor, should)* on each piece of paper. Have children make sentence murals by cutting out their sentences and gluing them onto the chart paper. Ask them to make sure that the High-Frequency Word used in the sentence matches the word on the chart paper.

Adjectives that Compare

Teach

Begin the lesson by displaying common classroom objects of three different sizes, for example, three pencils *(small, smaller, smallest)*. Describe the three objects, and write sentences on the chalkboard to point out the changes in the adjectives *small, smaller, smallest*. Help children to understand that the adjectives tell how things are different from each other. They *compare* objects.

Practice

Use words and concepts from *The School Mural* to practice using adjectives that compare. Write the following sentences on the chalkboard, and ask children to read them together. Ask children to underline the words *high, higher*, and *highest*.

Joe moves on a high swing.

Mara moves on a higher swing than Joe's.

Mei Lee moves on the highest swing of all.

Apply

Use other examples from the story so that children can apply what they have learned about adjectives that compare. Some examples follow.

Page 435 *"This gave her a <u>great</u> idea."* (great, greater, greatest)

Page 440 *"We'll need a really <u>big</u> wall for our mural."* (big, bigger, biggest)

Objectives

- identify adjectives that compare in the story
- write sentences with comparative forms

Materials

- Anthology: *The School Mural*

Review *The School Mural*

Ask children to review and retell *The School Mural*. After the retelling, have partners identify a problem in the story and tell how it was solved.

Day 4

Objectives

- drop the final *e* to write words with *-ed, -ing* endings
- read and write words ending in *-ed, -ing* in which the final *e* has been dropped

Materials

- large self-stick notes
- Phonics Library: *Fright Night*

RETEACH
SKILL FOCUS: PHONICS   25–30 MINUTES

Base Words and Endings
-ed, -ing

Teach

Say several words such as *jumped, painted, lunch, raced,* and *piles.* Have children raise their hand each time they hear a word ending in *-ed.* Repeat the procedure, substituting words with *-ing* endings.

Write *-ed* and *-ing* on large self-stick notes. Tell children that these endings may be added to base words. Write *greet* on the board, and read the word with children.

Place the self-stick note with the *-ed* ending next to *greet* and have children sound out each syllable and then the word. Repeat the procedure, using the note with the *-ing* ending. Have children use *greet, greeted,* and *greeting* in sentences.

Write *race* on the board and read it with children. Point out that this base word ends with the letter *e.* Explain that the *e* is dropped from *race* before *-ed* or *-ing* is added. To demonstrate, cross out the final *e* in *race* and place the *-ed* self-stick note over the crossed out letter. Have children sound out the word. Repeat the procedure, using the note with the *-ing* ending. Then remind children that the vowel sound of the base word stays the same when the *e* is dropped and the *-ing* ending is added.

Write *like* on the board and read it with children. Point out that this base word also ends with the letter *e.* Invite volunteers to show how endings are added to *like.* If necessary, remind them to look at the example you provided using *race.* Then have children sound out each word.

Practice

Make a 3-column chart on the board or chart paper. The column headings should be Base Word, Add *-ed,* and Add *-ing.* Under the Base Word heading, write *poke, bore, hope, chase, trade,* and *slice.* Read the words with children. Have children copy the chart on their own paper. Have them add *-ed* and *-ing* to each base word to complete the chart.

Base Word	Add -ed	Add -ing
poke	poked	poking
bore	bored	boring
hope	hoped	hoping
chase	chased	chasing
trade	traded	trading
slice	sliced	slicing

Invite volunteers to fill in the chart on the board and read all the words.

Apply

Have pairs of children find base words with final *e*, to which *-ed, -ing* have been added in *Will Holly Sing?* The words they should find are: *whined, sneezed, wheezed, skating, glided, raced, smiling, placing, waving, wiped, dazed, stroked, scraped, joked,* and *baked.* Each time children find a word, have them read it aloud while you write it on the board. Have volunteers come to the board, underline the base words, and circle the endings.

LITERATURE FOCUS: 10–15 MINUTES

Preview *Fright Night*

Preview *Fright Night.* Discuss the illustrations, name the characters, and use words from the story such as *cried, lived, spotlight, creature, spider,* and *spooky.*

Tell children to look at the picture on page 45. Ask: *What problem might someone dressed as a spider have?* Then say that children will read this story with the rest of the class.

Day 5

Objectives

- identify the problem and solutions in the story
- use the five-step problem-solving graphic organizer to evaluate problem solving

Materials

- Anthology: *The School Mural*
- Phonics Library: *Fright Night, Will Holly Sing?*

RETEACH

SKILL FOCUS: COMPREHENSION   25–30 MINUTES

Problem Solving

Teach

Ask children to brainstorm ideas for solving a problem, for example, losing a library book. Write children's ideas on the chalkboard. Then write the following problem-solving steps on the chalkboard as a summary of how the class solved the problem together.

> Define the problem.
>
> Consider the possible solutions.
>
> Examine possible solutions.
>
> Decide on the best solution.
>
> Carry out the solution.

Practice

Reread *The School Mural*. Discuss the events, guiding children to identify different problems in the story, such as Paul putting handprints on the mural by mistake. Discuss the steps that were taken to solve each problem. Have children review the problem-solving steps and evaluate how well they were used in the story to solve the problem.

Apply

Ask children to think about how they might have solved the problems in *The School Mural*. In pairs, have children work through the five problem-solving steps, brainstorming solutions that are not in the story, evaluating them, and making a decision to solve the problem. Then have the group compare their ideas.

Revisit *The School Mural, Fright Night*, and *Will Holly Sing?*

Page through all the stories with children, reviewing the illustrations and text in order to recall the problem solving that occurs.

Have children look through *The School Mural, Fright Night*, and *Will Holly Sing?* for High-Frequency Words *below, neighbor* and *should*, and for adjectives that compare.

Ask children to look for and say base words that end in *-ed* and *-ing* from the stories in the Anthology and the Phonics Library.

Short Vowels *a, i*

Put these letters together to write words that have the short *a* or short *i* sound.

1. h + i + l + l = _____

2. p + a + n = _____

3. h + a + t + s = _____

4. s + i + t = _____

Now use the words you wrote to complete these sentences.

5. Kitty and Brad _____ together.

6. Cindy and her cat wear big _____.

7. Jack and Jill went up the _____.

8. Phil and Fran cook eggs in a _____.

Short Vowels *a, i*

Put these letters together to write words that have the short *a* or short *i* sound.

1. g **+** a **+** s **=** _____

2. b **+** i **+** b **=** _____

3. b **+** a **+** g **=** _____

4. s **+** i **+** x **=** _____

Now use the words you wrote to complete these sentences.

5. The baby has food on her _____.

6. The cat has _____ kittens.

7. Tim cannot pick up the big _____.

8. The bus needs _____ to go.

Grade 2   Theme 1: Silly Stories

PMES 1-1

Story Structure

The Tortoise and the Hare

One afternoon by the pond, Hare began making fun of how slowly Tortoise walked. Tortoise didn't mind. In fact, he said he would race Hare around the pond. Hare agreed, and Tortoise began his slow and steady walk.

Hare looked at Tortoise and said, "He is so slow, I have time for a nap. Then I'll catch up with him and beat him to the finish line."

So Hare napped, and Tortoise walked on. When Hare woke up, he ran as fast as he could around the pond. But Hare was too late. Tortoise slowly crossed the finish line to win the race!

Who?	
Where?	
What happens? Beginning Middle End	

Name_____

Story Structure

One day at Han's house, his friend Sue said, "You like to draw. Draw a picture of me!" Han said, "You like to sing. Sing a song about me!" So Han drew a picture of Sue singing. She sang a song about Han and all of his crayons. They both had a lot of fun and kept on singing and drawing until it was time to go home.

Read the story and complete the following story map.

Who? _____

Where? _____

What happens?

Beginning _____

_____

Middle _____

_____

_____

End _____

_____

Short Vowels *o, u, e*

Dad has a big list:

    a truck for Ron

    a dress for a doll

    a drum for Dot

    a set of blocks for Bud

    a lap desk for Mom

Name_____

VCCV Pattern

Read the sentences.

Judd wants to make a <u>puppet</u>.

Pat has a pet <u>rabbit</u>.

Rob has a check-up with the <u>dentist</u>.

Jen needs a new <u>soccer</u> <u>ball</u>.

Look at the places in the building. Write the underlined words from the sentences to tell what people can see in the places.

4. _____

3. _____

2. _____

1. _____

Fantasy and Realism

Ana has three kittens—
Poppet, Moppet, and Stoppet!
Poppet likes bags. He
likes to blow them up like
balloons. Then he jumps on
the bags to pop them. The
pop makes Poppet laugh.

Moppet is always spilling things. She likes to
knock over a glass of milk or push over a water
dish. Then she yells, "I'll mop it!"

Stoppet gets into things. He messes up the
blankets on Ana's bed. He plays on Ana's
computer. Can you guess what Ana says to him?

Could Really Happen	Could Not Really Happen
_____	_____
_____	_____
_____	_____
_____	_____

Fantasy and Realism

Think about Ana's pets to answer the questions.

1. Which characters do make-believe things?

   _____

2. Name three things about Ana's pets that are make believe.

   _____

   _____

   _____

3. Name three things about Ana and her pets that are real.

   _____

   _____

   _____

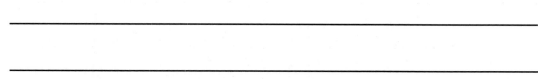

Long Vowels CVCe: *a, i*

Read the sentences. Draw a circle around each word that has a long vowel *a* or *i* sound.

1. We ride bikes and skate in the park.

2. We also wade to the side of the lake.

3. It is a safe place for ducks to glide and dive.

Now write each circled word under the word that has the same vowel sound.

lane	line
_____	_____
_____	_____
_____	_____
_____	_____

Name_____

Long Vowels CVCe: *a, i*

**Put these letters together to write words. Some words
will have a short *a* or short *i* sound. Some will have a long
a or long *i* sound.**

1. k **+** i **+** t **+** e **=** _____

2. k **+** i **+** t **=** _____

3. s **+** l **+** i **+** d **=** _____

4. s **+** l **+** i **+** d **+** e **=** _____

5. t **+** a **+** p **+** e **=** _____

6. t **+** a **+** p **=** _____

7. m **+** a **+** d **=** _____

8. m **+** a **+** d **+** e **=** _____

9. c **+** a **+** n **=** _____

10. c **+** a **+** n **+** e **=** _____

11. P **+** e **+** t **+** e **=** _____

12. p **+** e **+** t **=** _____

Now write the words under the correct vowel sound.

Short Vowel Sound	Long Vowel Sound
_____	_____
_____	_____
_____	_____
_____	_____
_____	_____

Predicting Outcomes

Anita likes to run. For a month, she has run the track after school. She has practiced very hard for her first meet. On the day of the meet, there are four other runners to race with. At the starting bell, she takes off and feels great!

What might happen?

1. _____

2. _____

3. _____

Name _____

Predicting Outcomes

Read the story. Write three things to tell what might happen next.

Sam likes music. He enjoys playing the flute and practices everyday. Sam hopes to be in the school band. On the day for school band try-outs, Sam plays his best. When he finishes, everyone cheers and claps.

What might happen?

1. _____

2. _____

3. _____

o, u, e in CVCe Patterns

cube	cute

That cub is so _____.

_____

Pete	These

_____ has a new pet.

_____

hole	hose

Use a _____ if you feel hot.

Name_____

Two Sounds for *g*

**Read the sentences. Circle each
word with the letter *g* in it.**

1. Grandma and I baked gingerbread
   cookies for the school fair.

2. We gave each cookie raisin eyes
   and a large smile.

3. Our grinning cookies were a huge hit at the fair.

4. People gently picked them up. Then people gobbled
   them down.

**Now write each circled word under the word that has the
same sound for *g*.**

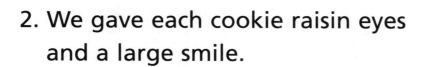

goat	giraffe
_____	_____
_____	_____
_____	_____
_____	_____

Compare and Contrast

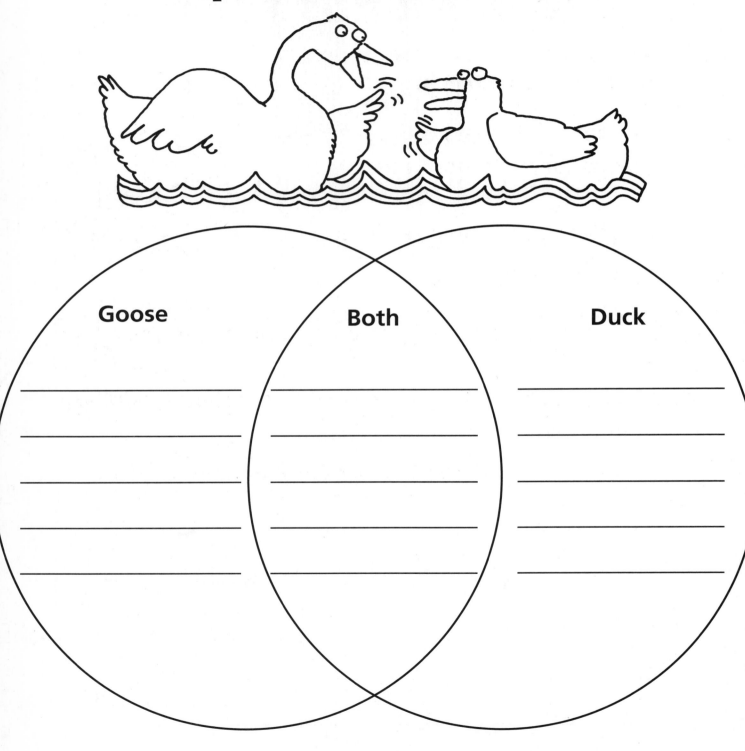

Goose   Both   Duck

_____   _____   _____

_____   _____   _____

_____   _____   _____

_____   _____

Name_____

Compare and Contrast

Read the story and look at the picture.

My Two Pets

Snowflake is my cat. He is all white with long fur. Midnight is my dog. She is all black with short fur. Snowflake and Midnight are both three years old.

Snowflake and Midnight are best friends. Midnight kisses Snowflake's nose. Snowflake rubs his head on Midnight's chin.

Fill in the chart to tell how the two pets are alike and different.

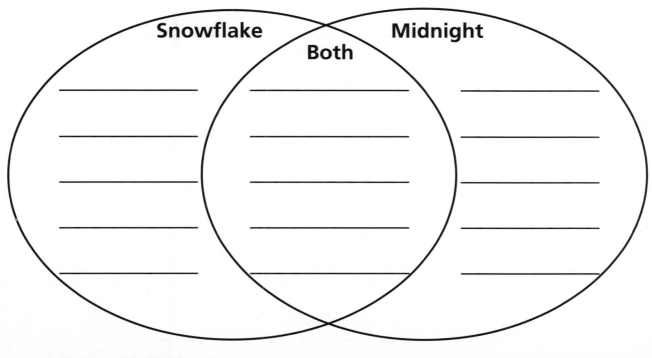

Consonant Clusters
r, l, s

"Help!" cried Fred. "This bug is a pest."

Fred shook his fist at the bug. "Stop flying here!"

Fred clapped to try to get rid of the bug.

The bug came to rest on Fred's chest.

Fred gave himself a slap.

The bug flew off.

"At last, it is gone!" said Fred.

l clusters	*r* clusters	*s* clusters

Name_____

Two Sounds for c

Read the sentences. Circle each word that has the letter c in it.

1. Dad and I drove the car out of the city.

2. We went to a place far out in the country.

3. It was a farm that sold nice red apples and sweet corn.

4. I also got a cold glass of fresh apple cider.

Now write each circled word under the word that has the same sound for c.

cup	cent
_____	_____
_____	_____
_____	_____
_____	_____

Fact and Opinion

_____   Birds have feathers.

_____   Birds are the best pets.

_____   Soccer is fun for everyone.

_____   Soccer is played with a ball.

_____   Apples are a kind of fruit.

_____   Apples taste good with peanut butter.

_____   A guitar has strings.

_____   Guitar music is too loud.

Fact and Opinion

Read about hermit crabs.

My Hermit Crab

A hermit crab lives in a shell. When it gets too big for its shell home, it moves into a larger shell.

It is easy to take care of a hermit crab. A hermit crab needs water and food pellets. I like watching my pet hermit crab. A hermit crab is a good pet for a small home.

Write two facts and two opinions about hermit crabs.

Facts:

_____

_____

_____

Opinions:

_____

_____

_____

Double Final Consonants

kick   kiss

Will the foot _____ the ball?

stiff   stick

Jump for the _____!

puff   puck

I see a _____ of steam.

full   fuss

The glass is _____.

Name_____

VCCV Pattern: Double Consonants

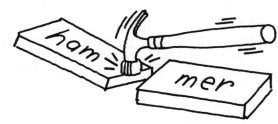

Read both words. Pick the one with two syllables. Write it in the sentence. Use a line to show where to break the word into syllables.

sudden sweet

What was that _____noise?

thick nickel

Five cents is a _____.

kitten kites

I like to play with my _____.

blade ladder

Step up on the _____.

Categorize and Classify

Living Things	Things Made by People	Sky Objects

Name_____

Categorize and Classify

Read each list. Cross out the
item that does not belong.
Tell what is alike about
the items that are left.

Example:

crow, sparrow, ~~worm,~~ robin _____birds_____

1. apples, hamburger, banana, orange _____

2. cake, milk, juice, soda _____

3. pond, lake, sea, boat _____

4. bee, housefly, horse, beetle _____

5. car, school, house, library _____

**Look at the pictures. Write a label to tell why they
belong together.**

_____

Grade 2   Theme 2: Nature Walk   **PMES 2–6**

Consonant Digraphs

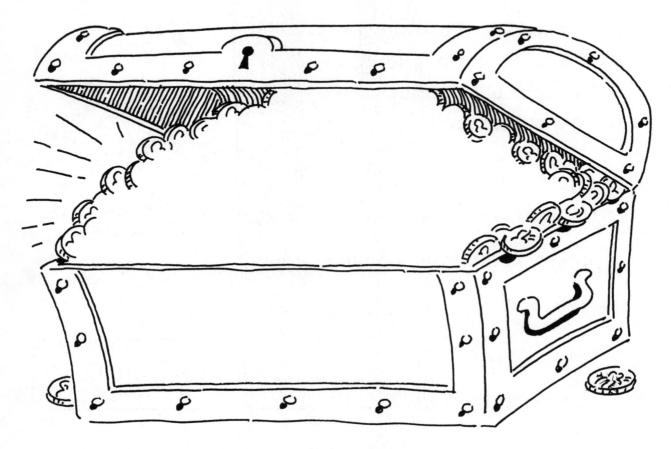

The ship was near the beach.

A man shouted, "Let's go to the shore."

He chose a small boat for the ride.

Waves crashed around the boat.

The man checked his map.

"We will dig for a chest of gold," he said.

Base Words and Endings
-er, -est

Read the sentences. Write a word from the box in each sentence.

nicer	tallest	cooler	bigger	sweeter	freshest

1. It is _____ in the shade than in the sun.

2. We'll have lunch under the _____ tree of all.

3. Mom took out a small jar and a _____ one.

4. "The drink in the small jar tastes _____,"
   she said.

5. We ate the _____ bread in the world.

6. A picnic is _____ than eating indoors!

Making Judgments

Things People in the Circus Do

Making Judgments

**Read the paragraphs.
Write answers to the
questions.**

There is a new water park in my town. It has great rides. Some rides are only for older children. A man checks to see how tall you are.

If you don't want to go on the rides, you can swim in a huge pool. There are many places to get snacks. You can even listen to a band play. Watch out if it starts to rain. The people in charge close the park. Everyone has to go home.

What do you like about the water park?

_____

_____

_____

What don't you like about the water park?

_____

_____

_____

Vowel pairs *ai, ay*

paint	pants	pail	past

sandy	saying	said	sailor

haystack	happen	hail	have

rocket	ranch	raid	railway

Bonus Word

_____

Compound Words

Read the words in each list.

Draw lines to connect words and make compound words.

rain	time
high	box
day	coat
mail	way
rail	road

Write the compound words you made.

_____

_____

_____

_____

_____

Topic, Main Idea, Details

Topic: _____

Main Idea: _____

_____

Details: You can find plump, round loaves of bread or thin, long loaves.

Some breads are flat such as pizza, pita, and tortillas.

There are special rolls made just to hold hot dogs.

Bagels are round with a hole in the middle.

Did you know pretzels and crackers are bread, too?

pic, Main Idea, Details

Read the paragraphs.
Then complete the chart.

We took a class trip to an apple farm. There are many interesting things to do and see at an apple farm. We saw rows and rows of apple trees. Some trees had red apples growing on them, others had green apples, and others had yellow ones!

We saw the apples go into a huge apple washer. Then they were sorted into big boxes. We even went into the apple cider room. A big crusher squeezed the apples. A man gave us some fresh cider to taste.

Topic: _____

Main Idea: There are many interesting things to do and see at an apple farm.

Details: Write details that tell more about the main idea.

_____

_____

_____

_____

_____

Vowel pairs *ou*, *ow*

Welcome to New Town!
Here are some of the many places to see!

Magic Fountain

Flower Park

Fair Grounds

High Tower

Downy Lake

Mile High Mountain

County Bridge

Scout Hiking Trail

_____   _____

_____   _____

_____   _____

_____   _____

Name _____

Suffix -*ly*

Read the words and the sentences.

Write a word from the box to complete each sentence.

cuddly exactly gently lonely quietly proudly

1. Nela knows _____ the kind of pet she wants.

2. She wants a _____ little puppy.

3. In the pet store, she sees a puppy that looks

   _____.

4. It sits _____ in a corner.

5. She pets it _____.

6. Nela _____ shows her friends her new pet.

Problem Solving

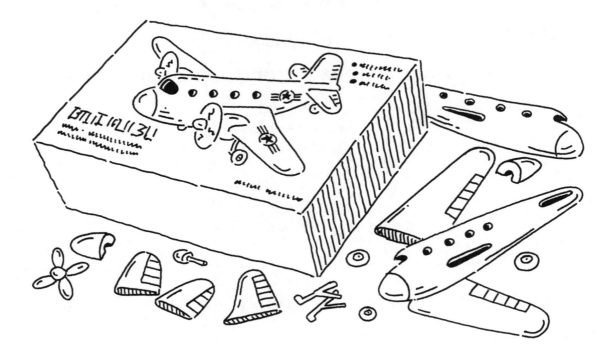

Problem:

Ben cannot put together his model airplane.

Solutions:

1. _____

2. _____

3. _____

Name_____

Problem Solving

Read the story. Then complete the chart.

Sara went downstairs for dinner. When she got back to her room, she said, "Oh, no! I must have left the cage door open. Now Mousey is gone."

Sara sat quietly and waited for Mousey to come back. That plan did not work.

Then she shouted "Mousey" as she looked all around. No luck.

Then, Sara remembered that mice like cheese. She put some cheese on the floor. Mousey came back!

Problem: Sara's mouse is missing.

Solutions — Put a star next to the one that worked.

1. _____

2. _____

3. _____

Vowel pairs ee, ea

Bean Bag Toss Game

asleep

speak

kettle

metal

self

wheat

wheel

present

deeply

meal

heat

Name _____

The Ending *-ture* in Two-Syllable Words

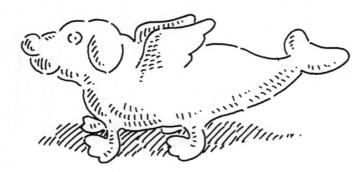

Read the words and the sentences.
Write a word from the box to complete each sentence.

mixture sculptures features nature creature picture

1. Ed likes to make clay _____ in art class.

2. He makes odd-looking _____.

3. They are a _____ of different animals.

4. The one you see has the _____ of a dog and a bird.

5. There is no such animal in _____.

6. Can you draw a _____ of what Ed will sculpt next?

Making Inferences

What Ray Is Like	Story Clues
_____ _____ _____	Ray studied hard. He missed a movie to study more.
_____ _____ _____	Ray waited quietly while other children got their tests back.
_____ _____ _____	Ray smiled and couldn't wait to show his parents his test.

Name _____

Making Inferences

Read the paragraphs and answer the questions.

Tammy had a busy day. She got up early to help her mom do the wash. After clearing the breakfast dishes, she went outside to ride her skateboard. That's when she saw her neighbor carrying lots of bags of food. Tammy took two small bags to carry.

What is Tammy like?

_____

_____

Max stood by the edge of the pool. He watched his friends link arms and dive in. They all were laughing and splashing. When they called to Max to jump in, too, he pretended not to hear what they were saying. Max just stared at the deep blue water.

What is Max like?

_____

_____

r-Controlled Vowels *ar*

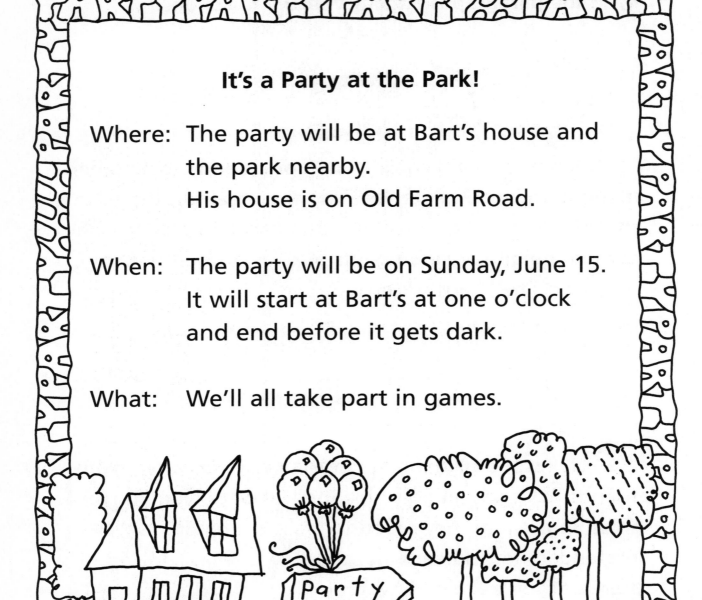

It's a Party at the Park!

Where: The party will be at Bart's house and
            the park nearby.
            His house is on Old Farm Road.

When: The party will be on Sunday, June 15.
            It will start at Bart's at one o'clock
            and end before it gets dark.

What: We'll all take part in games.

r-Controlled Vowels
or, ore

Use sounds you know to read the sentences. Draw a line to match each sentence with the correct picture.

1. Carl is tall, and his sister is short.

2. They will pick the corn.

3. She finds shells at the shore.

4. The trees blew in the storm.

Drawing Conclusions

Mort likes to paint pictures and shape clay into animals. Sometimes he makes little books.

What I Think Mort likes to spend time in the book corner.
Mort likes to spend time in the art room.

Clues

_____

_____

_____

Name _____

Drawing Conclusions

**Read each story. Look for clues that will help
you draw conclusions. Put an X by your choice.
Then circle the clues in the story.**

Tuffy is our pet. He is black and white. He likes to play
fetch with a stick. He likes to hide a bone in the yard.
Tuffy always wags his tail and barks when I get home.

What is Tuffy?   _____ Tuffy is a cat.

                              _____ Tuffy is a dog.

                              _____ Tuffy is a skunk.

Mom has the day off. She wants to do something for
fun. She packs food in a basket. She packs cool drinks,
too. She adds plates and napkins.

Where is Mom going?   _____ Mom is going on
                                           a picnic.

                              _____ Mom is going to
                                           the store.

Final Consonant Clusters *nd, nk, nt*

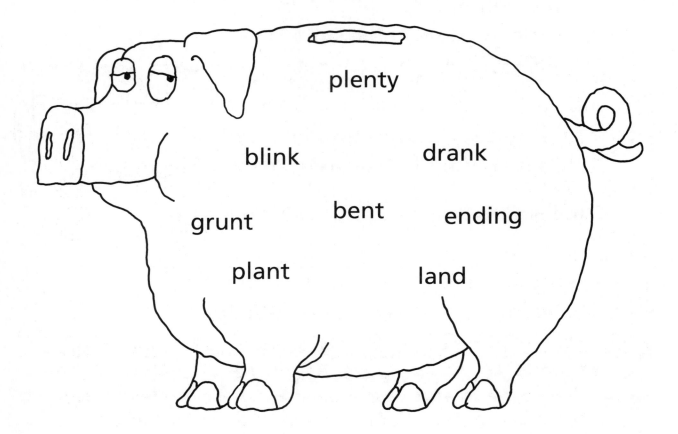

plenty

blink   drank

bent   ending

grunt

plant   land

1. The girls will _____ some seeds.

2. What is the _____ of your story?

3. The plane will _____ soon.

4. He _____ a glass of cold milk.

Base Words and Endings: *-es, -ies*

Use sounds you know to read the questions.
Circle Yes or No to answer each question.

1. Are kittens and puppies animal babies?   Yes   No

2. Can you find shells at beaches?   Yes   No

3. Can cars and buses fly?   Yes   No

4. Do watches tell the time?   Yes   No

5. Can you pay for things with pennies?   Yes   No

6. Are cherries sweet?   Yes   No

7. Are bushes as tall as trees?   Yes   No

8. Can bunnies hop?   Yes   No

Text Organization

Read the information. Then read the main idea.
Underline details in the paragraph that tell more
about the main idea.

Animals need doctors, too. These doctors
check dogs and cats for fleas and ticks. They give
animals shots and pills to keep them well. Some
can mend birds' broken wings. I would like to help
animals some day.

Main Idea: Animal doctors do many things to
help animals.

What does the picture tell you an animal
doctor can do?

_____

_____

Name_____

Text Organization

Read the information. Then read the main idea. Use the caption for the picture and the details in the selection to tell about the main idea on the lines below.

Birds carry what they need to make nests.

Birds build nests as their homes. Some nests are in trees. Others are on the ground. Most nests are made of grass and twigs. Some nests are large, but others are small.

Main Idea: Birds build nests. _____

Detail: _____

Detail: _____

Detail: _____

Detail: _____

Detail: _____

Vowel pairs *oa, ow*

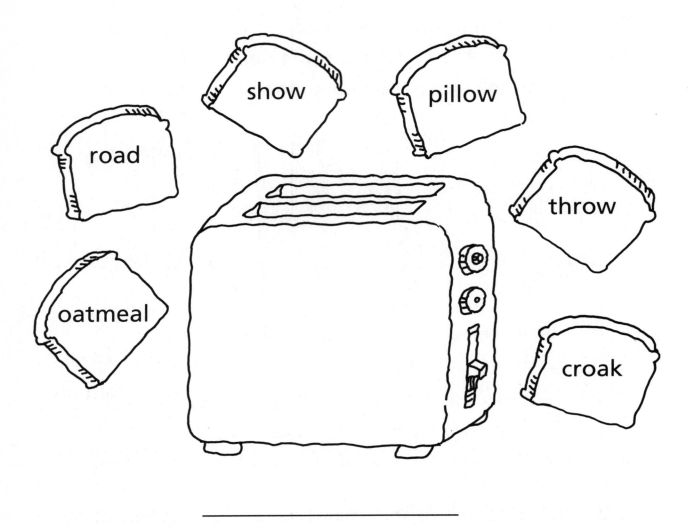

show

pillow

road

throw

oatmeal

croak

_____

1. Catch the ball when I _____ it!

2. Let's walk on this _____.

3. The cat naps on a fluffy _____.

4. She will sing in the _____.

Name_____

Vowel pairs **oa, ow**

Use sounds you know to read the story. Then find all the words with the long *o* sound in the story. Write them on the lines.

A toad and a crow had a contest. The goal was to show who could make a plant grow faster. The crow put his plant in the sun and gave it water. The toad yelled at his plant, "Grow, grow!" The crow's plant grew. The toad just got a sore throat from yelling.

_____   _____

_____   _____

_____   _____

Cause and Effect

    Today is a special day for Juan. His mom and dad invited his friends and family to their home. Juan wants to help out, so he and Dad make colorful decorations to put on the walls. Then he helps Mom make a cake. Soon all the guests arrive and say, "Happy Birthday!"

Why do Juan's parents invite his friends and family to their home?

_____

_____

Why does Juan make decorations with his dad?

_____

_____

Cause and Effect

Read what happens. Then check the circle next to the sentence that tells why it happens.

What Happens

Why It Happens

Bird cannot fly.
She must hop from place
to place.

○ Bird wants to move
like Rabbit.

○ Bird broke her wing.

Bear goes into the woods
to pick ripe berries.

○ Bear needs to find a
new cave.

○ Bear is hungry.

Bat does not know which
road to follow. He is lost.

○ Bat left his map at
home.

○ Bat forgot to take his
backpack.

The *-er* Ending in Two-Syllable Words

The storm started at dinner time. Thunder boomed and boomed. Our dog hid under the bed. Mom said we had better close all the windows. She did not want to get rain on the rugs. After we ate, we put on our robes and slippers and watched the rain.

Name_____

The -*er* Ending in Two-Syllable Words

Each word names a thing. Write the word from the box that goes with that thing.

| hammer | member | butter | letter | water | finger |

1. soap _____

2. stamp _____

3. hand _____

4. toast _____

5. nails _____

Making Generalizations

Generalization:
Little children can get into big trouble.

Supporting Details:

1. _____

2. _____

3. _____

4. _____

Name_____

Making Generalizations

Read each paragraph. Then read the generalization.
Write a word to finish it.

Six children in Mrs. White's class live in apartments.
Twelve children live in houses. One girl lives in a trailer.

Generalization: Most of the children in the class
live in _____.

There are three girls in Nora's family. Nora is on a softball
team. Her sisters Tessie and Jill play tennis.

Generalization: All the girls in the family play _____.

Our club collects books. Some members like funny books.
Others like books that give facts about animals.

Generalization: The club members like to _____.

In our house, Mom shops and cooks. Dad cleans and does
yard work. My brother and I set the table.

Generalization: Everyone in the family does _____.

Contractions

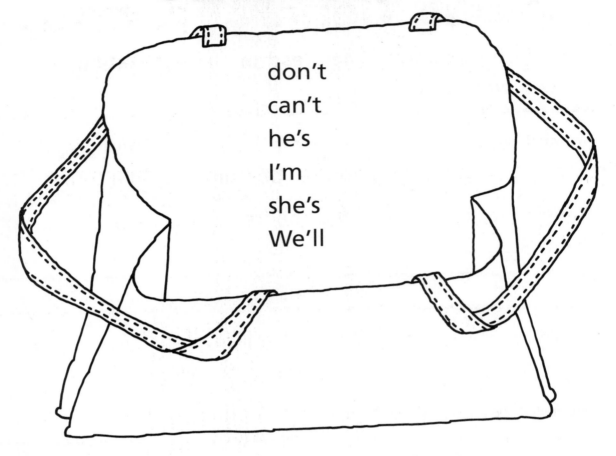

don't
can't
he's
I'm
she's
We'll

What's in the bag? _____

1. Tom looks as if _____ not happy.

2. Mom said, "_____ all eat here."

3. I _____ find my backpack.

4. "_____ the winner!" Joan boasted.

5. They _____ want any pie.

6. Pam will call if _____ late.

Name_____

The -*le* Ending in Two-Syllable Words

Read the sentences. Write a word from the box in each sentence.

mumble	candle	giggle	puddle	apple	puzzle

1. Blow out the _____.

2. She'll _____ when she hears the joke.

3. The rain left a big _____ on the street.

4. We're trying to solve the _____.

5. I can't hear you when you _____.

6. The _____ is red and juicy.

Following Directions

Celery Stuffers

What I Need: _____

_____

What I Will Do:

First, <u>wash the celery and dry it.</u> _____

Next, _____

_____

Then, _____

Last, _____

Following Directions

The pictures show the steps for making a fruit smoothie.

Look at them as you write directions someone can follow.

First _____

_____

Then _____

_____

Next _____

_____

Last _____

_____

Sound of *y* at the End of Longer Words

Vera was tired of the rainy weather. The yard was all muddy. She couldn't go outside.

Vera's mom had an idea. "Let's make berry ice cream," she said. "It is tasty." Vera smiled. Vera helped her mom.

Later the whole family had ice cream. They ate every last bit of it. It was very good!

The Prefix *un-*

Circle the word to finish each sentence. Write the word on the line

1. The stacks of books are _____.

   unable   uneven

2. An icy road can be _____.

   unsafe   unsaid

3. Our team is _____!

   unlike   unbeaten

4. I like _____ carrots.

   unhooked   uncooked

5. He looked for an _____ pencil.

   unreal   unbroken

Draw an unhappy face in the box.

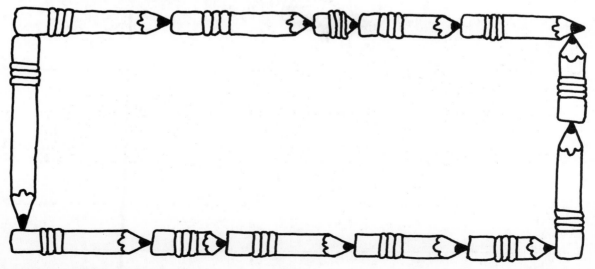

Making Judgments

Opinion of Reggie: _____

_____

Reasons: _____

_____

_____

Opinion of Reggie: _____

_____

Reasons: _____

_____

_____

Making Judgments

Read each story. Finish each sentence.

Ned has a bag of apple chips.
He goes into the shed to eat
the chips because he does
not want to share them.

I think Ned is _____.

I think that because _____.

Jen wants to finish her
puzzle. She knows it's almost
time for dinner. She gets up
to help Dad set the table.

I think Jen is _____.

I think that because _____.

_____.

Base Words and *-ed*, *-ing* Endings

flapping
shutting
dripping
shopped
dropped

a bucket of _____

1. The boy _____ for a pair of pants.

2. The little bird is _____ its wings.

3. I am _____ the window.

4. The glass broke when Dad _____ it.

5. Water is _____ from the pipe.

Silent Consonants *gh, k* in *kn,* and *b* in *mb*

Read the sentences. Draw a line to match each sentence with a picture.

1. The kitten climbs the ladder.

2. He slipped and hurt his knee.

3. Mom is cutting with a small knife.

4. She taught her dog a trick.

5. There is a big knot in the rope.

Sequence of Events

Henry's Day

Beginning

Henry woke up.
He ate breakfast and got dressed.

Middle

_____

_____

_____

End

_____

_____

_____

_____

Sequence of Events

The sentences in the box are in the wrong order. Read them, and then write them in the right order.

Nela makes a snack at home.
The teacher waves goodbye to Nela.
Nela rides the school bus home.
Nela goes to Bonnie's house.
She writes a note that says, "I've gone to Bonnie's house."

_____

_____

_____

_____

_____

_____

Vowel pairs *oo*, *ew*

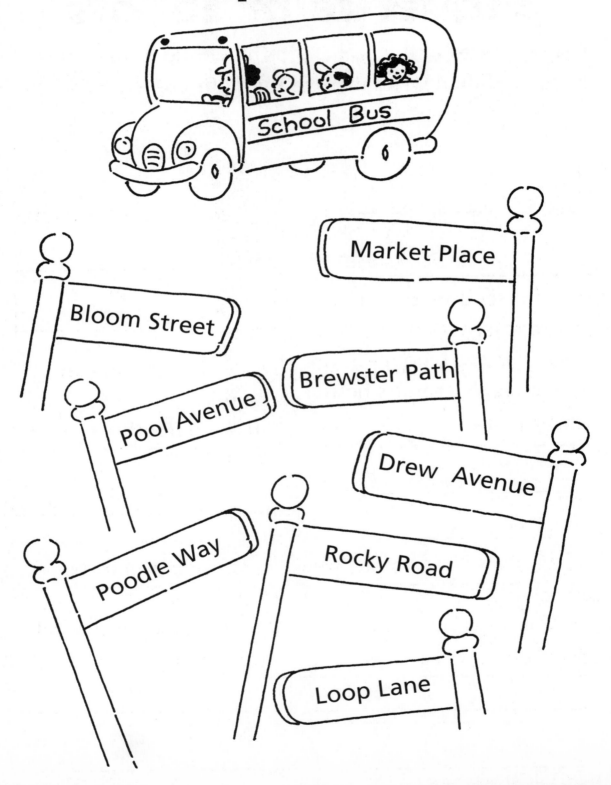

Vowel pairs oo, ew

Read the riddles. Answer each one with a word from the box.

pool	newspaper	boot	stew

1. I'm a tasty food.
Eat me with a fork or spoon.
What am I?

_____

2. I'm something you
can read.
I'm not a book.
What am I?

_____

3. I'm something to put on
a foot.
I'm not a sock or slipper.
What am I?

_____

4. I'm something you
can swim in.
I'm not a lake or a pond.
What am I?

_____

Author's Viewpoint

What the Story Says

_____

_____

_____

_____

_____

What the Author Probably Thinks About Cats

_____

_____

Author's Viewpoint

Read the story. Then circle the answer to the question. Draw lines under sentences in the story that helped you answer the question.

Hi! My name is Quan. I like to walk in the woods. I take a notebook with me and sometimes a camera to make notes and take pictures of the trees. I use my notes and pictures to give reports in class.

One day I told the class that there are many kinds of trees. I told them that people and animals need trees for food and that trees are homes for some animals, too. I told how trees help keep our air clean.

"I'm glad we have trees," I said at the end of my report. The class agreed with me.

How does the author feel about trees?

The author thinks trees are important.

Long *i* (*igh*)

A Frightful Night

What a storm! What a night! I was reading
when the lights went out. It was very, very dark. I
couldn't see. I could only hear an odd rap, rap,
rapping high over my head. I was frightened, but I
went up the flight of stairs. In a flash, the lights
came back on. What a sight! An open window was
rap, rap, rapping. I sighed a happy sigh.

Name_____

Long *i* (*igh*)

| frightening | high | fight | light | tight | night |

Read the words in the box and the numbered clues.
Write the word from the box that goes with each clue.

1. not low, but   _____

2. a lamp gives   _____

3. not loose, but   _____

4. people at war do this _____

5. something scary is   _____

6. not day, but   _____

Write clues that would help someone guess the word
***bright*.**

_____

_____

Noting Details

Tonya thinks she has a good chance to be voted the best second-grader.

Tonya is a whiz at math.

_____

_____

Tonya is the best in gym class.

_____

_____

Tonya helps in the community.

_____

_____

Name_____

Noting Details

Read the story. Then answer the questions.

Perry and Jerry are twins. The boys look alike and they dress alike, too. People sometimes get them mixed up, but their mom never does!

Perry likes to read and play video games. Jerry likes to be outdoors. Nothing frightens him. He climbs to the top of the huge tree in the yard.

1. Why do people get the twins mixed up?

    _____

2. Who can always tell the boys apart?

    _____

3. Which twin likes outdoor adventures?

    _____

4. What are some things Perry likes to do?

    _____

More Words with -ed or -ing

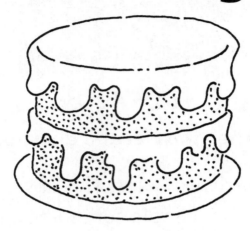

1. He _____ some friends to visit.

   inviting   invited

2. Now he is _____ a cake.

   baking   baked

3. First, he mixed the batter and _____ it.

   tasted   tasting

4. When the cake was ready, he _____ it.

   slicing   sliced

5. He is _____ his friends will like it.

   hoping   hoped

6. Yes, his friends _____ the cake!

   liked   liking

More Words with -ed or -ing

Read the sentences. Draw a line to match each one with a picture.

1. The dog is shaking to dry off.

2. The runner raced to the finish line.

3. She is placing the book on the shelf.

4. They are hiking on the trail.

5. She smiled when she got the prize.

Problem Solving

Problem:
_____
_____
Solution:
_____
_____

Problem:
_____
_____
Solution:
_____
_____

Name_____

Problem Solving

Read each paragraph. Think about the problem the character has. Circle the solution that is not a good one.

Mike wants to go camping with his friends
Jamal and Ken. Mike never went camping before,
and he doesn't know what to pack. What can he do?

Mike can ask his friends for help.
Mike can read a book about camping.
Mike can hope his friends will lend him things.

Meg slept too long. Her alarm did not ring.
She missed the school bus. It is too far to walk
to her school. What can she do?

Meg can ask her mom to drive her to school.
Meg can go back to bed.
Meg can ride her bike to school.

A	E	I	M	R	V
A	E	I	N	R	W
A	E	J	N	S	W
B	F	J	O	S	X
B	F	K	O	T	X
C	G	K	P	T	Y
C	G	L	P	U	Y
D	H	L	Q	U	Z
D	H	M	Q	V	Z

Letter Cards

a	e	i	m	r	v
a	i	i	n	r	w
a	e	j	n	s	w
b	f	j	o	s	x
b	f	k	p	t	x
c	g	k	p	t	y
c	g	l	p	u	y
d	h	l	q	u	z
d	h	m	q	v	z

Letter Cards

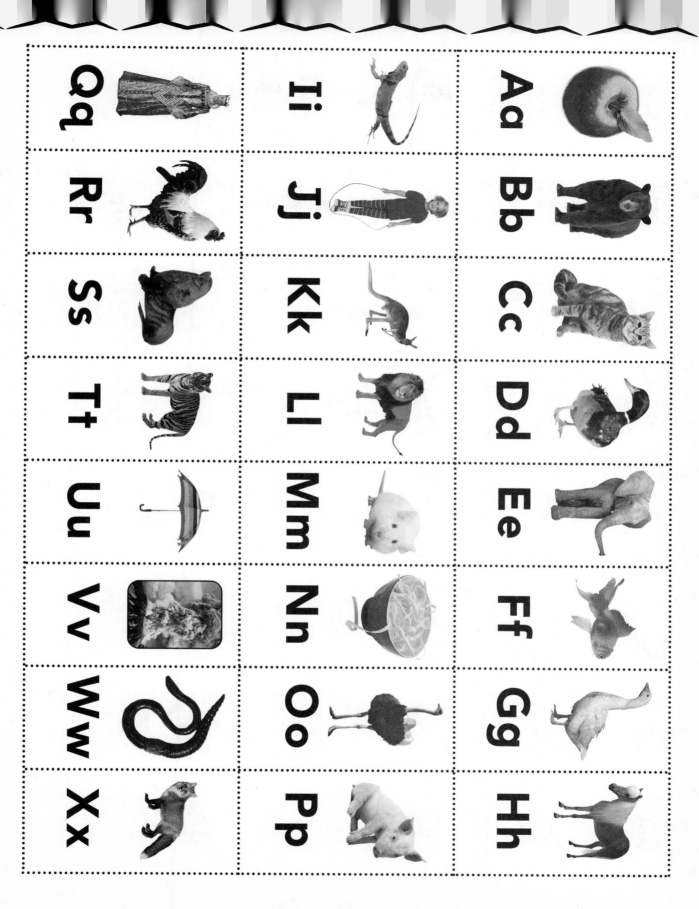

Aa	Bb	Cc	Dd	Ee	Ff	Gg	Hh
Ii	Jj	Kk	Ll	Mm	Nn	Oo	Pp
Qq	Rr	Ss	Tt	Uu	Vv	Ww	Xx

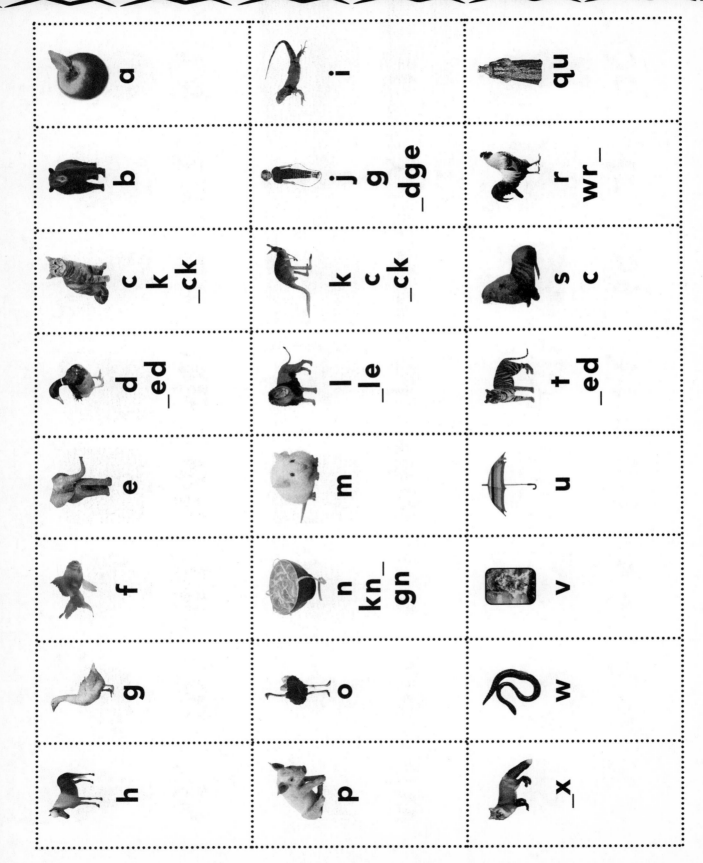

a

b

c k _ck

d _ed

e

f

g

h

i

j g _dge

k c _ck

l _le

m

n kn_ gn

o

p

qu

r wr_

s c

t _ed

u

v

w

x _

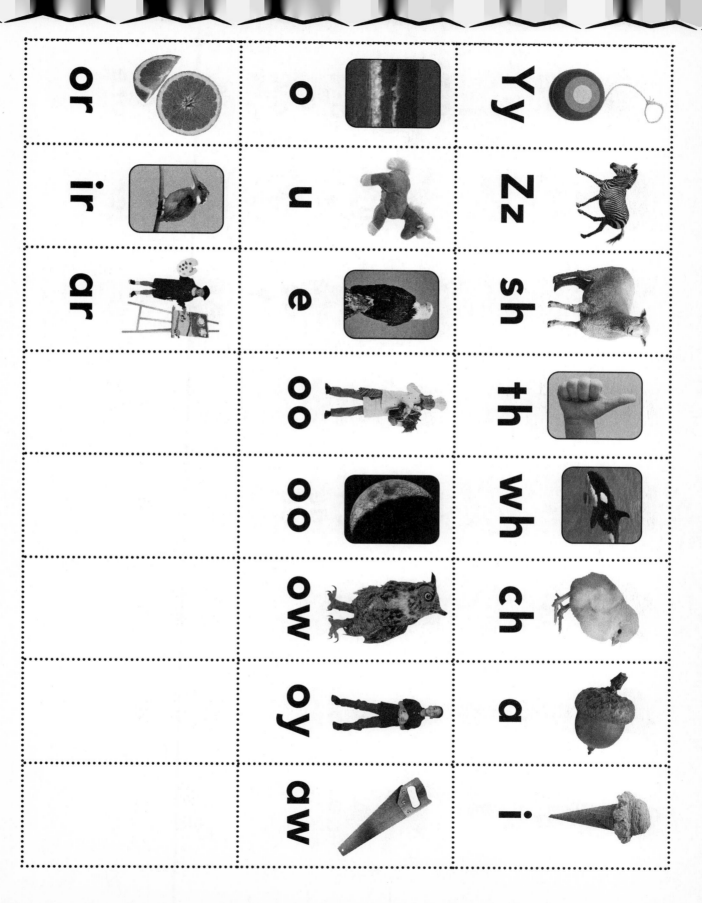

or	o	Yy
ir	u	Zz
ar	e	sh
	oo	th
	oo	wh
	ow	ch
	oy	a
	aw	i

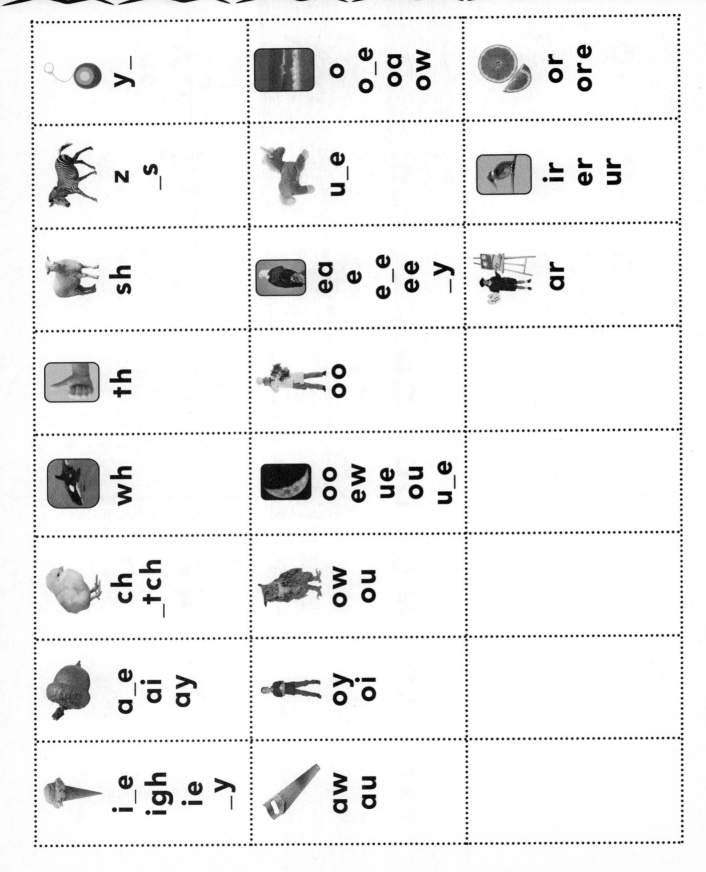

y_	o / o_e / oa / ow	or / ore
z / s_	u_e	ir / er / ur
sh	ea / e / e_e / ee / _y	ar
th	oo	
wh	oo / ew / ue / ou / u_e	
ch / tch / _tch	ow / ou	
a_e / ai / ay	oy / oi	
i_e / igh / ie / _y	aw / au	

Blending Routine 1
Continuous Blending

Procedure	Example: *sat*
1. Display the letter cards or write the letters for the word.	**Display *sat*.** `s` `a` `t`
2. Have children listen as you blend the sounds of the word, "stretching out" the word while pointing to each letter in a sweeping motion. Then say the whole word naturally.	**Point to *sat* and say *sssăăăt*, *sat*.** `s``a``t` →
3. Repeat step 2, this time having children blend the word with you.	**Children blend *sat* with you, saying *sssăăăt*, *sat*.**
4. Have children blend the sounds on their own and then say the whole word naturally.	**Children blend *sat* on their own, saying *sssăăăt*, *sat*.**
5. Now have children blend the word silently, in their heads. After they say the whole word aloud, have them use it in a sentence.	**Children look at the letters and then:** • blend the sounds in their heads, saying *sssăăăt* • say the whole word *sat* aloud • use *sat* in a sentence

Blending Routine 2

Sound-by-Sound Blending

Procedure

1. Display or write the letter or letters that stand for the first sound in the word. Point to the letter as you say the sound.

2. Have children say the sound as you repeat it.

3. Display the letter or letters for the next sound and say the sound. Then have children say it with you.

4. Model blending the displayed letters, pointing to the letters in a sweeping motion as you say the sounds. Then have children repeat this with you.

5. Display the letter or letters for the third sound and say the sound. Children say it with you. Have children listen as you blend the sounds so far; then blend together. Add any remaining letters, one by one, and continue this procedure.

6. Model blending the whole word, pointing to the letters in a sweeping motion as you blend the sounds. Then have children blend the word silently in their heads. Finally, have children say the whole word naturally and use it in a sentence.

Example: *mask*

Display *m* and say /m/.

m

Children say /m/.

m

Add *a* to display *ma*. Point to *a* and say /ă/. Children say /ă/ with you.

m a

Model blending *ma*, saying *mmmăăă*. Repeat. Children blend *ma* with you.

m a →

Add *s* to display *mas*. Point to *s* and say /s/. Children say /s/ with you. Model blending *ma* and *s: mmmăăăsss*. Children repeat. Now add *k* and say /k/. Children repeat.

m a s →

m a s k →

Model blending *mask*, saying *mmmăăăsssk*. Children blend *mask* silently in their heads. Children say the whole word *mask* and then use it in a sentence.

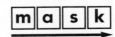

Blending Routine 3

Vowel-First Blending

Procedure

1. Display or write the letter that stands for the vowel sound in the word. Point to the letter as you say the sound.

2. Have children say the sound as you point to the letter and say the sound again. Explain that when you come to this letter as you blend the word, you will remember to say that sound.

3. Display the letter for the first sound in the word and say the sound. Then have children say it with you.

4. Model blending the word through the vowel, pointing to the letters in a sweeping motion as you say the sounds. Then have children repeat this with you.

5. Display the letter for the final sound and say the sound. Then have children say it with you.

6. Model blending the whole word, pointing to the letters in a sweeping motion as you blend the sounds. Have children blend the word with you and then silently in their heads. Have children say the whole word and use it in a sentence.

Example: *sat*

Display *a* and say /ă/.

`a`

Children say /ă/ as you point to the letter *a* and say /ă/. Say: *When we come to this letter in the word, we will say /ă/.*

`a`

Display *s* and *a*. Point to *s* and say /s/. Have children say /s/ with you.

`s` `a`

Model blending *sa*, saying *sssăăă*. Repeat, having children blend *sa* with you.

`s` `a` →

Add *t* to display *sat*. Point to *t* and say /t/. Then have children say /t/ with you.

`s` `a` `t`

Model blending *sat*, saying *sssăăăt*. Repeat, having children blend *sat* with you. Children blend *sat* silently in their heads, then say the whole word. Have a volunteer use *sat* in a sentence.

`s` `a` `t` →